WELL IT'S **O N E**
FOR THE MONEY,

T W O
FOR THE SHOW,

T H R E E
TO GET READY,

N O W
GO, CAT, GO!

ROCKABILLY

You pick the tune
And you slap the bass
I'll play the rhythm
And I'll set the pace
But we gotta get with it
Ain't no time to waste!

—Charlie Feathers, "Get With It,"
1956

I got a rocket in my pocket
and the fuse is lit . . .

—Jimmy Lloyd,
"I Got a Rocket in My Pocket," 1958

ROCKABILLY

THE TWANG HEARD 'ROUND THE WORLD

★ The Complete Illustrated History ★

FOREWORD BY SONNY BURGESS

Featuring

GREIL MARCUS ★ PETER GURALNICK
LUC SANTE ★ ROBERT GORDON
DEKE DICKERSON ★ DAVID MCGEE
CRAIG MORRISON ★ RANDY MCNUTT
DAN FORTE ★ GARTH CARTWRIGHT
VINCE GORDON ★ AND MORE

Voyageur
Press

WITH INTERVIEWS + REMINISCENCES FROM

BRIAN SETZER ★ WANDA JACKSON

CARL PERKINS ★ CHARLIE FEATHERS ★ BILLY RILEY

CLIFF GALLUP ★ SCOTTY MOORE ★ REV. HORTON HEAT

THE CRAMPS ★ TAV FALCO ★ HEAVY TRASH

GLEN GLENN ★ DALE HAWKINS ★ ROSE MADDOX

BARBARA PITTMAN ★ JIM DICKINSON ★ PAT CUPP

PAUL BURLISON ★ RONNIE HAWKINS ★ RAY CAMPI

JOHNNY CARROLL ★ JOE CLAY ★ MAC CURTIS

ROLAND JANES ★ SONNY CURTIS ★ NARVEL FELTS

JOE LEE ★ JIMMY LLOYD ★ MARCUS VAN STORY

and many more. . .

MICHAEL DREGNI, EDITOR

CONTENTS

By Sonny Burgess

Sonny Burgess with red hair, red tux, and red Telecaster leads the red-hot Pacers in 1957.
Michael Ochs Archives/Getty Images

ARMORY
TRENTON - TENN. 8:00 P.M.
SAT FEB 2
WTUC PRESENTS
ROCK AND ROLL SHOW & DANCE
STARRING
WARREN SMITH
"UBANGI STOMP"
JERRY LEE LEWIS
"AT THE END OF THE ROAD"
AND THE SENSATIONS
SONNY BURGESS AND THE PACERS
DON'T DARE MISS IT

Concert poster, Armory, Trenton, Tennessee, February 2, 1956.
Pete Howard/Poster Central

I NEVER HEARD THE TERM "rockabilly" back then. Nobody did. Everybody said, "Where'd that term come from?" I don't know. We never really pinned it down, where that term came from. When people asked what music we played, we were rock 'n' rollers. We didn't think about "rockabilly." We were rock 'n' rollers.

It was shocking music to people at the time. Elvis, Johnny Cash, Jerry Lee Lewis, Warren Smith, Billy Riley, Roy Orbison, Carl Perkins, Johnny Burnette and the Rock 'n' Roll Trio—we played shows together all over the country. It was wild back then.

Sonny Burgess and the Pacers—we had a real *show*. We used to have these 50-foot-long cables for our guitars which would allow us to jump off stage and play out in the crowd. We had the cables specially made. One night back in '56, we were playing a show with Marty Robbins, Ray Price, and the Maddox Brothers and Rose at Robinson Auditorium in Little Rock, Arkansas. My guitarist Joe Lewis, our bassist Johnny Ray Hubbard, and I all jumped off the stage and we didn't look before we leaped. Usually stages were about 12 inches up to three foot high. We just assumed this was the same, so we jumped off and there was an orchestra pit and we went *down*. We must have dropped 10 foot. Johnny Ray's upright bass just came all to pieces. But the show had to go on, and so we climbed back up on stage and kept on playing.

Another time, I tried to dye my hair *white*. It was black and I wanted to dye it white. Perkins was blue with his blue suede shows. Elvis was

pink and black. I wanted a color, too. I was reading about a guy named Shell Scotty, a detective in pulp magazines, and he had white hair with black eyebrows. I thought that would be really cool, different. Me and my wife, Joann, we decided we'd do it— but it turned out *red*. It was *really* red. We were heading out to California that week to join the tour with Cash in '57. So the Pacers and I all got red tux jackets with black shirts, black ties, and black pants. I had that red tuxedo and got red shoes, red socks, and played a red Telecaster and red Stratocaster. I sure stood out.

My band also had a trumpet player, Jack Nance. Adding a trumpet to the band was actually good for us, because nobody else had a trumpet—they all had saxophones. We *wanted* a sax player, but couldn't find one. We already had Russ Smith playing drums; Jack Nance was also a drummer but he was also a music major and played a little bit of everything. He had an old trumpet and that's how we wound up with a trumpet player. In clubs, it was fantastic, you could play it *loud*! It turned out great for us. But Jack would get hit a lot. See, people would reach up to touch us and hit his trumpet and he had false teeth—young guy, but he had false teeth—which put things out of whack.

We were in Truman, Arkansas, one night at the Cotton Club, drove up there in a our old green Cadillac, and we had a big crowd and we was really going strong. Jack and Johnny Ray had got themselves some Prince Albert smoking tobacco and some cigarette papers and they took aspirin tablets, ground them up, and rolled them cigarettes with this aspirin in it. Boy, they got *wild.* I've never seen anyone do that before or since, but they got wild. Jack was playing that horn so bad, Joe Lewis finally took it away from him. Jack said, "You can't do this—that's the best I've ever played in my life!" We had to send Jack and Johnny home.

Our band also did the bug dance. We got the bug trick from Orbison. He played the Silver Moon in Newport, Arkansas, in 1955 along with Warren Smith, Eddie Bond, and us. He had a guy named Big Jack playing the upright bass and a little guy named Willie playing rhythm guitar; Roy's playing guitar, then he had a mandolin player and a drummer. Anyway, they done this bug dance. Big Jack and the little guy. They'd reach down on the floor and pick up this "bug" and throw it on each other. That's where we got it. So four of us would do it and we outdid them on it. We had four of us, throw it on each other, shake around, try to catch it, and then throw it on the next guy.

Playing those shows on the road became our life. Marcus Van Story was the bass player for Warren Smith. He couldn't wait to get on the road. Our pianist, Smoochy Smith, accused Marcus of hanging his clothes up out on the tree in his front yard two days before he left the house. He loved the road—and he put on a show, rolling on his back, playing his bass behind his head.

Warren Smith had a couple good records. As soon as he got "Ubangi Stomp" and "Rock and Roll Ruby" out, he thought he was *the* star, but we'd blow his ass off the stage because we had a *show.* It wasn't just a couple songs, it was a *show* we had.

Orbison was a good guy, and we toured with him a lot. See, the Teen Kings quit him when they got paid for "Ooby Dooby" in '55—it was a big seller; sold about 400,000, and that was pretty big back then. Well, they got their money and Little Willie and Big Jack, they thought *they* were stars, so they said, "We're going to go back to Texas and become stars ourselves." So they all left Orbison there in Memphis. Now, Bob Neal was booking us all then, so he put us and Orbison with Cash, because Cash was big then in '56, '57 because he had "Folsom Prison Blues" and he just kept getting bigger and bigger and was pulling huge crowds. Orbison traveled with us a million miles and never bought a nickel's worth of gas! We'd get a cheap room in a motel and there'd be four of us, two guys to each bed. And Orbison would pay just $5 and get a rollaway bed and roll in there with us.

Jerry Lee was different than anyone else who ever came along. I love Jerry Lee's piano playing; he's *so* good. He's a little bit crazy, but he's allright crazy.

We crossed paths with the Rock 'n' Roll Trio all the time. Johnny Burnette used to come to the Silver Moon and watch us—always had three or four gals with him. The Trio didn't make much of an impression back then, because there was so much of those little bands back then. But they were nice

guys—and they liked to fight. We'd play Memphis three or four times a year, Paul would always come play those deals with us. And years later, we became the Sun Rhythm Section together, an all-star band.

My first record came out on Sun Records in '56, "We Wanna Boogie" and "Red Headed Woman." When Sam Phillips recorded us, he just sat up there and rolled tape. He just let us set up our equipment wherever we wanted to, just like we were on stage. He had that one good mic, an RCA 77, in the middle of the room and we'd all stand around that mic. Sam didn't say anything; he just sits up there and turned that machine on and we'd play like he was the audience, playing like he was 10,000 people out there. We were a-beating and a-banging around in there, just like we do on stage. And he'd say, "Well, go through it again." When he got the one he felt was right and sounded good to him, that's what he put out. He had a talent for putting out stuff that was different, that felt good.

Jerry Lee recorded "Whole Lotta Shakin'" with just him, drummer J. M. Van Eaton, and guitarist Roland Janes on it. Billy Riley was setting around there somewhere, maybe playing bass. In the middle of that song, if you listen real close, J. M. gets off—he tries to take a drum roll and he gets off; he gets out of time but gets back in it real quick. But it sold over 12 million records—*ha!* That was Sam's talent, capturing that.

Nowadays they want it too pretty. Everything's got to be perfect. They have machines that will put you in tune if you sing out of tune or put you back in time. And I think that's where music has lost its soul. There's no feeling to it any more.

Back then we didn't have any sort of feeling we were doing anything revolutionary—or we would have put out more records! We weren't even trying to make a dollar—there was no money to be made back then. That wasn't why I was in it, to make money. You had a lot of fun. And you'd meet a lot of gals.

We did it for fun. You felt good playing it. You got your high off the music. You didn't have to have whiskey or drugs. It was just fun, and you'd get high off that music.

"We Wanna Boogie" called it exactly like it was. Sonny Burgess' first single on Sun records was released in August 1956 and reportedly sold more than 90,000 copies. Presumably, others wanted to boogie as well.

OPENING RIFF

INTRODUCTION

ROCKABILLY CAME AND WENT LIKE A SATURDAY NIGHT.

It's arrival can be pinpointed: July 5, 1954, the night Elvis Presley, Scotty Moore, and Bill Black recorded "That's All Right" in Memphis' Sun Studios.

Its departure is a bit more foggy: Some say it was March 24, 1958, the day Elvis was issued his dog tags and entered the U.S. Army as Private Presley. Others claim February 3, 1959, the infamous "day the music died" when Buddy Holly, Ritchie Valens, and the Big Bopper lost their lives in the plane crash in an Iowa cornfield. Or the May 1958 derailment of Jerry Lee Lewis' first career due to outrage over his polygamous marriage to his 13-year-old cousin. Or the April 17, 1960 death of Eddie Cochran in a car accident in England, a crash that Gene Vincent just barely survived.

Whatever the date, rockabilly was a flash in the pan, burning with a brilliant intensity, but lasting just three or four or five years in its glory days. But oh what a fire it sent spreading through the musical world—and popular culture at large. Almost by accident, almost like a joke, just as Elvis had joshed around recording "That's All Right."

ROCKABILLY WAS TRULY THE TWANG HEARD 'ROUND THE WORLD.

CLASSIC ROCKABILLY GUITAR
A 1956 Gretsch Model 6120 Chet Atkins Hollow Body.
Steve Catlin/Redferns/Getty Images

Elvis Presley at Sun Records
1954–1955

CHAPTER 1

ELVIS' "THAT'S ALL RIGHT" WAS A HARMONIC CONVERGENCE.

There was Sam Phillips with his open eyes and ears seeking something special in music and with the means to go with it if and when he found it. There was Scotty Moore and Bill Black—part of the traditional Starlite Wranglers country band—who were willing, eager, and able to make a new music. And there was of course Elvis himself.

It was more than mere symbolism that "That's All Right" would not have been possible without five previous years of Sun Studios. Sam Phillips had been shocking listeners with his recordings, from Howlin' Wolf to B. B. King, Bobby Bland to Junior Parker, Jackie Brenston and Ike Turner, and many more. These past records were more than just inspirations and influences. They were revolutionary in their own right.

THEY ALSO SET THE STAGE FOR THE FUTURE, FOR ROCKABILLY.

ELVIS PRESLEY AT THE DAWN OF ROCKABILLY
With Scotty Moore on guitar and bassist Bill Black just out of the picture to the right, the trio performs at Fort Homer Hesterly Armory in Tampa, Florida, on July 31, 1955. *Michael Ochs Archives/Getty Images*

Born Tupelo, Mississippi, on January 8, 1935; died August 16, 1977

Young Elvis Presley poses for a family portrait with his parents Vernon Presley and Gladys Presley in Tupelo, Mississippi, in 1937. *Michael Ochs Archives/Getty Images*

Elvis' birthplace in Tupelo, Mississippi.

FROM THE VERY BEGINNING, the need to label Elvis spoke of his fans and critics' urgent need to understand and define the power of his music, which itself lacked a name. On the heels of his first Sun singles, newspapermen and radio disc jockeys were seeking labels, scrounging through what they knew to define this new blast.

In 1954 and 1955, they began calling him The Memphis Flash, which denoted some sort of sense of civic pride.

Or they termed him The Boppin' Hillbilly. "Hillbilly" was a popular description, as it spoke of something backwoods and unknown, a mysterious force brewed out there in the beyond, like potent white lightning moonshine, unleashed on the unsuspecting good citizens of the civilized city.

Others labeled him The Hillbilly Cat. Or simply The Cat, as at that time there was only one. Soon, they were writing about him as The Pied Piper of Rock 'n' Roll. And as his music seemed the perfect soundtrack for the dawn of the atomic age, he was billed as The Nation's Only Atomic Powered Singer. His early manager, Bob Neal, hung the moniker of The King of Western Bop around his neck. From there, it was little stretch to simply regal him as The King.

They struggled as well to find a name for the music—a label to denigrate it for do-gooders and moral watchdogs; a code name for the adherents to recognize each other. Elvis' audience in the early days was mostly country fans—albeit a younger country fan and, more and more, a female one as well. His music was labeled country bop or hillbilly bebop, blending that sense of backwoods mysticism with the hottest and wildest jazz then making the rounds.

Some few newspaper and magazine writers called it "rockabilly," but it was not common coin back then. Still, it proved a fine term, distinguishing this Southern white country music from the rock 'n' roll perpetrated by Little Richard and Fats Domino in New Orleans, Ike Turner and Jackie Brenston, Chuck Berry and Bo Diddley laid down in Chicago, and even the Tin Pan Alley rock 'n' roll of Bill Haley and His Comets.

Others simply called it vulgar, animalistic, jungle music—and worse.

Elvis' rags to riches story is so perfectly American, it's almost pure cliché.

He was born in a two-room shotgun house in the poor white section of Tupelo, Mississippi, to Gladys Love and Vernon Elvis Presley. His identical twin brother, Jesse Garon Presley, was delivered stillborn 35 minutes before him—a fact that would haunt Elvis throughout his life.

The family attended a Pentecostal Assembly of God church. Here, he was schooled in Southern gospel music, which became a love that never left him.

From a pastor at church, as well as some uncles, Elvis received basic guitar lessons. He had been given the guitar for his tenth birthday, but it was not a present he relished; he had been wishing for a bicycle or rifle. As he later recalled, "I took the guitar, and I watched people, and I learned to play a little bit. But I would never sing in public. I was very shy about it."

In November 1948, the family moved to Memphis, living at first in rooming houses and later in a public housing complex known as the Courts. Here, he began practicing guitar regularly under the tutelage of neighbor Jesse Lee Denson. Two other brothers—Dorsey and Johnny Burnette—also lived in the Courts and played music.

His interest in musical styles was expanding as well. He was a constant presence in record stores, listening to recordings on jukeboxes and in listening booths. He favored the country music of Ernest Tubb, Hank Snow, Roy Acuff, Jimmie Rodgers, and Bob Wills; expanded his love of gospel music, including Sister Rosetta Tharpe and Jake Hess; and had his ears open to the blues and R&B of musicians from Mississippi Delta bluesman Arthur "Big Boy" Crudup, Memphis' own Rufus Thomas, and the up and coming B. B. King. In April 1953, Elvis fought his shyness about performing and competed in a minstrel show talent contest, playing the recent country hit "Till I Waltz Again With You." He loved the bit of attention the performance brought him among schoolmates.

Elvis was also developing a distinct sense of personal style. He began to stand out among his high school classmates due to his look: He combed back his hair and styled it with rose oil and Vaseline while also growing out his sideburns. And he had an eye for sharp clothes: He visited Lansky Brothers, a tailor's shop on Beale Street at the heart of Memphis' African American community to dream about the flashy Saturday-night garb.

In August 1953, Presley strolled into the offices of Sam Phillips' Memphis Recording Services at 706 Union Avenue on the corner of Marshall. He carried cash in hand to pay for studio time and a single acetate disc of himself as a gift for his beloved mother. He sang two songs, "My Happiness" and "That's When Your Heartaches Begin."

Phillips was not impressed by Elvis' singing, but there was something about him that did linger in the back of his mind. Receptionist Marion Keisker asked Elvis what kind of singer he was, to which Elvis responded, "I sing all kinds." When pressed on whom he sounded like, Elvis proudly answered, "I don't sound like nobody." Still, on Phillips' request, she noted next to Elvis' name, "Good ballad singer. Hold."

Elvis tried out for several other local groups, but was consistently turned down. He failed an audition for the Songfellows, a vocal group. He was rejected by Eddie Bond, the bandleader for vocalist Ronnie Smith's group. His acquaintances, the Burnette brothers, never invited him into their band either.

In June 1954, Phillips called Elvis and invited him back to the studio. He had a balled that he believed would fit Elvis well, a tune called "Without You." Again, the audition was not fruitful. But still, something intrigued Phillips.

Phillips dialed up a local guitarist, Scotty Moore, who played in a country band called the Starlite Wranglers. The band seemed to be going nowhere, and Moore was always seeking something new, hounding Phillips for projects. Now, Phillips asked Moore to try jamming with Elvis and see if they could work something up.

On the evening of July 5, 1954, Moore rounded up bassist Bill Black and Elvis and set up in the Sun Studio. They had played together at Moore's house and had a couple ballads, gospel tunes, and country songs they hoped would inspire Phillips. But the session was flat: They went through tune after tune, each one being rejected by Phillips.

As they were taking a break late into the night with their hope mostly gone, Elvis began fooling around, strumming his guitar and clowning his way through an old blues tune, "That's All Right Mama" that Arthur Crudup had first cut back in 1946.

It was almost as if he were speaking in tongues. When Elvis played "That's All Right," he was channeling all of the music he had grown up on—gospel, country, blues, R&B, and more. Given his Pentecostal Assembly of God upbringing, glossolalia—the Biblical "gift of tongues"— was part of his world. Thus, it was not a stretch to speak in musical tongues.

As Scotty Moore remembered in a 1955 interview, the trio was "just jamming, just cutting up" when it rocked and rolled the old blues

Elvis Presley poses for one of his first promotional portraits in 1954.
Memphis Brooks Museum/Michael Ochs Archives/Getty Images

"That's All Right" was more than just all right—it was the song that jumpstarted rockabilly. The story of the session has become legend: Derived from Mississippi Delta bluesman Arthur "Big Boy" Crudup's 1946 recording, "That's All Right, Mama" Elvis and the erstwhile Starlite Wranglers created rockabilly ground zero. As Brian Setzer would state decades later, the guitar sounded like a country musician trying to rock. And doing it. Bill Black's bass was textbook slapping, providing the bottom end and percussion at the same time. The single was released on July 19, 1954.

number: "We went into the studio primarily for an audition . . . Bill [Black] and I only went in with [Elvis] to have just some kind of meager accompaniment with him, so he wouldn't be standing alone in the studio, you know. . . . we went through two or three different songs, more or less taking a break, having a coffee, or coke, and Elvis started clowning around. Just picked up his guitar and started kibitzing, singing 'That's All Right' and clowning around the studio dancing, just cutting up in general, and Bill picked up his bass, started slapping it, and clowning also . . . I joined in with just a rhythm vamp. Sam was in the control room, the door was open. He came out and said, 'What are y'all doing?' Said, 'That sounds pretty good.' We said, 'We don't know . . .' He said, 'Well, see if you can do it again the same way. Let's put it on tape, see what it sounds like.'"

Phillips cut an acetate of the best take and three nights later brought it to Memphis' wildman radio DJ Dewey "Daddy-O" Phillips. Despite the shared surname, the two were related only by a love for music. Dewey spun "That's All Right" on his locally famous Red, Hot & Blue show on radio WHBQ. Listeners instantly began calling in, raving about the performer. Many assumed he was African American, due to both the song choice and the delivery. Over the next two hours of his show, Dewey continued to play the disc while someone went to pull Elvis out of a movie theater for an on-air interview. Dewey began by asking what high school he attended, a not-so subtle point that proved to listeners he was a local white boy who could certainly sing the blues.

When Elvis began performing on stage, he developed a nervous tick. He, Scotty, and Bill played in public for the first times on July 17, 1954 at Memphis' Bon Air Club and later that month outdoors at the Overton Park Bandshell. It was in part due to sheer nervous stagefright, but also in part to the music's deep rhythm: Elvis' legs twitched and shook, and his stylish, wide-cut pants only emphasized what looked to the crowd like a dance. Young women in the audience began to scream. Scotty was shocked; as he told Elvis biographer Peter Guralnick, "During the instrumental parts he would back off from the mike and be playing and shaking, and the crowd would just go wild."

Elvis almost immediately proved to his bandmates that he was natural showman. Throughout that summer and fall of 1954, the trio played frequently at Memphis' Eagle's Nest club. At each show, Elvis developed his performance. As Scotty remembered, "His movement was a natural thing, but he was also very conscious of what got a reaction. He'd do something one time and then he would expand on it real quick."

And the young women only screamed louder.

Elvis made only one appearance on Nashville's on-air barn dance *The Grand Ole Opry*, broadcast over WSM–AM radio. The Opry was the bastion of country music correctness, as dictated by many of Elvis' long-time heroes, such as Ernest Tubb. It was a show that often defined country music—and in turn carried with it many rules, from not allowing electrified instruments in the early days to not permitting drums on stage. After Elvis' performance there on October 2, 1954, Opry manager Jim Denny politely told Sam Phillips that his singer was "not bad," but did not fit the show. Elvis and Sam couldn't have agreed more.

Instead, Elvis was booked onto the *Louisiana Hayride*. Broadcast from Shreveport, Louisiana, over KWKH–AM, the show was well-known for its more adventuresome spirit, serving as a launching pad for future stars like Hank Williams, Webb Pierce, and many more. Here, drummers were indeed allowed, and house drummer D. J. Fontana backed Elvis' trio during their first performance later in October 1954. Fontana would soon make the trio a quartet.

With the success of his first *Louisiana Hayride* show, Elvis was hired for a year's worth of Saturday-night shows. During the weekdays, his new manager, Bob Neal, kept him booked on the road, playing as far as the group could travel before making the dash back to Shreveport.

Between the radio broadcasts and the weekday shows, Elvis's rockabilly was spreading across the South. Along the way, he was outraging moralists, stoking fires of passion in young women, angering jealous teenaged boys, giving concerned parents ulcers, upsetting the country-music old guard, inspiring other would-be rock 'n' rollers, and changing music forever.

SUNDAY - FEB. 6
TWO SHOWS ★ 3:00 p.m. & 8:00 p.m.
AUDITORIUM
MEMPHIS, TENN.

FARON YOUNG
★ "IF YOU AIN'T LOVIN"
MARTHA CARSON
★ BEAUTIFUL GOSPEL SINGER
FERLIN HUSKEY
THE HUSHPUPPIES
Doyle and Teddy
WILBURN BROTHERS
Plus... MEMPHIS' OWN
ELVIS PRESLEY
SCOTTY and BILL
He'll Sing "HEARTBEAKER" - "MILK COW BOOGIE"
MANY MORE...

Elvis was toying with sacrilege when he cut "Blue Moon of Kentucky" as a rockabilly shuffle. The original song was a waltz penned by bluegrass pioneer Bill Monroe and much loved by fans. Looking for a B-side to "That's All Right" several nights later, Elvis, Scotty, and Bill jumpstarted a jam through the classic. Their revision was so right, so swinging, that even Monroe himself would re-record the tune in an upbeat tempo.

Kentucky's Bill Monroe was hailed as the father of bluegrass music for his hard-driving, heavily rhythmic style.

"'Blue Moon of Kentucky' came about the same way. After we did 'That's All Right,' Sam said, 'Okay, we have to have a B-side,' and again we went in and everybody was scratching their brains trying to think of songs to try. And this time Bill—again during the break—started 'Blue Moon of Kentucky.' It was originally a waltz. But he started singing it up-tempo in a high falsetto voice, just mimicking Bill Monroe. Elvis knew the song so he started and we all just fell in again.

"Everything we did on Sun was done the same way. We had absolutely no material going in. We'd just go in and start kicking things around. Sam would mention some of the R&B stuff he had done, and we'd try some of that. You know, 'That's All Right' was just something Elvis had heard on the radio and knew, but every session we did on Sun was done the way—just through trial and error until something would just finally click. You didn't know what you'd come out with. And there were a few times when you didn't get anything, and we'd just come back the next day or two."

—Scotty Moore as told to John Floyd,
Sun Records: An Oral History, 1998

IN THE BEGINNING, this new music had no name. It grew out of country, the blues, gospel, bluegrass, big-band swing, jump blues, western swing, boogie woogie, R&B—a bastard child of musical miscegenation. And yet it was a music all its own and clearly defined in its style.

There was the slapped string bass providing both the bottom end and percussion, as drums were rarely part of the music at the start. There was an electric guitar picked with a combination of traditional country style—Mother Maybelle Carter's "Crunch" by way of Merle Travis—blended with a raucous new intensity. There was the frantic fast tempo, the frenetic singing, the whoop, the holler, the sense of youth and an undercurrent of rebellion—at least from the music that had come before. And it all resounded with that slapback tape echo and distortion.

At the start, this was Southern music. And even more so, regional music. It came of course from Memphis, but soon spread across the South from Alabama to Mississippi to Arkansas and Louisiana and on to Texas. Then inspired by Elvis, there was soon rockabilly being cut in California, even in the cold north from Washington to Minnesota to Massachusetts—and across the ocean to France and Great Britain—anywhere the germ could travel.

Hailing from southwestern Virginia, the Carter Family helped define American folk and country music during their reign from 1927 to 1956. Their recordings of songs like "Wildwood Flower," "Wabash Cannonball," "Will the Circle Be Unbroken," and "Keep On the Sunny Side" made them country standards, and they exerted a profound influence on country, bluegrass, and gospel music—as well as rockabilly. Mother Maybelle Carter's self-taught and unique "Carter Scratch" style of playing the guitar's bass and melody lines simultaneously was an inspiration to country guitarist Merle Travis' picking, which in turn influenced Scotty Moore and every rockabilly guitarist thereafter.

"I grew up on the Carter Family. Beginning in 1927, when they made their first recordings for Ralph Peer, a talent scout for the Victor Recording Company of New York, in an improvised studio in Bristol, Tennessee, their music filled the air in the South (and elsewhere). It's difficult, in fact, to overemphasize their importance and influence on American country, folk, and pop music."

—Johnny Cash,
Cash: The Autobiography, 1997

MADDOX BROS. AND ROSE

Many rockabillies spoke of the influence of the Maddox Bros. and Rose. Nicknamed "America's Most Colorful Hillbilly Band," they had a long run stretching from the 1930s to the 1950s creating rollicking country music. Originally from Boaz, Alabama, the family rode the rails and hitchhiked to California during the Great Depression, where they made their careers.

ROSE MADDOX: "I started in 1937 in Modesto, California, with my brothers. Our family moved from Alabama to California during the Depression, so I was really raised on the coast. I was only eleven years old when I started singing professionally with my brothers, who were all older than I. We were called hillbilly singers. No, none of this country music then; people just called us hillbilly. It took people in our field years and years just to get to the point where we were called country singers. After recording for Four Star Records for about six years, starting in 1946 or '47, we went over to Columbia Records, which offered us a good deal. We recorded many things with Columbia in the '50s, and the label offered me the opportunity to record as a single, too. Naturally, I accepted the offer. When the band broke up in '57, I stayed on the label by myself. People tell me that I was one of the first women to sing what I sang—country boogie. I guess I was. There was no rock 'n' roll in those early days, before 1955. Only country boogie. In the mid '50s, I threw a little rock into the act. We did all our recording in California, except for my first session as a single, which was done in Nashville. And sometimes we recorded in Texas. But California was our base for recording the Maddox Brothers and Rose. I was always a different kind of singer. Nowadays, all the girl singers sound alike. I sounded like nobody else, and I guess that's why I was so distinctive."

-Interview by Randy McNutt
Los Angeles, California, July 1987

Jackie Brenston and Ike Turner's "Rocket 88" was recorded in Sun Studios in March 1951, then licensed to Chess Records. It was one of the first rock 'n' roll songs; Sam Phillips knew what he wanted to hear even then.
Pete Howard/Poster Central

BIG 4TH OF JULY DANCE

AMERICAN LEGION HALL
125½ E. 9th ST. - CHATTANOOGA

WED. JULY 4
9 P.M. TIL 1 A.M.

JACKIE BRENSTON
SINGING "ROCKET 88"
FEATURING
IKE TURNER
KING OF THE IVORIES
"I'M LONESOME BABY" - "HEARTBROKEN AND WORRIED"

ADMISSION: ADVANCE $1.25 - AT DOOR $1.75
TICKETS ON SALE AT USUAL PLACES

SOUTHERN POSTER PRINTING CO. ATLANTA, GA.

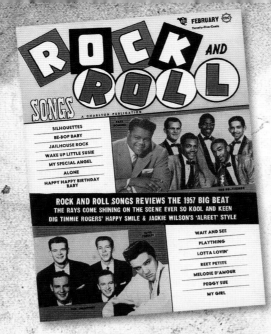

Antoine Dominique "Fats" Domino was a pure product of New Orleans. His influence on early rock 'n' roll was paramount: From 1949 to 1962, he waxed more than sixty early rock 'n' roll singles for the Imperial label, with 40 songs in the R&B charts top ten and scoring eleven top ten pop singles.

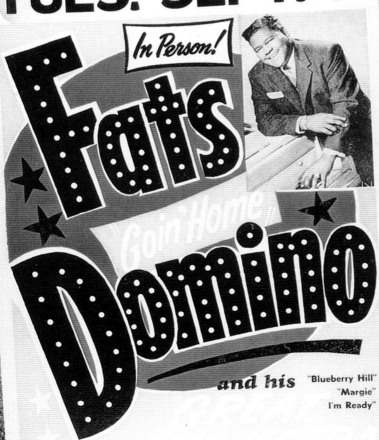

Sam Phillips also recorded Howlin' Wolf in 1951. As Phillips later said of Wolf's music: "This is where the soul of man never dies."

Few shocked the world like Richard Wayne Penniman, better known as Little Richard. From his clothes and makeup to his piano pounding and vocal acrobatics, he led the way from R&B to rock 'n' roll.

Little Richard — Worlds Greatest Male Singer

22

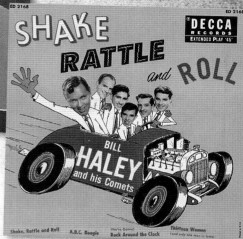

Bill Haley and His Comets' "Rock Around the Clock" was pure Tin Pan Alley rock 'n' roll. Released in 1954, it didn't catch on until it was used behind the credits of *The Blackboard Jungle* in 1955. Like Haley himself, with his perfect spit curl, his brand of rock 'n' roll was spit-polished to a high sheen—the opposite of Elvis' Sun singles.

Elvis Presley leads his trio on October 16, 1954, during a weekly radio broadcast of the *Louisiana Hayride* at the Shreveport Auditorium just three months after Elvis left home for the first time. *Michael Ochs Archives/Getty Images*

Among those Elvis copied were Roy Brown and his 1947 tune "Good Rockin' Tonight." Yet one of Brown's main inspirations was Bing Crosby, and they don't come much whiter than Bing. And so the influences crossed over, and then back again.

Elvis' second single was a cover of R&B singer Roy Brown's "Good Rockin' Tonight," backed with "I Don't Care If the Sun Don't Shine." The single was released on September 22, 1954.

"Milkcow Blues Boogie" begins with a moment of pure show-biz schmaltz—that faux false start that doesn't "move" Elvis until he gets "real gone." But from then on, it's hot-rodded blues all the way. Like many of Elvis' other early hits, this too was a cover, this time of Georgia bluesman Kokomo Arnold's 1930s "Milk Cow Blues." As Elvis shouts in charging Scotty's solo chorus, "Let's milk it!" He'd milk the schmaltz again, too. The single was released on January 8, 1955.

Elvis Presley sings on stage before a predominantly female audience in early 1956.
Frank Driggs Collection/Getty Images

Released on April 25, 1955, "Baby Let's Play House" immediately became Elvis' most imitated song—a blueprint for rockabilly thereafter. The guitar lines sear, the bass bops like a racing heartbeat, and Elvis is pure vocal exuberance. He stutters and hiccups and sings of the pink Cadillac famous forever more. The original song was written and recorded by bluesman Arthur Gunter in 1955 on Excello Records. It became Elvis' first song to appear on a national chart, reaching #5 on the *Billboard* Country Singles chart in July 1955.

THIS WAS ROCKABILLY GROUND ZERO. Sam Phillips' Memphis Recording Service studio at 706 Union Aveune on the corner of Marshall in Memphis was nothing but a 20x30-foot room, covered in cheap acoustic tile, with a tiny control booth on one end. But in this studio, Phillips created a magical alchemy of sound that forever changed music.

Advertisement for Phillips' Memphis Recording Services. *GAB Archive/Redferns/Getty Images*

"Sam was everything back then. The producer, the engineer, he set up all the mikes. He did it all. Sam was good to work for. He was real pleasant and was very straightforward. He'd tell you what he liked and didn't like. He didn't hem and haw about it."

—Malcolm Yelvington as told to John Floyd, *Sun Records: An Oral History*, 1998

Sam Phillips at the controls in the control booth at Sun Studios, circa 1960. *Colin Escott/Michael Ochs Archives/Getty Images*

"See, Sun Records was a dream for almost every artist of that era. It was a label that would be a dream for almost anybody to be on. Not just because of Elvis and the other people involved with it—Carl Perkins and everybody else—but because the sound they were getting was so unique for that era. The echo and the quality of the recordings. I mean they rocked. There were a lot of rock and roll things out there then, but nothing that rocked like the Sun Records stuff."

—Johnny Powers as told to John Floyd, *Sun Records: An Oral History*, 1998

The restored Sun Studio at 706 Union Avenue, Memphis. *Library of Congress*

"The man that did it all was Sam. Without Sam there wouldn't have been any of those guys. I would've never had an opportunity to do it and a lot of other people wouldn't have, either. Sam is someone that, he's gotten a lot of recognition, but you stop and think about the people he got started in the business. He's amazing. I'm talking about the musicians and engineers and producers, not to mention the great artists. He had an ear like nobody in the world. I think the most important thing I learned from being around Sam was, the thing I was most amazed by, was his ability to handle people, to get the most out of people, to put people at ease and get the most out of them. And the fact that he was strictly his own man, he was not afraid. When he had it right, he knew it. I remember one time I told him, 'Mr. Phillips, I made a mistake in that,' and he said, 'Don't worry about it. The feel,' he says, 'it's got the feel. That's the cut I want.' And I'm not going to tell you which record it was, but over the years I've never had someone come up to me and say, 'Hey man, you made a mistake on that record.' I've heard people say, 'Man, that was a great record,' so the man knew what the hell he was talking about."

—Roland Janes as told to John Floyd, *Sun Records: An Oral History*, 1998

The recording studio at Sun measured a mere 20x30 feet.

ARENA BUILDING
Cape Girardeau, Mo.
WEDNESDAY - JULY 20th
8:30 P.M.

Presenting...
ELVIS
PRESLEY
★ "Blue Moon"
with... ★ "Good Rockin'"
SCOTTY AND BILL
WANDA JACKSON
BUD DECKELMAN
JOHNNY DAUME
AND HIS OZARK RIDGE RUNNERS

Concert poster, Arena Building, Cape Girardeau, Missouri, July 20, 1955. *Pete Howard/Poster Central*

Pete Howard/Poster Central

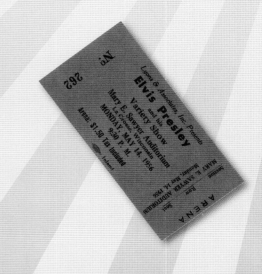

Program from Elvis' sole appearance on Nashville's *Grand Ole Opry*, on October 2, 1954. *Opry* manager Jim Denny told Sam Phillips that Elvis was "not bad," but that he didn't suit the program.

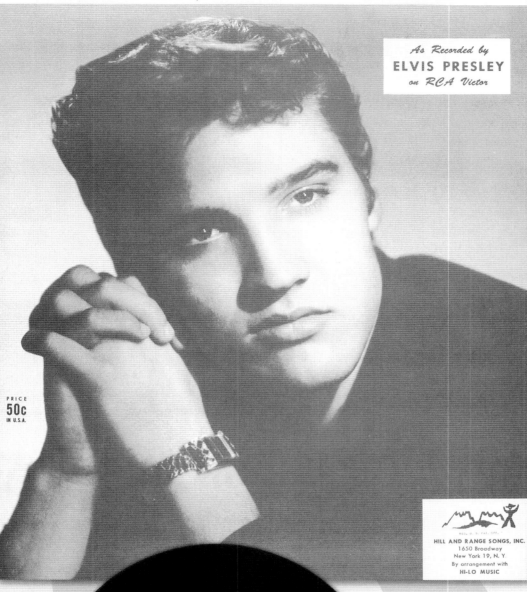

MYSTERY TRAIN

Words and Music by SAM C. PHILLIPS and HERMAN PARKER, JR.

As Recorded by
ELVIS PRESLEY
on RCA Victor

PRICE
50c
IN U.S.A.

HILL AND RANGE SONGS, INC.
1650 Broadway
New York 19, N. Y.
By arrangement with
HI-LO MUSIC

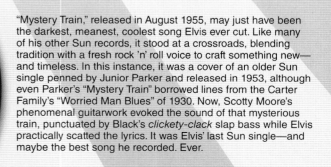

"Mystery Train," released in August 1955, may just have been the darkest, meanest, coolest song Elvis ever cut. Like many of his other Sun records, it stood at a crossroads, blending tradition with a fresh rock 'n' roll voice to craft something new— and timeless. In this instance, it was a cover of an older Sun single penned by Junior Parker and released in 1953, although even Parker's "Mystery Train" borrowed lines from the Carter Family's "Worried Man Blues" of 1930. Now, Scotty Moore's phenomenal guitarwork evoked the sound of that mysterious train, punctuated by Black's *clickety-clack* slap bass while Elvis practically scatted the lyrics. It was Elvis' last Sun single—and maybe the best song he recorded. Ever.

THE ELVIS PRESLEY SHOW

STARRING IN PERSON

ELVIS PRESLEY

WITH AN **ALL STAR CAST**

THE JORDONAIRES
PHIL MARAQUIN
FRANKIE CONNORS
BLUE MOON BOYS & Others

RCA Victor Recording Star
HEAR HIM SING
"HEARTBREAK HOTEL"
"HOUND DOG"
AND HIS OTHER GREAT
RECORDING HITS

FLORIDA THEATRE
JACKSONVILLE - FLORIDA
FRI · SAT AUG 10 - 11
MATINEE AND NIGHT SHOWS

Concert poster, Florida Theatre, Jacksonville, Florida, August 10–11, 1956.

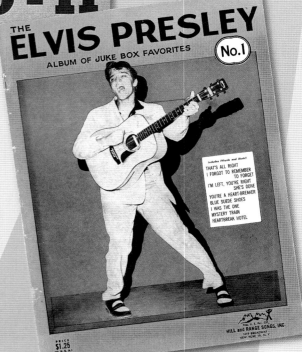

ELVIS PRESLEY SHOW
Cleveland Arena — Cleveland, Ohio
Friday, November 23, 1956
THIS TICKET GOOD 4 P.M. SHOW ONLY
SPECIAL ADVANCE SALE ADM. — $2.00
Federal, State and local taxes, if any, included
NO REFUNDS
SHOW RAIN OR SHINE
Nº 2199

ELVIS PRESLEY SHOW
Hobart Arena — TROY, OHIO
Saturday, November 24, 1956
THIS TICKET GOOD 8 P.M. SHOW ONLY
SPECIAL ADVANCE SALE ADM. — $2.00
Federal, State and local taxes, if any, included
NO REFUNDS
SHOW RAIN OR SHINE
Nº 3177

THE **ELVIS PRESLEY**
ALBUM OF JUKE BOX FAVORITES
No. 1

Includes (Words and Music)
THAT'S ALL RIGHT
I FORGOT TO REMEMBER
TO FORGET
I'M LEFT, YOU'RE RIGHT
SHE'S GONE
YOU'RE A HEART-BREAKER
BLUE SUEDE SHOES
I WAS THE ONE
MYSTERY TRAIN
HEARTBREAK HOTEL

PRICE $1.25
(M.U.S.A.)
HILL and RANGE SONGS, INC.

ELVIS PRESLEY

Blue Suede Shoes • Tutti Frutti • I Got a Woman • Just Because

EPA-747

RCA VICTOR
A "NEW" ORTHOPHONIC HIGH FIDELITY RECORDING

ELVIS PRESLEY

After three major labels bid up to $25,000 for Elvis' contract, his manager, self-appointed Colonel Tom Parker, and Sam Phillips struck a deal with RCA–Victor on November 21, 1955, for an unprecedented $35,000 plus payment of back royalties. RCA released Presley's self-titled debut album on March 23, 1956. It included five previously unreleased Sun recordings and seven new tracks. It became the first rock 'n' roll album to top the *Billboard* chart, a position it held for ten weeks.

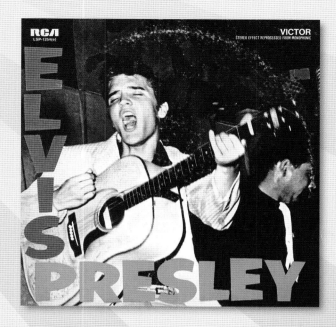

RCA   VICTOR
LSP-1254(e)   STEREO EFFECT REPROCESSED FROM MONOPHONIC

ELVIS PRESLEY

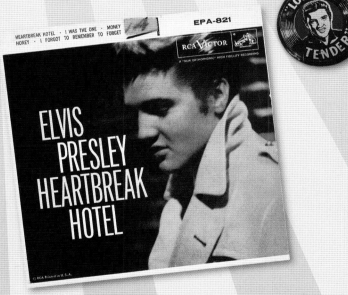

HEARTBREAK HOTEL • I WAS THE ONE • MONEY
HONEY • I FORGOT TO REMEMBER TO FORGET

EPA-821

RCA VICTOR
A "NEW" ORTHOPHONIC HIGH FIDELITY RECORDING

ELVIS PRESLEY HEARTBREAK HOTEL

Elvis first recorded for RCA in Nashville on January 10, 1956. Along with his usual backing group of Moore, Black, and Fontana, RCA enlisted guitarist Chet Atkins, pianist Floyd Cramer, and three background singers, including Gordon Stoker of Elvis' favorite Jordanaires quartet. The session produced the moody "Heartbreak Hotel," released as a single on January 27, 1956.

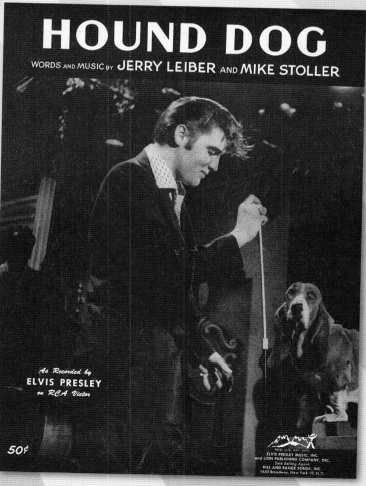

HOUND DOG
WORDS AND MUSIC BY JERRY LEIBER AND MIKE STOLLER

As Recorded by
ELVIS PRESLEY
on RCA Victor

50¢

ELVIS PRESLEY MUSIC, INC.
and LION PUBLISHING COMPANY, INC.
Sole Selling Agent
HILL AND RANGE SONGS, INC.
1650 Broadway, New York 19, N.Y.

"Hound Dog" sheet music, featuring Elvis singing to a bona fide hound dog on *The Steve Allen Show*. To appease critics and moralists, TV producers forced Elvis to sing just to the dog, hoping thus to hold his hips from gyrating and outraging the viewing audience.

Looking dapper in pink and black, Elvis Presley performs on stage in 1956. *Michael Ochs Archives/Getty Images*

By Sigrid Arnott

ELVIS INVENTED ROCKABILLY. He also invented Rockabilly Style.

Looking back at Elvis' slicked-back pompadour, two-tone shoes, baggy pants, and too-sharp suits in pink and black, he personified the classic 1950s rockin' look. But before Elvis became famous, his style was considered so outlandish and weird that it was downright shocking. As Elvis' guitarman, Scotty Moore, remembered, "When I first met Elvis, when he came to my house on that Sunday afternoon, he had on a pink shirt, pink pants with white stripes down the leg, and white shoes. And I thought my wife was gonna go out the back door. Again, just the shock, because people just weren't wearin' that kind of flashy clothes at the time. He had the sideburns and the ducktails—just a lotta hair." Kids like Elvis who were born during the austere years of the depression, and grew up during the war-obsessed 1940s, came of age with the time and opportunity to dress up—and the money in their pockets to buy the clothes. Yet adults designed the fashions marketed toward teens, which were often just sized-down, grown-up fashions, or sized-up children's play clothes. As a teen culture developed, teenagers increasingly began to create their own styles by altering or exaggerating existing fashions. Some boys might dress like their fathers did on weekends in preppy slacks and colorful casual shirts, but the more popular look of the early 1950s was rolled up drainpipe jeans or work pants, T-shirts, and boots. This look was popularized by Marlon Brando in the movies *On the Waterfront* and *The Wild One* and James Dean in *Rebel Without a Cause*, but it originated with young World War II veterans who kept wearing their tough, government-issued white undershirts, trousers, and leather flight jackets in a rebellious, anti-authoritarian way.

Teens were trying to differentiate their looks from adults, yet most kids dressed pretty much alike. So when a shy boy named Elvis showed up for shop class dressed in ruffled shirts and tailored pants, he stood out, to say the least. Classmate Red West recalled in Peter Guralnick's *Last Train From Memphis*, "He would wear dress pants every day—everybody else wore jeans, but he wore dress pants. And he would wear a coat and fashion a scarf like an ascot, as if he were a movie star. Of course, he got a lot of flak for this, because he stuck out like a sore thumb. People thought 'that's really weird.' It was like he was already portraying something he wanted to be."

Sam Phillips once said that he felt the genius of Elvis was that he had no internal boundaries: "He had the most intuitive ability to hear songs without ever having to classify them—or himself—of anyone I've ever known outside of Jerry Lee Lewis and myself . . . He didn't draw any lines. And . . . you have to be an awful smart person or dumb as hell (and you *know* he wasn't dumb) to put out that kind of thinking."

Marlon Brando's white t-shirt and leather jacket in 1953's *The Wild One* set a style for simple cool with 1950s men.

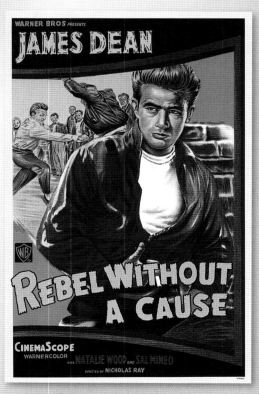

James Dean's slouch and simple red jacket made rebellion real in 1955's *Rebel Without A Cause*.

Elvis' music was more than blues songs sung by a hillbilly, or country music with an R&B feel—his best songs came because he indiscriminately steeped himself in the sounds of all the music he could find. But before Elvis had figured out how to make the "hillbilly bop" music that confused all categories, he was starting to mix up his own fashion style. Just as he equally loved gospel, country music, blues, and opera, his sartorial inspirations had no boundaries—movie stylings, work wear, cat clothes, even "feminine" ruffles and colors. After ushering at the downtown Memphis theater Loews (and no doubt admiring, maybe even studying, the movie star look) Elvis liked to walk around the corner to window shop down Beale Street. At that time, Beale was lined with churches, restaurants, night clubs, and shops, all of them owned or frequented by African-Americans. On Saturday nights, the sound of blues and R&B music poured from the local park where up-and-coming musicians played for free, or out the club doors from where big-name musicians like B. B. King performed to crowds.

It was pretty rare, however, for a white boy to walk alone down that street. As childhood friend Jerry Schilling put it, "It was dangerous for us to go down Beale Street. Our parents would have grounded us forever if they found out. It was a totally segregated society. Beale Street was black. Main Street was white." Elvis didn't go in for the night clubs or other vices—it was the sharp fashions displayed in the windows that attracted him.

The flashiest store was Lansky's, where an immigrant Jewish family from Kiev had turned a basic Army–Navy surplus store into the highest-fashion haberdashery in town. Bernard Lansky and his brother, Guy, hand-picked and later hand-tailored the sharpest fashions to attract an African-American clientele that wanted to look hot on Saturday night. And the Lanskys found their market—not just with those looking for dress up for good times—but with customers such as Count Basie, Duke Ellington, and B. B. King himself.

Bernard Lansky remembered, "As you know, Beale Street was an all ethnic street. We had all the blues singers and bands. You had the theatres down here. People used to come and walk up and down Beale Street. So, I started doin' windows. I knew how to dress windows. I started makin' real sharp windows."

In the mid 1950s, Lansky began noticing a lone white boy particularly drawn to the window but too shy to come in. "It was very seldom to see a white dude come down Beale Street to look and see what's happening. He was there 'cause he was interested in seeing what we had in the window." Finally, Lansky went out to the street and invited him in. Soon, Elvis was a regular, spending a good bit of his weekly pay on flashy shirts, bolero jackets, ruffled shirts, and dress pants. Lansky even made Elvis his first pink-and-black combos—a color pairing which at that time was considered appropriate only for women's clothes and Cadillac cars, not men's clothes.

By the time he was 18, Elvis had a job and more spending money from driving trucks for Crown Electric. He was still shy, but his clothes were definitely attention-getting. His first sweetheart, Dixie Locke, noticed him at a Christian Ambassadors meeting wearing a pink-and-black outfit with his long hair greased back, and thought, "He was just so different. All the other boys were like replicas of their dads." Dixie hinted she might want to see him again. The next time they crossed paths, he was impossible to miss attired in a black bolero jacket, black pegged dress pants with a pastel pink stripe down the side, and a ruffled shirt. Dixie saw past the flash to a rather sweet boy, but it horrified Dixie's mom who questioned how she could to go out with a boy "like that." Another family member offered her money so Elvis could get a haircut.

Elvis swept his long front hair up with pomade for a movie star look, and trained the back into a ducktail with wax. Then, in a subversive nod to his job and background, he grew out his sideburns to look all the more like a truck driver. For years, high school teachers found they just had to get used to the constant fiddling, combing, and slicking Elvis required to train his hair into his do. Still, his first employer out of school ordered Elvis to cut his hair or lose his job. What looked normal to everyone else embarrassed Elvis so much he didn't want to be seen. For his next job, Elvis found employers who liked him even after they were warned about his "off-putting" looks. They even sent him to a hairdresser, perhaps to expedite the constant grooming sessions.

In 1954, when Elvis started to perform, African-Americans were wearing flashy zoot suits they bought at stores like Lansky's, but most white musicians were either playing country music and wearing elaborate country suits, or singing pop or gospel in dress clothes. Scotty Moore and bassist Bill Black were still wearing the country suits from their former band the Starlite Wranglers as they began playing the hillbilly bop behind the ruffle-shirted Elvis. They wore their hair and sideburns closely cropped.

Black-and-white spectators became the shoes to be seen in after Elvis. These 1950s licensed shoes helped rockabillies keep the faith.

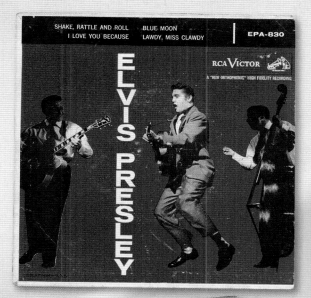

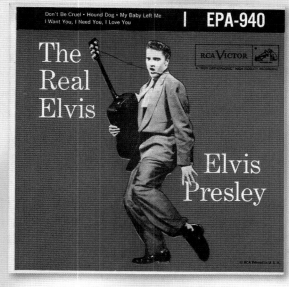

Penned by Otis Blackwell, "Don't Be Cruel" was released by RCA in 1956, backed with "Hound Dog." Within weeks, "Hound Dog" reached #2 on the pop charts, selling more than a million copies. It was overtaken by "Don't Be Cruel," which hit #1 on all three main charts—pop, country, and R&B. Between them, both songs remained at #1 on the pop chart for a run of eleven weeks. Elvis was here to stay.

Elvis Presley performs on *The Milton Berle Show* in Burbank, California, on June 4, 1956. *Michael Ochs Archives/Getty Images*

When Elvis was first on radio, his interviewers would ask him the name of his high school so listeners would not mistake him for a black man. Likewise, his producers worried that his cat clothes would alienate white audiences. For his first gig playing for a "pure redneck" crowd, Sam Phillips knew "you had better be careful looking like Elvis did and not singing hillbilly songs [if] you want to live." In one of the very first publicity photographs of Elvis, someone besides Bernard Lansky must have dressed him: He wore a plain white shirt, conservative bow tie, and an ill-fitting western shirt-jac that all looked as if it was borrowed to make him appear more acceptable to contemporary eyes. But Elvis looks determined to be himself, with his signature greased-back black hair, sideburns, and clearly visible eye liner.

With one of his first checks from Sun Records, Elvis went to Lansky Brothers to buy clothes and jewelry. Guy Lansky remembers that although Elvis had been a customer for some time, he was reluctant to cash the paycheck because of Elvis's appearance. He ran the check to the bank to make sure it was good.

Within a year, Elvis was back, asking Bernard Lansky to clothe him for his first TV appearances.

At this time Lansky didn't know "what the hell he did," but he knew his money—and his word—was good, and advanced him the clothes on credit.

Elvis's music was already gaining popularity on the radio and in traveling shows, but when the images of a leg-shaking, mascara-wearing Elvis clad in a black shirt, white tie, and loud tweed jacket was televised back to the Memphis, Lansky said, "That's my man, this guy's got to be something!"

More appearances followed in lavender shirts, alligator shoes, loud suits, baggy "booty pants" pants, and co-respondent two-tone shoes. Elvis was a white boy wearing black cat clothes in women's colors with eye make-up and hick sideburns. Sometimes handlers considered taking his appearance into their own hands, but as New York RCA producer Steven Sholes said about Elvis' sideburns—and his style in general, "I guess you don't tamper with success, I guess we'll leave them on the kid."

Elvis's "weird" clothes ended up becoming Rockabilly fashion, just as his hybrid sound inspired a whole wave of musicians to play their own boundary-breaking music. By 1957, he was named the worst-dressed man on TV. Half the world was shocked. The other half the world was ready to imitate the Hillbilly Cat. Rockabilly style had arrived—and the eyeliner was there to stay.

Elvis polishes his first Cadillac in 1956. Even when working on his car, he dressed in style. *Michael Ochs Archives/Getty Images*

With RCA on board, Colonel Tom Parker stepped up the marketing and sale of Elvis Presley as never before. Toy Elvis guitars were a hot item for youths with rock 'n' roll dreams of their own.

For the true Elvis fan, a rockabilly skirt was the height of fashion, circa 1956.

EMENEE MUSICAL TOYS
EASY TO PLAY - NO LESSONS NEEDED
ELVIS PRESLEY Guitar

I LOVE ELVIS

Song Hits MAGAZINE
OCTOBER 25¢
HIT SONGS
WIN $1,000.00 IN PRIZES
PRESLEY PUZZLER CONTEST

CORRECT LYRICS BY PERMISSION OF COPYRIGHT OWNERS

SONG HITS of Today | Leading The Way DORIS DAY | SONG HITS of Tomorrow

MY PRAYER
DON'T BE CRUEL
STRANDED IN THE JUNGLE
CANADIAN SUNSET
HOUND DOG
MORE
WHEN MY DREAMBOAT COMES HOME
YOU DON'T KNOW ME
I ONLY KNOW I LOVE YOU
GIVE US THIS DAY
BE-BOP-A-LULA

ELVIS PRESLEY

FEVER
I ALMOST LOST MY MIND
I PROMISE TO REMEMBER
SOMEBODY UP THERE LIKES ME
YOU'RE SENSATIONAL
RIP IT UP
LOVE LOVE LOVE
GLENDORA
MAMA TEACH ME TO DANCE
AFTER THE LIGHTS GO DOWN LOW
IN THE ALPS

CROWNING THE 1956 "KING OF THE BARITONES"
THE FOUR ACES — THE TOP OF THE MUSICAL DECK

ELVIS PRESLEY FAN CLUB

Elvis Presley

- MORE THAN 100 PICTURES
- PRESLEY'S COMPLETE LIFE STORY
- TRIPLE DYNAMO
- FROM MEMPHIS to TV
- EXCLUSIVE ELVIS' FIRST SCREEN TEST
- MORE THAN 100 PICTURES

25¢

WAY BACK AT THE DAWN of rock 'n' roll history in July 1954, those first notes of Sun Records #209 came blasting out of your radio like a hound dog hit by lightning. The sound of Elvis Presley's supercharged hillbilly voice singing "That's All Right" was backed by Scotty Moore's twanging golden guitar. The world would never be the same.

Plucking his Gibson ES-295, Scotty's style was part country, part Travis picking, part something totally new. Whatever you called it, that twang reverberated far beyond the radio waves. Every aspiring rockabilly had to slow down Elvis' Sun Records to 16rpm and make those sounds. And many of them saved their pennies for an ES-295.

Scotty's choice of the golden guitar seemed just right to jumpstart a new music. In the early 1950s, men wore gray

The ES-295 that made history: Scotty Moore picks his golden ES-295 backing the King in 1955.

flannel suits, Betty Crocker was the homemaker's heroine, and tailfins on cars were just a gleam in some mad designer's eyes; Gibson stood for big band jazz, Fender for country and western, and pedal steels were hot sellers. And then along came this audacious golden archtop at a time when guitars were only supposed to be *au naturel*—or painted with a funky "sunburst" if they didn't look good in their birthday suits. Whoever played a golden guitar was just asking for trouble. Gibson never planned it this way, but the ES-295 became the first rock 'n' roll guitar, as outrageous as the music it stood for.

As with many things in the guitar universe, it was Les Paul who sparked the development of the ES-295. Back in 1951, Les asked Gibson to spray one of its stock ES-175 archtops in gold lacquer for an ailing World War II veteran who was a fellow fretter. Les tells the tale:

"Mary Ford and I were playing at Wood Hospital in Milwaukee in 1951 for injured war veterans. We would carry our guitars and amps from room to room. I was playing my Epiphone 'Clunker' and Mary sang.

"One vet named Dean Davis had his head all bandaged up from a brain tumor operation, and he was propped up so he could see us. He said, 'I am a guitar player but I'll never play again because I am paralyzed down one side of my body.'

"I said, 'It is possible to play with one hand,' and told him of my car accident and how I had my arm cast in plaster so I could still play.

"I asked him what song he wanted to hear and he picked a difficult one in the key of F#, 'Just One More Chance.' I turned my amp way up and I tapped out the chords with just one hand on the fretboard, and tears rolled down his face.

"I told him that I would have a guitar made for him, any kind he liked. He said he would like a golden archtop guitar.

"Out in the hallway, the doctor told me that the vet's case was terminal and he probably wouldn't last one week. I called Ted McCarty at Gibson immediately and said I needed a guitar right now—take an ES-175 and paint it gold. He said he would make it and ship it directly to the hospital. There was no publicity intended; it was just a gift.

"Well, the guitar arrived but the vet never saw it. He died shortly after we visited him. His wife received the guitar and sent it back to me with a letter explaining of the vet's passing."

Les parked the golden ES-175 at his house for years until a friend borrowed it for just one night, during which it was lost in a nightclub fire. That guitar was serial number #A9196, registered on December 4, 1951. It was pure serendipity, but that spray-painted jazz-player's archtop became the prototype of the first rock 'n' roll guitar.

Nothing more came of that sole one-off golden guitar, although subsequently at least two other ES-175s—serial numbers #A10137 and #A10474—were given the Midas touch in early 1952. Spraying a perfectly good 175 in gold paint was either sacrilegious or just downright silly,

depending on your point of view. But then Les Paul liked things in the guitar world of the early 1950s that most people couldn't comprehend.

Still, a handful of golden ES-175s was not a production run. The true inspiration came once again from Les Paul's helping hand.

Throughout the late 1940s and early 1950s, Les had hounded Gibson to produce a solid-body electric guitar based on his own homebuilt "Log"—"the broomstick with the pickups on it," as he remembers CMI-Gibson president Maurice H. Berlin calling it. When Gibson finally changed its corporate mind and hustled to catch up with that upstart Leo Fender, Les remembers Berlin telling him that they would put his name on the solid-body and build it to his specifications. Les again:

"M. H. asked me what I wanted, and I just spurted out 'gold!' as if I'd been rehearsing it. Well, if I'd had a bomb and thrown it, it couldn't have been any worse.

"The shop foreman stood up and said, 'That's the most god awful color you could pick!'

"And I said, '*Metallic* gold!' That was even worse.

"Berlin said, 'Hold it. Now Les, why do you want gold?'

"I said, 'Gold means rich. Gold means the best.'

"Berlin said, 'Gold it is.'"

And golden it was. The new Les Paul Model was officially added to the Gibson line in March 1952.

Following in the glare of the Les Paul, Gibson created an archtop version of its solid-body electric—or a golden version of its ES-175. Thus was born the ES-295, ES standing for

Golden guitar: 1954 Gibson ES-295.

Electric Spanish and the number designation denoting the price tag of $295. The first production ES-295s—serial numbers #A10554 and #A10555—were listed on May 14, 1952, some three months after the Les Paul debut.

The ES-295 was an ES-175 with the radical features of the Les Paul Model. It used the 16-inch laminated maple archtop body of the ES-175, the same 19-fret neck with double parallelogram inlays, and the 175's cutting-edge Florentine cutaway. But here the similarities ended.

Whereas the 175 was only available in 1952 with a single P-90 single-coil pickup, the 295 featured two, covered in ivory-colored Royalite to harmonize with the gold lacquer body and gold-plated parts. In a backflip of inspiration, the twin-pickup 295 would later prompt Gibson to create its double-pickup ES-175-D in 1954.

Like the Les Paul Model, the ES-295 featured Les' combination bridge–tailpiece, a long-reach tail with the bar bridge bolting directly to the guitar top. Les had created the tailpiece in search of added sustain but a design snafu on the solid-body routed the strings *underneath* the bridge and any advantages of the new bridge were dampened. On the 295, however, the strings went over the top and added the kind of hollow-body sustain Chet Atkins would later strive for with his aluminum bridge and nut on the Gretsch 6120.

Optional features could be custom-ordered for your ES-295. A gold-plated Bigsby vibrato could be substituted for the Les Paul tailpiece, usually accompanied by a Tune-o-matic bridge. At least one 295 was fitted with black-cover Alnico pickups from the factory. And in an odd twist, several 295s exist with factory sunbursts instead of gold paint, presumably conservative-minded custom orders for twin-pickup guitars before the advent of the ES-175-D.

Les Paul remembers those early Les Paul and ES-295 guitars with fondness: "Gold was a pretty outrageous color in 1951. It didn't make you play any better—it just made you look better."

It was that look that hooked Scotty Moore: "When I was in the Navy, buddies and I would buy Japanese guitars that were so bad, the frets would wear out in three months. I came out of the Navy in January 1952, and said I'm going to buy me a good guitar.

"The first thing I found was a Fender Esquire and a little Champ amp, but I didn't keep them too long. I just couldn't hold on to that guitar—it was always getting away from me.

"I walked into the O. K. Houck Piano Company in Memphis and I saw that ES-295 all gold and shiny and I said, 'Wow, I got to have that!' I traded in the Esquire for the ES-295, which was brand new, a late 1953 or early 1954 model.

"I had the ES-295 during the whole Sun period. In July 1955, I traded in the ES-295 for a blonde L-5 at O. K. Houck.

"The ES-295 was pretty far out in looks. Everyone thought it was just neat."

But "neat" was in the eyes of the beholder. The golden archtop was outrageous when introduced in 1952, and in 1959, Gibson decided the declining sales of the ES-295 were due to that gold paint. Production was halted.

The first variant of the 295 with P-90s was built from 1952 to 1957, during which time a twentieth fret was added in 1955. The second 295 variant was built in 1958 with humbucking pickups. According to Gibson shipping totals, a total of 1,770 ES-295s were shipped and probably only forty-nine of those were of the second, humbucking variant. The sales of ES-295s were minuscule. In 1957, for instance, Gibson was selling 891 ES-175s of all type and 4,012 Les Paul Models in standard, Deluxe, and Junior form.

Subsequently, Gibson attempted to breath new life into the ES-295 by trying out some new color schemes. Gibson records show that four ES-295s were built for the music-industry's summer 1959 convention: two were sprayed Cherry Red (#A30224 and #A30225) and two in Argentine Gray (#A30226 and #A30227). But the times were still not deemed right, and the ES-295 was laid to rest.

By 1988, times had changed, and Gibson introduced an ES-295 reissue, although now fitted with chrome-plated parts, a Tune-o-matic, and Bigsby. Scotty Moore was approached concerning a Scotty Moore Replica, but nothing came of it. For several years afterwards, the ES-295 was part of Gibson's Historic Collection along with a budget Epiphone version.

The 295 fit into an odd moment in music history. In 1952, you could have bought one of those newfangled solid-body Fender Telecasters or a Les Paul Model, but they were pretty far out to invest your hard-earned dollars in. Or you could have opted for an ES-5, but they were a bit behind the times if you were playing that new music. Better off buying something traditional but with added pizzazz, like the 295. That's what Scotty Moore did, and with his golden guitar he set a style for rockabillies following in his footsteps from Sonny Burgess and Ersel Hickey to Danny Gatton and Matt Verta-Ray of Heavy Trash.

By the time rock 'n' roll was established, the solid-body concept had also been accepted, and everyone from Buddy Holly to Hank Marvin put their money down for a Fender Stratocaster. And one of the first custom colors for a Strat was Shoreline Gold.

But in the early 1950s, the choice was clear. The ES-295 had style and it had twang.

BATTLE AXE: Danny Gatton's well-worn, well-traveled, and well-loved Gibson ES-295. He bought the guitar in a Memphis shop in honor of Scotty Moore. *Steve Gorospe*

By Deke Dickerson

THE HISTORY OF ROCKABILLY music is like the other types of great American folk music—the story lies in the people who made it. Rockabilly was a burst of swagger, attitude, and unique characters, and left its mark like a meteor crater on rock 'n' roll's musical landscape.

However, if Rockabilly has its version of the Holy Grail, a physical object surrounded with mystery and intrigue, it is the EchoSonic amplifier, made by the Ray Butts Music Company of Cairo, Illinois.

The EchoSonic amp was a handmade, expensive, fragile, and temperamental device made in exceedingly small quantities for a brief time in the 1950s. The unique quality the amp had to offer was a built-in tape loop echo, and as such was one of the first commercially available guitar "effects." After testing the device, inventor Ray Butts went to Nashville to demonstrate the amp. Chet Atkins, "Mr. Guitar" of country music, bought one and immediately started using it on recordings and the radio, including his hit instrumental version of "Mr. Sandman."

Scotty Moore, who had been playing with an upstart from Memphis named Elvis Presley for about a year, heard Chet playing the amplifier live on the radio. As soon as he heard it, he said to himself—"What is it, who made it, and where can I get it?" Within a month, Scotty was in the studio recording "Mystery Train" with his new EchoSonic amplifier.

Truly obsessed scholars of rockabilly music can talk about tape echo for hours. From the regurgitating echo on Sam Phillips' Presto tape recorder to the combination of Ampex tape recorder echo and water-tank reverb on Duane Eddy's "Twangy" guitar, it's another one of those subjects that seems innocuous to the average listener, and yet holds layers of subtlety to those who can focus their ears on this important aspect of rockabilly's recorded oeuvre.

Scotty Moore's guitar sound was a seductive, mysterious thing—and completely and utterly unique. Listen to the guitar solo on "Heartbreak Hotel," the spooky intro lick to "I Want You (I Need You, I Love You)," the warped genius of the solo in "Too Much." These tracks are the Rosetta Stone of rockabilly guitar, with the EchoSonic amplifier doing its mysterious thing on these tracks. Nothing had sounded like it

before or since. Simply put, there was something magical that occurred when Scotty Moore combined his fingers with a Gibson guitar and the EchoSonic amp.

Though the specter of Elvis is always present on these recordings, it doesn't diminish the magic Scotty brought to the table—listen to Scotty's unappreciated solo on Thomas Wayne's "You're The One That Done It," and get the same goosebumps.

Chet and Scotty's influence sold quite a few amplifiers for Ray Butts, despite the fact that the EchoSonic amplifier was $500 in 1956, when one could buy a top-of-the-line Fender Twin amplifier for less than $300. Other rockabilly luminaries such as Roy Orbison, Carl Perkins, and Johnny Cash's guitarist Luther Perkins all bought EchoSonics, but none became as identified with the device as did Scotty Moore.

Within a few years of its introduction, cheaper, stand-alone tape echo devices became available, and soon thereafter, spring reverb became a standard option on most guitar amplifiers. Reverb was universally accepted as the newest guitar gizmo, and working musicians largely discarded tape echo. The EchoSonic amplifier, once regarded as an expensive luxury item for America's top guitarists, became a relic of the past, forgotten.

Like the proverbial Holy Grail, the lack of information, and the absence of physical examples made the EchoSonic a mystery, even for those intrigued with the subject. As of this writing, there has still never been a complete, working example of an EchoSonic come up for public sale, on eBay or otherwise.

After becoming friends with Scotty a few years back, he sold this author his Number Two EchoSonic amplifier, an amp few people knew existed, one he had kept as a spare.

There I was, standing with Yoda, in his studio nestled in the Tennessee hills above Nashville, and the man himself was showing how he cared for and maintained the delicate tape echo mechanism. I felt like I was in the presence of Benjamin Franklin, showing me how to use a quill pen. It was hard to breathe.

When I got the amp home, I just looked at it for about a week. Finally, I worked up enough nerve to dig out a Gibson guitar and plug it in. The 55-year-old box of wood and wires spoke back to me as I played "Heartbreak Hotel."

There it was. There was the unmistakable and unforgettable tone. It was magic, conjured out of Mississippi mud and Cadillacs and Southern preachers and wild men slapping upright basses and the smell of female and other things so intangible and yet instantly recognizable. I had found the Holy Grail.

Deke Dickerson (left) and Scotty Moore with Moore's backup EchoSonic amplifier. *Rick Malkin*

WHOLE LOTTA SHAKIN'

Carl Perkins, Johnny Cash,
Roy Orbison, and Jerry Lee Lewis

BRUNO
of
Hollywood
N·Y·C

CHAPTER 2

SAM PHILLIPS NEVER CAST HIS LOT SOLELY ON ELVIS' ASCENDING STAR.

Even when Elvis was at his zenith with Sun, Phillips continued recording and releasing sides by others. And amazingly, his other discoveries during just the years 1955 to 1956 included the likes of Carl Perkins, Johnny Cash, Roy Orbison, and Jerry Lee Lewis. Any other label would have been thrilled to find even one of these artists.

Still, even with hits on the charts by all his stars, Phillips never had the cash to juggle all their musical careers. On November 21, 1955, he sold Elvis' contract to RCA–Victor for $35,000 plus payment of back royalties to Elvis—a small sum only in retrospect but all-important to Sun at the time.

Perkins, Cash, Orbison, and eventually much later Lewis, would all leave Sun behind for larger labels and brighter lights.

STILL, ARGUABLY THE BEST MUSIC THEY EVER RECORDED COME OUT OF THE TINY SUN STUDIOS.

Carl Perkins in 1956 with the fancy Gibson ES-5N Switchmaster guitar he bought with earnings from "Blue Suede Shoes."

Born Tiptonville, Tennessee, on April 9, 1932; died January 19, 1998

By David McGee

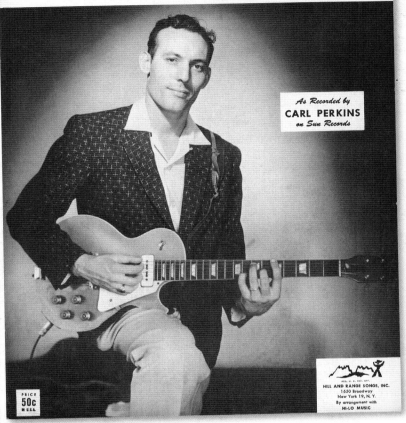

BLUE SUEDE SHOES

Words and Music by CARL LEE PERKINS

As Recorded by
CARL PERKINS
on Sun Records

PRICE 50¢
IN U.S.A.

HILL AND RANGE SONGS, INC.
1650 Broadway
New York 19, N. Y.
By arrangement with
HI-LO MUSIC

Original 1956 sheet music for Carl Perkins' hit "Blue Suede Shoes," featuring Perkins playing one of his Gibson Les Paul goldtops.

IN DECEMBER 1955, Carl Perkins stood at the edge of hope and despair, both emotions battling for primacy as his fortunes rose and ebbed in the music world. Two singles for the Sun label had failed to make any noise nationally, but had been well received in his native South. He and his band—his brothers Jay and Clayton, along with W. S. "Fluke" Holland—had steady, if dangerous, employment at the honky tonks in the Jackson, Tennessee, area, but the financial pickings of such gigs were slim indeed. Carl, his wife Valda, and their three toddler children were scraping by, with Valda taking in ironing to generate a few more dollars. Christmas was approaching, and Santa was hurting, so to speak. Carl knew he had come a long way from the cotton fields of west Tennessee, where he had spent his youth and where, at age six, had been taught the

rudiments of guitar. He was proud of his two Sun singles, but restless, in part due to his diminishing finances, but more to his sense of having written a song with the potential to change the Perkins family's life forever, and for the good. The wait to record it and let it loose on the land was excruciating.

Born April 9, 1932, in the west Tennessee cotton country of Tiptonville, with the Mississippi River almost within sight of his sharecropper family's shotgun shack that housed him, his older brother Jay, younger brother Clayton, and father Buck and mother Louise, he had come from deepest poverty to having wedged his foot in the door of the music business he thought would be his salvation from the fields, where he and the other Perkinses (picking cotton was indeed a family affair) would earn, at most, 50 cents each a day. At age six, crazy about *The Grand Ole Opry* that his father tuned in every Saturday night on the radio, and about Roy Acuff's "Great Speckled Bird" specifically, he had been teaching himself guitar on a makeshift instrument Buck had fashioned from a broomstick and cigar box. Then a fellow field hand, John Westbrook (affectionately known to Carl as "Uncle John"), befriended him, taught him his first chords and, more important, the secret of expressing his soul through his fingers: "Lean your head down on that guitar. Get down close to it. You can feel it travel down the strangs, come through your head and down to your soul where you live. You can feel it. Let it vib-a-rate." From Uncle John, an elderly black man, he

> "One day I was listening to a disc jockey, Bob Neal, from Memphis play 'Blue Moon of Kentucky' sung by Elvis Presley. Elvis was brand-new on the country scene, and I was astonished to hear the new twist to the old Bill Monroe tune. I turned up the radio and shouted to [my wife] Val, 'That sounds just like us playing! I'm goinna find out who put that record out.'"
>
> —Carl Perkins,
> *Disciple in Blue Suede Shoes*, 1978

"Blues Suede Shoes" was released in December 1955 backed with "Honey Don't."

A PRODUCT OF SUN RECORD CO., INC., MEMPHIS, TENNESSEE

learned some blues; in the fields and on the radio he was absorbing gospel and country and Bill Monroe's hard driving new music that would one day be called "bluegrass"; and on his own was meshing all these styles into something new and strange, at least to those in his immediate vicinity—such as father Buck, who recoiled the evening his second-born son proudly cut out on an energetic rendition of "Great Speckled Bird," declaring, "You're ruining Roy Acuff's music, and Bill Monroe's along with it. That ain't the way they play. You just put that guitar back up on that nail."

Instead of putting the guitar "back up on that nail," Carl continued to develop his unusual approach to expressing his soul through his fingers. Eventually Jay took up the guitar, too—as enamored of Ernest Tubb's raw-boned western swing as Carl was of Roy Acuff's traditional country and Bill Monroe's revved up country—and began working up duet numbers with Carl. The Perkins family left Tiptonville for what Buck hoped would be more fruitful labor at the Bemis Bag Co. in Bemis, Tennessee, a company community about 70 miles southeast of Memphis, abutting the larger burgh of Jackson. But Buck's poor health excluded him from the promised land of Bemis. To help support the family, Carl took a morning delivery route with Day's Dairy, a mere diversion from the big plans he and Jay had formulated, centered on an opportunity they created for themselves in a bare cinder-block structure with the words "Cotton Boll" painted in colorful cursive script on one wall. There, in the decrepit honky tonk plopped down in the middle of a cotton field, Carl, all of 14, persuaded the owner to give the newly named Perkins Brothers Band a tryout playing their music for the patrons. They went over like gangbusters, as the hard

partying "red dogs"—poor white southerners with short tempers on the best of days—ate up the bopping, thumping music Jay and Carl were laying down: sprightly treatments of Ernest Tubb's "Walking The Floor Over You," sung by Tubb dead-ringer Jay; Bill Carlisle's wildly shuffling "Rattlesnake Daddy"; even Carl's own song, "Movie Magg," a buoyant straight country ditty about working class dating mores in the deep south, received enthusiastic responses.

The Perkins Brothers' success at the Cotton Boll led to more tonk bookings in and around the Jackson area, and a rabid following for the band's "good time music," as Carl's wife Valda termed it. By 1954 the Perkins Brothers Band had expanded to include younger brother Clayton slapping a mean doghouse bass, and Clayton's good friend W.S. "Fluke" Holland beating out a solid, percussive rhythm on the side of Clayton's bass; the band's sound, too, had gelled as the result of Carl replacing his electric hollow-body Harmony—purchased years earlier on a dollar-a-week installment plan—with the most desired new instrument on the market, a Les Paul-designed solid-body, gold-colored electric from the Gibson company, purchased on a five-dollar-a-week installment plan. Experimenting with the Les Paul's multitude of tonal colors, Carl found the stinging, ringing voice that would become his signature. As these positive changes were occurring in Carl's musical pursuits, he came home one evening to news from Valda of a new record out by a Memphis artist whose approach was uncannily reminiscent of the Perkins Brothers'. The artist was Elvis Presley, and his first record, released on the Sun label, featured on one side "That's All Right Mama," an Arthur Crudup blues, and on the other, Bill Monroe's "Blue Moon of Kentucky"—the latter being performed in an arrangement similar to one Carl had worked up and used in the tonks since 1947.

"Presley nailed it," Carl recalled years later in his biography. "He jumped right in the middle of what I was doing, and the minute I heard it I knew it. I started knowing that I had a shot then, because, you know, if you record 'Blue Moon of Kentucky' by Elvis, you might record it by me, too."

Carl and the band packed up and headed to Memphis, hoping to get an audition for Sam Phillips, owner of the Memphis Recording Service studio, and the Sun label, on Union Avenue. It was October 1954. Unimpressed with Jay's Ernest Tubb-like voice ("There's already an Ernest Tubb out there."), he perked up when Carl performed "Movie Magg," describing it as "a little different type of country," and asking Carl to come back with another uptempo song in the same vein. The song was already written—"Honky Tonk Gal," a jaunty 2/4 mover the band had been playing in the tonks for some time, Carl making up verses as he went along, "thousands and thousands of verses," he recalled. Unimpressed with a stripped-down original called "Honky Tonk Gal," Sam decided he needed a country ballad to back "Movie Magg." A couple of weeks later, Carl returned with a textbook ode to tortured longing, "Turn Around," much

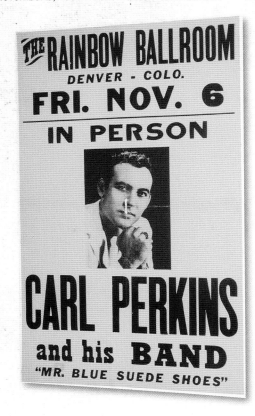

Concert poster, Rainbow Ballroom, Denver, Colorado, November 6, 1956. *Pete Howard/Poster Central*

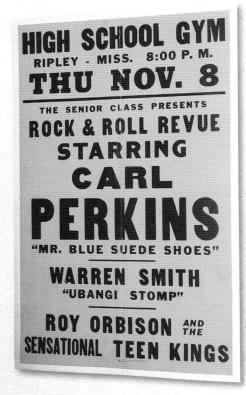

Concert poster, High School Gym, Ripley, Mississippi, November 8, 1956. *Pete Howard/Poster Central*

in the vein of a Hank Williams tearjerker, with Carl even emulating some of Williams's bluesy phrasing as he sang. Adding Bill Cantrell on fiddle and Stan Kesler on steel guitar—two of his most reliable session players—Phillips got the prototypical country weeper he was hoping for, and Carl got his first professional recording contract. Thus did the Perkins Brothers band name recede into history, to be replaced simply with "Carl Perkins" on the label and in concert bookings. At the same time, "Fluke" Holland bought his first set of drums, which would lead eventually to him being referred to as "the first rock 'n' roll drummer" by Johnny Cash, his eventual employer for more than three decades after Holland left Carl's band.

Released in February 1955, "Movie Magg"/"Turn Around" had picked up some promising airplay in the south (and in Memphis had been embraced by the town's most important disc jockey, WHBQ's wild man Dewey Phillips, the first to play Elvis on the air). With momentum gathering for Carl's debut, Sam released a second Perkins single in August, pairing the honky-themed love ballad "Let the Jukebox Keep On Playing" with "Gone Gone Gone," an uptempo burner of the sort the Perkins Brothers Band was trading on in the tonks. Compared to Carl's other Sun recordings, "Gone Gone Gone" had blown in from nowhere, a rowdy, crude, swaggering bit of hillbilly-fired R&B, pockmarked by Carl's scatted nonsense lyrics, drunken exhortations, and, for good measure, a couple of his preternatural guitar solos, which he signaled in advance by hollering to the band, "Let's go, cats!" Sam had been reluctant to let Carl record this kind of sizzling cut, fearing it was too close to Elvis's style and would result in the two artists canceling each other out commercially. But he couldn't resist the feral energy of "Gone Gone Gone," and issued it as the B side of Sun single 224. Visiting radio stations in order to promote the single, Carl heard DJ after DJ extol "Gone Gone Gone" as "the kind of music the younger people are eatin' up." From the tonks to the kids' ears—Carl knew he was on to something.

Sam's fears of his top two artists canceling each other out were short lived. Near the end of '55 RCA and Hill and Range Publishing had swooped in and, in the most famous buyout in music history, had paid Phillips $35,000 for Elvis's contract, which sum enabled the continued existence of financially bereft Sun Records.

Booked together for a show in Parkin, Arkansas, in the fall of '55, Carl and his new best friend (and new Sun labelmate) Johnny Cash sat backstage talking songwriting. Cash offered as to how an old Air Force buddy of his, one C. V. White ("I asked him what the C. V. stood for," Cash remembered, "and he said, 'Champagne Velvet.'"), was quite particular about anyone soiling his dress blues—not his parade uniform but rather his blue suede shoes.

"I had an idea you oughta write a song about blue suede shoes," Cash offered.

Finding the idea uninspired, Carl shrugged. "I don't know nothin' about them shoes, John."

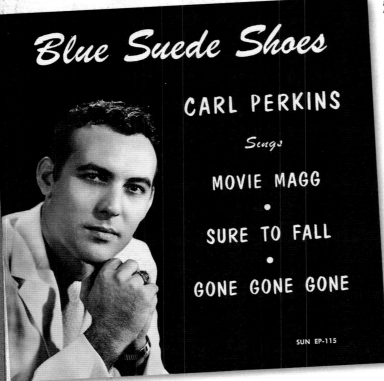

potatoes, he grabbed a pencil and began writing as fast as
the lyrics were coming to him:

But don't you
Step on my blue swade shoes.

Then, straight out of the Perkins Brothers Band's tonk experiences, came a verse:

Well, you can knock me down
Step on my face
Slander my name all over the place
Do anything that you wanna do
But uh-uh, honey, lay off my shoes
Now don't you
Step on my blue swade shoes.

In short order, another verse:

You can burn my house
Steal my car
Drink my liquor from an old fruit jar
Do anything that you wanna do
But uh-uh, honey, lay off my shoes.

Valda gave the new song her unbridled approval when Carl
played it for her at breakfast the next morning, and also cor-
rected his spelling of "swade" in the written lyrics. Carl then
brought Jay, and Jay's guitar, over from across the street to
hear the tune. Jay had trouble hitting the two-beat stop-time

A quick learner, Carl better understood C. V. White's sense
of propriety about his choice of footwear come October 21,
when the band played a Union University school dance held
at the Supper Club, an upscale Jackson nightspot. Before a
packed house of well-dressed, fresh-scrubbed college students, Carl and the band blazed away on some rockabilly to
get the room shaking. The energy coming off the dance floor,
Carl later recalled, was "electrifying."

While regrouping between songs, Carl was startled to
hear the angry voice of a young man standing near the front
of the stage, upbraiding his chagrined date: "Uh-uh! Don't
step on my suedes!"

Good gracious! Carl thought. *A pretty little lady like that
and all he can think about is his blue suede shoes.*

Returning to his home in Apartment 23D of Jackson's
Parkview Courts early the next morning, Carl couldn't
unwind. In his mind's eye he replayed the scene of the boy
lashing out at his date for stepping on his suedes. Then he
remembered Cash urging him to write a song about blue
suede shoes.

Creeping out of bed, down the cold, concrete stairs into
the living room, he made a beeline to his unamplified Les
Paul, strummed an A chord and hummed a melody he'd
been kicking around, then softly sang to it the words of the
children's rhyme, "One for the money/two for the show/
three to get ready/four to go!" Adding stop-time passages
between each phrase, he transformed "four to go" into a
slangy phrase he had been hearing the young patrons use in
the tonks: "Now go, man, go!"·

Breaking into a boogie-woogie rhythm, Carl found the
song writing itself. Emptying a brown paper bag of its Irish

The dapper Tennessee rockabilly. As Sam Phillips described Carl Perkins, he was "one
of the greatest plowhands in the world . . . There was no way Carl could hide that pure
country in him—although pure country can mean an awful lot of soul."

CARL PERKINS
SUN RECORDS

GENERAL ARTISTS CORPORATION
NEW YORK CHICAGO BEVERLY HILLS CINCINNATI DALLAS LONDON
MANAGEMENT
STARS, INC.

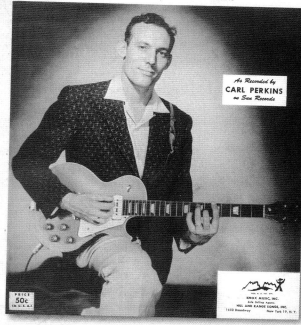

Released in February 1957, "Matchbox" was another traditional blues song revamped rockabilly style. This time, the song was adopted from an old Blind Lemon Jefferson twelve-bar blues, recorded in 1927—although Jefferson likely adapted it from earlier minstrels, too.

pauses, but eventually got them down, and at the band's next tonk shows "Don't Step On My Blue Suede Shoes" was an instant hit with the crowd, resulting in the quartet playing it eight times in one night, which had the added effect of giving the musicians a chance to lock into the arrangement. Before that show an excited Carl had called Sam and sung the opening and first verse to him over the phone.

"Sounds good," Sam said in his matter-of-fact way. "But the title's too long; it'll take up the whole label. We'll call it 'Blue Suede Shoes.'"

Carl was ready to record "Blue Suede Shoes" and get it out, but Sam counseled him to bide his time while "Let the Jukebox Keep on Playing"/"Gone Gone Gone" ran its course.

With the holiday season approaching, and he and Valda barely getting by, a humbled Carl returned to the one place where he knew he could hire on for a few days' work, take his wages and walk away. As he drove toward the Jackson city limits, he hated himself, hated his life, hated what he had to do, hated that all his years of hard work had brought him back to a cotton field. About ten miles out of town he parked, took a sack off a wagon, and headed out to pick from daybreak to sunset, "from can to can't," in the pickers' lexicon.

As Carl made his way down a row, he felt the other pickers' eyes boring in on him. "You look like that sanger," drawled one of the older ones. At the end of the day, with fifteen dollars

in hand from his labors, Carl headed home, humiliated and bitter.

"I worked on that froze ground and my hands bled," he remembered. "If that don't callous you; if that don't hurt about as bad as anything, to have some ol' farmer recognize you out there. 'Course I'd been singin' around here for years. I'd been in the tonks, everybody around here had seen Carl Perkins, everybody around here was proud Carl Perkins had a record called 'Turn Around.' Every disc jockey around here played it. And when I pulled cotton before Christmas 1955 I had *two* records. As far as the cotton pickers in this part of the country was concerned, I was a big shot. And it was embarrassing for me to hear them say, 'You just out here for the exercise?' I pulled cotton for my kids' Christmas."

On December 19, Phillips summoned Carl to the studio. The timing was right all around. A year earlier, when Carl had upgraded to a Les Paul guitar, Sam had dispensed with his Presto 6-N lathe and Presto turntable in favor of two Ampex 350 recorders, one a console model, another rack-mounted behind the console. Bouncing an audio signal between the two machines created a split-second pause, resulting in an echo effect peculiar to Sun recordings. Although he cut Elvis with heavy echo, Sam preferred Carl's vocals crisp but employed other tricks to spice up the soundscape. During Carl's second session, Sam placed cardboard boxes over the amplifiers, turned them toward the corner where two walls met and miked them from the rear. Cutting a hole in one of the boxes created a crude fuzz effect from the rattling sound. The mic placement, as Sam explained to Carl, brought sound in from the back and from the waves reflecting off the wall.

"He was right," Carl said. "It was a little hesitation, coming out of that speaker back through the amp, and the speaker was throwing the sound out against the walls. It was hittin' between those walls. He said, 'It won't do if you just put it against a flat wall. It won't sound the same.' It was picking up a little rumble sound as it made its way out. Sam was a good sound man. He'd fooled with it for a good while before he started making records with us, fooled with it with blues people, and he knew about recording. Sun Records had a little different sound to 'em. And it wasn't the room, it was the players and the equipment he had. It wasn't high-priced equipment, but there was always a little roar about the records. It's not a noticeable roar, but it's a little roar. I've always heard it in Sun records. Those cheap microphones were being overworked, probably."

The first take of "Blue Suede Shoes" was tentative, stiff. Carl changed his original lyric of "Go, man, go!" to "Go, boy, go!" and added "I don't care, baby, just what you do" before singing "but uh-uh, lay offa my shoes." Searching for some fire but managing only faint sparks, he fashioned a tepid, sloppy run on his first guitar solo. After the second verse he shouted to the band, "Go now!" and cut out on a solo equal parts chordings and single-string runs. Those once-faint sparks suddenly burst into a crackling fire, goosing the song into overdrive.

Phillips kept rolling tape. On Take 2 Carl altered his lyrics again; "Go, man, go!" and "Go, boy, go!" were transformed into the exuberant cry of "Go, cat, go!" (in recent years stories have surfaced in which reporters have attributed this lyrical change to a suggestion from Sam, but such a claim was never asserted in either Carl's or Sam's lifetimes), and the superfluous words at the end of the first verse were eliminated to produce the flowing "do anything that you wanna do, but uh-uh..." During his tough solo on the first break Carl was excited enough to exclaim, "Aaahhh, go cat!" in the middle of it all. Before launching himself into orbit on a second solo that was even hotter than his second solo on the first take, he barked out a single-word command to the band—*Rock*!" Vocally, Carl was cutting loose, singing with an easy but driving swing made all the more infectious by his total commitment to the moment. The lyrics were tighter, the instrumentalists better synchronized with each other, and the feel was fresh and lively. "Blue Suede Shoes" had the abandoned quality of "Gone Gone Gone," but also vitality quite distinct

from any other Perkins recording. Jay, Clayton and W. S. backed Carl with a bedrock rockabilly rhythm attack, and Carl's soloing was reflecting all the sources he had absorbed in sculpting this new music—country, blues, R&B, western swing, even pop. A third take proved mediocre, closer in feel and performance to the first than the second. Carl picked a rousing second solo, as he had done on the previous takes, and shouted out, "Yeeeeaahh, *them blue suede shoes*!" but then got carried away at the end of the song. Instead of chanting "*blue, blue, blue suede shoes*," hammering home the image as he had been doing all along, he varied the rhythm and reframed the chant as "*I said my blue suede shoes/Don't you step on my blue suede shoes/I said my blue suede shoes*." He was trying too hard, adding filigree where none was needed.

Carl Perkins rocks out on "Glad All Over" for the movie *Jamboree* with his band, from left, Clayton Perkins, Carl, W. S. "Fluke" Holland, and Jay Perkins.

When it was over Carl pleaded with Sam for another take, saying he had erred in shouting out "go, cat, go!" and had made "some bad guitar mistakes in there." Brooking no dissent, Sam cued up one of Carl's hot guitar solos, and announced: "Smash, smash, smash—this record's a smash." He even rang up Dewey Phillips at WHBQ and shouted into the receiver, "Carl Perkins has got a smash! *Do you hear me, Phillips!? Do you hear me!?*"

Hearing the playback of Take 2, Carl suddenly sensed the magic that had so captivated Phillips, and his objections faded away. Take 2 was beautiful: "I felt I had the best rockabilly song I had ever written. I liked the beginning and I liked the way I sang, 'Blue, blue, blue suede shoes, mmm-hmmm, blue, blue, blue suede shoes.' That was jive; that was in the pocket, shakin' 'em lose, gettin' 'em ready to play it again. I felt really good when it was played back through those cheap speakers at Sun. I had a tingle that had never been there before. I looked at Jay and Clayton and W. S. with, I know, a different look. I had to. That was the moment I had really searched for all my life. We pulled away from the studio that night aching to hear that song again. We talked about it all the way home. Jay said, 'That one might do it. You may have cut something that's gonna get someplace, Carl.'"

More significant for Carl, seventeen years of his life, from the time he had first strummed a guitar at age six, had

Concert poster, Al's State Line Club, Hobbs, New Mexico, November 22, 1956. *Pete Howard/Poster Central*

Concert poster, Strater Club, Martin, Tennessee, February 16, 1956. *Pete Howard/Poster Central*

culminated in a precious few seconds in the Sun studio. The wisdom that had guided him as a youngster—"Let it vib-a-rate"— "Keep prayin', Carl, God will hear you"—the distant dreams, the hand-to-mouth life of the tonk musician, the pursuit of the elusive commercial grail— all of it poured out onto the fretboard of the Gibson Les Paul as Carl's fingers found each note that would tell his story, make his statement in the most personal and most dramatic terms, guided, he believed, by a Divine hand. "I went off into deep water on the neck of that guitar on the second solo. Way over my head. I only knew, *Here's my shot. This is my song. It's cookin'. Get somethin' outta this box you ain't never got before.* And I did. I never had played what I played in the studio that day. Never. I know God said, 'I've held it back, but this is it. Now you get down and get it.' I felt all kinds of things going on in me, and I tore into brand-new territory. I was so nervous when it was over. When Sam played it back, it just made my fingers tingle. I'd done

pulled my guitar off and looked down at it, much to say, 'I thank my own guitar for what it did.' I felt that: 'Thank you, boy. We connected.' I knew it."

The special feeling washing over Carl as he listened to the playback of "Blue Suede Shoes" stayed with him the rest of the night. Early the next morning he walked into the apartment where he had written the song, climbed the stairs and embraced the woman he loved, rousing her from sleep. "Carl, did it come out good?" a groggy Valda queried.

Hesitating, as he listened again to the song in his mind, Carl smiled. "Valda, I've done it. I wish you could hear it."

They held each other tight, and waited.

Released on January 1, 1956, "Blue Suede Shoes" took off, a "smash, smash, smash," as Sam had boasted. Cleveland was the bellwether market, requesting another 25,000 copies no sooner than it had aired (southern disc jockeys initially were programming the single's other side, the more countrified swinger, "Honey Don't," but popular Cleveland disc jockey Bill Randle was featuring "Blue Suede Shoes" instead, to immediate, overwhelming listener response both in terms of requests and sales). There was no letup: the

MATCH BOX
YOUR TRUE LOVE
BLUE SUEDE SHOES
BOPPIN' THE BLUES
ALL MAMA'S CHILDREN

DANCE ALBUM OF ★ ★ ★ CARL **Perkins**

single kept selling and climbing the charts, on into April, peaking at #2 nationally in March with a four-week run on the Billboard Singles chart, topping many regional country charts (where it was jockeying for #1 with Elvis's first RCA single, "Heartbreak Hotel"), and becoming the rare country-to-R&B crossover hit as well. Elvis so respected Carl and his hit single that he resisted the importuning of RCA and his manager, Col. Tom Parker, to cut it as his next single; instead, RCA released it not as part of a double-sided single but initially on a four-song 45 rpm EP single and later on Elvis's debut album. Elvis's guitarist, Scotty Moore, a close friend of Carl's, confirmed his boss's intention not to steal any of Carl's thunder while "Blue Suede Shoes" was hot. "He did ['Blue Suede Shoes'] more as a tribute thing than anything else," Moore explained.

Every time Carl played the song for teen audiences, he knew that "Blue Suede Shoes" mattered in some important way even he did not completely understand. Unlike the very available Elvis, Carl, at 23, was a married father of three and far removed from the emerging teen culture embracing the new rhythmically charged music coming of age in post-war America. He understood the energy behind it, remembered the charge he got as a youngster hearing the field hands' gospel raveups and Bill Monroe's "Blue Moon of Kentucky" on *The Grand Ole Opry* broadcasts. What was unusual, what neither Carl nor anyone else had seen before, was a song of such ample dimension. Carl's exhortation to "go, cat, go!" was at once an astute summation of America's new spirit and an entire generation's rallying cry. "Blue Suede Shoes" evoked a phenomenon bigger than, but inseparable from, the music itself.

Carl had given voice to his young audience's growing fascination with fashion as personal statement, as metaphor even, much akin to James Dean's striking red jacket in *Rebel Without a Cause*. Symbols and attitudes of a new sensibility were encoded in the lyrics. However simple, the choice of words was complex in subtle ways. Drinking liquor from a fruit jar was an image straight out of the rural Tennessee of Carl's youth, whereas the proper use of "slander" in describing oral defamation was fairly highbrow for a rockabilly lyric.

Moreover, in celebrating the simple pride of ownership of a single item of clothing, the song spoke the language of the working class poor, irrespective of race, of anyone who had struggled and kicked and clawed and scratched to have one good thing, a solitary shard of beautiful light cutting through poverty's degrading, suffocating darkness. The singer drinks moonshine, not the choice beverage of the privileged, and indicates by subtext that his house and car aren't worth burning or stealing, so go ahead, knock yourself out. But the shoes—not leather but *suede*, fine, soft, elegant suede, make the man one to be reckoned with, if for no other reason than right here, right now, they are his. See and believe. Go, cat, go!

Carl and the band hit the road to promote the single, playing throughout the south and on up the east coast,

destination New York City, where they were booked for their first national TV appearance, a March 24 date on *The Perry Como Show*. Feeling the surge of "Blue Suede Shoes" at every stop, Carl was both buoyant and incredulous. He was playing bigger venues, drawing sellout crowds with no Elvis on the bill—he was doing it on his own. "The song was carrying its weight out there and they were coming to see the guy who did the record. It was my name that was on those marquees that was drawing those kids in there, and they was hollerin' and screamin' and jumpin' up for me, just like they had been for Elvis. It was *me*."

Sam dispatched Memphis disc jockey Stuart Pinkham (known as Poor Richard on the air) to drive the band from Memphis to New York in a rented Chrysler limousine, with a stop in Norfolk, Virginia, for a March 21 show. In the early morning hours of March 22, following the Norfolk show (where Carl was introduced to an aspiring rockabilly named Gene Craddock, who would soon hit it big as Gene Vincent singing the song Carl heard him perform that night, "Be Bop a Lula"), on a flat stretch of highway in an unpopulated area outside Dover, Delaware, Pinkham fell asleep at the wheel and slammed into the back of a pickup truck, killing the truck's driver instantly and launching the Chrysler into a roll. After four flips and the demolition of a guardrail, the Chrysler plunged over a bridge and landed right side up on the banks of a stream. Jay was knocked unconscious, but came to with his torso hanging out a window. Despite having fractured vertebrae in his neck and suffering severe internal injuries, he managed to climb out of the car and up the bank, where he was sitting when he was approached by "Fluke" Holland, who had awoken to find himself prostrate in the middle of the road. Other than some minor lacerations, Clayton and Pinkham were in good condition. Thanks to Fluke's quick action, Carl, unconscious and face down in the stream, was saved from certain drowning. His numerous injuries included a broken collarbone, a severe concussion, and lacerations all over his body. All were taken to the Dover hospital, where Fluke and Clayton were treated and released. When Carl was able to go home in April, his career momentum was shot. He recovered quicker than anticipated and was out on the road again by late April, with Jay's rhythm guitar spot filled by Ed Cisco, an old friend who occasionally sat in with the Perkins Brothers Band back in the Jackson tonk days.

Never again would Carl rule the Hit Parade roost as he did in the first quarter of 1956, although much of his best work at Sun occurred after his return to the active list and on through 1958, when he signed with Columbia Records. "Dixie Fried" (1956) and "Matchbox" (1957—recorded at the Perkins session that was halted when Elvis walked in, fresh from his

first, and disastrous, Las Vegas performances, and turned into the fabled Million Dollar Quartet summit) were as good as rockabilly or rock 'n' roll could get; if seen as a literary endeavor, the Perkins Sun catalogue is a vivid sociological chronicle in music of the lives, values and cultural traditions of poor southern working class whites. Instrumentally, Carl was nothing less than one of the major architects of rock 'n' roll guitar, on a par with Chuck Berry and Scotty Moore. For many years he insisted to interviewers that he had written far better songs than "Blue Suede Shoes"—"Dixie Fried" was always his personal favorite—but in 1994, four years before his death in 1998 from a series of strokes, he finally acknowledged the impact his signature song had made on his time.

"I'm so proud that a black man's nickel played my record on a Wurlitzer jukebox just like any other fella's. And I'm proud that song relieved some of their tension, even if it was only two minutes and forty-five seconds long. 'Cause I don't think anybody worried about anything when they

Sam Phillips' presents Carl Perkins' with the keys to his first Cadillac.
Michael Ochs Archives/Getty Images

was listening to 'Blue Suede Shoes.' in 1956. That song was just a very simple little ol' thing that I heard a boy say to a girl, but it was at a time in this country when the teenagers were ready for their kind of music. If it did anything to change the course of history, so be it. Maybe it made it to happen. I think it was time the engine got off idle. Some of the preachers around the south and the disc jockeys breaking our records were saying, 'This music's got to go,' or, 'It was sent here by the Devil.' I was hurtin' because I knew it wasn't. I say it makes people happy, brings back memories, plants a thought. I knew in my soul there was nothing wrong with kids getting out on a floor, dancing and getting their frustrations out through the beat. I loved it—there ain't nothing prettier than two clean teenagers out there jitterbugging. And if they want to jitterbug at my funeral to 'Blue Suede Shoes,' I might just raise up and say, 'Go, cat, go!'"

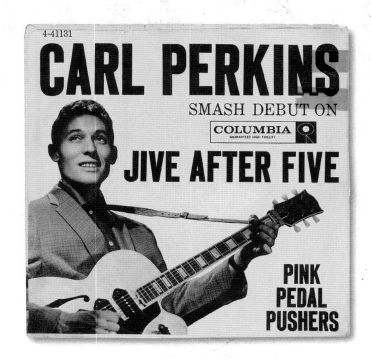

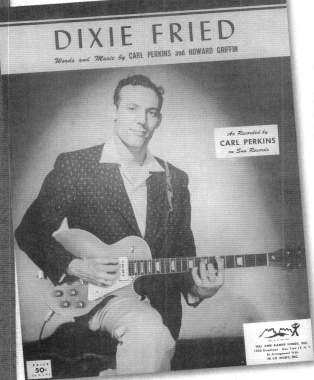

"Dixie Fried" was Carl Perkins' other masterpiece—and perhaps summed up rockabilly culture better than any song ever. Perkins joyfully sings about a Saturday night of bar-hopping, drinking, dancing, and a good rowdy fight, with the chorus an all-out shout to keep the good times rolling: "'Rave on, children, I'm with ya!/Rave on, cats,' he cried/'It's almost dawn, the cops are gone/Let's all get Dixie fried.'" Released on August 3, 1956, Perkins was obviously singing from experience. *John Ritchie Collection*

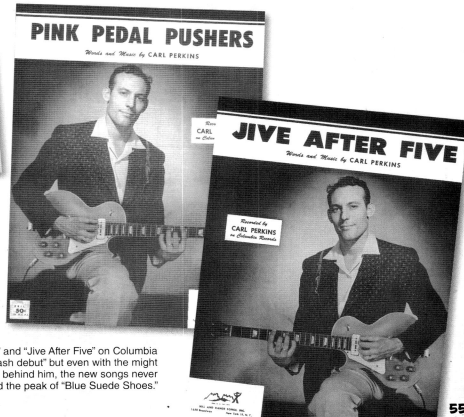

Carl Perkins' "Pink Pedal Pushers" and "Jive After Five" on Columbia may have been promoted as a "smash debut" but even with the might of Columbia's promotional machine behind him, the new songs never reached the peak of "Blue Suede Shoes."

Born Kingsland, Arkansas, on February 26, 1932; died September 12, 2003

Door-to-Door Appliance Salesman Makes Good

JOHNNY CASH

Johnny Cash tells it like it is. The faithful Luther Perkins was always at his side, armed with his favored Fender Esquire. Cash, the failed door-to-door appliance salesman, and Perkins, the auto mechanic, were a perfect pair, teamed with bassist Marshall Grant. *GAB Archive/Getty Images*

IN NEARLY FIFTY YEARS of recording and performing, Johnny Cash collected millions of admirers who included working stiffs, suits, squares, saints, felons, and freaks. Cash's mind-bendingly diverse fan base could be chalked up to his humble "Man in Black" persona, his booming vocals, and his redemption narrative, which rivaled anything from Greek mythology. But consider, too, the breadth of genres encompassed by his work.

Despite a deep knowledge of old-time gospel and his celebrated covers of modern-rock heroes recorded with Rick Rubin in the last decade of his life, "Cash, Johnny" will forever be filed under "Country." He achieved true superstar status in Columbia's country division beginning in 1958. Even the Cash catalog most admired among rockabilly fans, that amassed on his first label, Sun Records, prominently features songs by the likes of Hank Snow, Don Gibson, and especially Hank Williams—hardly surprising for a white southerner raised on prewar broadcasts from the Grand Ole Opry. What is surprising is that Cash's most successful Sun sides were original compositions (the exception being "Folsom Prison Blues," a "rewrite" of Gordon Jenkins' "Crescent City Blues") that climbed the country charts despite brilliantly stripped-down arrangements at a time when steel guitars, fiddles, and drum kits were as essential to the C&W trade as Nudie suits and Nocona boots.

In early 1955 Cash was just a few months out of the Air Force and living in Memphis when he gathered the courage to turn up on Sam Phillips' Sun Records doorstep with Luther Perkins and Marshall Grant—armed with an electric guitar and stand-up bass, respectively. (A steel guitar–playing friend, Red Kernodle, came along for that first session but left after one cut, never to return; Cash's backing band, the Tennessee Three, became the Tennessee Two.)

The trio's first release, "Hey Porter" b/w "Cry, Cry, Cry" (Sun 221) featured the sound that would most resonate among rock 'n' rollers through the ages (the first-person accounts in songs like "Folsom Prison Blues" and "Cocaine Blues" notwithstanding). Phillips' tactical use of a tape echo accentuated Cash's barrel-chested vocals. The producer and label boss also recalled threading a piece of paper through the strings of Cash's guitar to achieve a snare effect, but the world's introduction to Perkins' much lauded boom-chicka-boom rhythm tracks was equally monumental. Grant once said that the tick-tock rhythm wasn't a stroke of genius, but the only way they knew how to play. More blatant attempts at rockabilly would seem to bear this out. Cash's own recording of "You're My Baby," which he wrote for label-mate Roy Orbison, finds the songwriter falling all over the intro's stop rhythms.

By 1957 Cash was bristling in the studio under Phillips' new house producer, Jack Clement, who began arranging Cash's recordings in a manner which Phillips, ironically, had steered away from two years earlier. Cash would move on to Columbia, but not before leaving behind a selection of songs that would prove touchstones of both country and rock. At Sun, Cash didn't pander to the youth market with songs about hot rods, fast underage girls, and knife fights (he was married with a young daughter, after all), but the recordings he made in Memphis and the mythos he built subsequently have cemented his place among the giants of American music.

THE ARMORY
KLAMATH FALLS

THUR. NOV. 28
dance! show!

NATION'S No. 1 COUNTRY SINGING SENSATION

JOHNNY
CASH
and his
TENNESSEE TWO

PLUS ALL-STAR SHOW
CARL BLUE SUEDE SHOES PERKINS
and his BAND

TOUR DIRECTION, STEW CARNALL, 33 RAMETTO RD., SANTA BARBARA, CALIF.   COLBY POSTER PRINTING CO., 1419 W. Pico Blvd., Los Angeles

Concert poster, Armory, Klamath Falls, Oregon, November 28, 1957. *Pete Howard/Poster Central*

"Big River" was one of Johnny Cash's rockingest tunes from his Sun days, released in December 1957.

HIGH SCHOOL AUDITORIUM
West Monroe, La.
MONDAY NIGHT - APRIL 1
8:00 P.M.
★★★ KUZN Presents ★★★
THE
JOHNNY CASH
SHOW
"I Walk The Line" - "There You Go"
THE TENNESSEE TWO
Added Attractions...
JERRY LEE LEWIS
"Crazy Arms"
ONIE WHEELER
PAUL DOUGLAS

Concert poster, High School Auditorium, West Monroe, Louisiana, April 1, 1957. *Pete Howard/Poster Central*

"The boom-chicka-boom instrumental style suited me, and it came naturally to us. Marshall Grant was mostly right when in later years he said that we didn't work to get that boom-chicka-boom sound—it's all we could play. But it served us well, and it was ours. You knew whose voice was coming when you heard it kick off."

—Johnny Cash,
Cash: The Autobiography, 1997

Johnny Cash's first LP, released on Sun in 1957. The album was Sun's first long player.

The famed Tennessee Two: Marshall Grant (left) and Luther Perkins.

Concert poster, Minneapolis Auditorium, April 22, 1958.

Concert poster, KRNT Theater, Des Moines, Iowa, April 17, 1960.

Luther Perkins' well-travelled and well-worn 1955 Fender Esquire.
© Christie's Images, Limited 2010

THE FENDER TELECASTER was the working man's guitar par excellence. It was simple—two wooden boards, a pickup or two, some wires, knobs, tuners, frets, and a handful of screws. It was cheap. It was plentiful. And it had that sound. It's thus little wonder the Tele became one of the great rockabilly guitars.

It's also one of the great guitars, period. Perhaps no other guitar has made so much music in so many players' hands in so many styles of music. From country to jazz to blues, rockabilly to rock 'n' roll to punk

The story of the genesis of the Tele has taken on near-biblical import in the world of music due to its seminal significance as the first mass-produced solid-body electric guitar. It was by no means the first solid-body built—there were numerous predecessors, including Adolph Rickenbacher's "Frying Pan" and Electric Spanish of the 1930s, the Slingerland from Chicago, machinist genius and motorcycle tuner Paul Bigsby's pseudonymous guitars debuting in 1947–1948 to Merle Travis' design; and homemade wonders like O. W. Appleton of Brulington, Iowa, and his App guitar from 1942. And of course there was Les Paul and his "Log" of 1939–1941.

But Leo Fender's guitar was the first to be produced in volume. And thus it changed history.

It also saved Fender's fledgling company. Fender began repairing radios and then building steel guitars and a line of amplifiers that would also revolutionize music. But in the late 1940s, the company was on the verge of bankruptcy.

Leo Fender launched his solid-body electric savior as the Esquire with a first prototype in 1949. The guitar was revised and first manufactured as a production model in April 1950. Both single-pickup and twin-pickup versions were made, although the Esquire would later be offered solely with one pickup.

The twin-pickup version became the Broadcaster in November 1950. A warning from Gretsch, which had been selling a Broadkaster drumkit, forced Fender to seek a new name for its guitar. In the meantime, workers simply trimmed the words "Broadcaster" for the headstock decals and the guitar became known by later collectors as the "Nocaster." The dual-pickup version soon became known as the Telecaster.

Thanks to its trebly voice, the Esquire and Tele were ideal for cutting through the sound and fury of a band. Luther Perkins of Johnny Cash's Tennessee Two became an early proponent. Sonny Burgess traded in his Gibson ES-295 for a Tele, which he later painted his favorite color, red. Russell Willaford of Gene Vincent's Blue Caps played one, as did Paul Burlison of the Rock 'n' Roll trio, Rusty York, and Al Hobson of Warren Smith's band.

It was likely James Burton, a young guitarslinger from Minden, Louisiana, who got the most out of a Telecaster, both in terms of his own virtuosic picking and in the range of tones he was able to extract from the simple working man's guitar.

"When I first met [Luther Perkins], in 1954, he had a Fender Telecaster that had lost the plate where the heel of your hands rests and a little Fender amplifier with an eight-inch speaker, the rig he used on my records at Sun, laying his right hand on the strings to mute them as he played. That's where boom-chicka-boom came from, Luther's right hand."

—Johnny Cash,
Cash: The Autobiography,
1997

Playing alongside rockabilly singer Robert Gordon, Danny Gatton picks his 1953 Fender Telecaster onstage at the Ritz in June 1981. At various times he modified the guitar with a Charlie Christian-style pickup or a custom-made Joe Barden pickup in the neck position *Ebet Roberts/Redferns/Getty Images*

The Fender Custom Shop's relic reissue of the 1951 Nocaster. *Fender Musical Instruments Corporation*

Waylon Jennings' 1950 Fender Broadcaster. © *Christie's Images, Limited 2010*

Born Vernon, Texas, on April 23, 1936; died December 6, 1988

Roy Orbison with trademark glasses and quiff.

ROY ORBISON'S LEGACY is forever tied to ethereal vocals and wistful lyrics of the sort introduced with "Only the Lonely," released in 1960. Coming across as a sophisticated take on Bill Monroe's "high lonesome" sound, Orbison's singular voice perfectly complemented his modern ruminations on loss and loneliness. Heavyweight arbiters like working-class millionaire Bruce Springsteen and self-styled hipster Tom Waits have famously name-checked the pride of Wink, Texas, as a primary influence.

Such was the power and popularity of his 1960s work that Orbison's Sun recordings with his band the Teen Kings, all made in 1956 and 1957, are often treated as a collective footnote. Disassociate yourself from Orbison's later pop masterpieces, however, and take a moment to spin his early rock chestnuts like "Mean Little Mama" with its growled title, quavering vocal delivery, and chiming guitar break. The big drum sound propelling "Rock House," a re-read of Elvis' take on "That's All Right," is an utterly libidinal racket underscoring the power of a road-tested outfit that had honed its chops in the roadhouses of west Texas. The touchstone of Orbison's Sun catalog, however, is "Ooby Dooby"/"Go! Go! Go!." The former

was a rave-up penned by two of Orbison's frat brothers at North Texas State. Orbison and the Teen Kings' late-1955 recording of the track in Clovis, New Mexico, at the studio of Buddy Holly's manager, Norman Petty, convinced Sun boss Sam Phillips to lure Orbison and his band to Memphis. In terms of pure energy, the platter known as Sun 242 rivals anything released on the label.

Even during his tenure at Sun, hints of Orbison's future fragile balladry were evident. "Domino," the tale of a JD archetype credited to Phillips, is as close as he came to menacing, but the excitement that prevails among Orbison's Sun cuts is enough to grant him a pass on Inspiration Point fodder like "A True Love Goodbye."

A series of personal tragedies and a career downturn dogged Orbison in the late '60s. By some accounts, he began revisiting his early work around 1970. Whether Creedence Clearwater Revival's amped-up reading of "Ooby Dooby" on their stellar *Cosmo's Factory* LP of the same year triggered Orbison to reexamine his roots is open to speculation. Certainly, though, it confirmed that rock's next generation hadn't entirely forgotten the seminal work of the unassuming Texan with the Colonel Sanders horn rims.

Sheet music for Roy Orbison's rocking Sun single "Go! Go! Go!" *John Ritchie Collection*

"Ooby Dooby" by the Teen Kings
on Jewel Records

Roy Orbison and the Teen Kings' "Ooby Dooby"
on Sun, released in May 1956.

"Go! Go! Go!" was the flip side of "Ooby Dooby" and
certainly more of a rockabilly tune than the A-side
dance ditty.

OXFORD ARMORY
WED. 8:00 P. M. NOV. 14
ROCK & ROLL SHOW & DANCE
IN PERSON
"MR. BLUE SUEDE SHOES"
CARL PERKINS
ADDED ATTRACTION
ROY ORBISON
& THE TEEN KINGS
"OOBY DOOBY"
3 HOUR SHOW AND DANCE

Concert poster, Oxford Armory, Oxford, Mississippi, November 14, 1956.
Pete Howard/Poster Central

Autographed Sun Records promotional photograph of Jerry Lee Lewis, circa 1957. Even smiling pretty for the camera, he looked every inch the Killer.

JERRY LEE LEWIS

...t of Shakin' Going On" was first recorded by b... ...r Big Maybelle in 1955 before co-author and rockabilly pianist Roy Hall cut his own version later that same year. But those earlier covers pale in comparison with Jerry Lee Lewis' single, released on March 15, 1957. As Lewis later "apologized" for the song: "If that's risqué, well, I'm sorry."

IN SEPTEMBER 1956, fired by conflicting senses of Godliness and rock 'n' roll hellfire, Jerry Lee Lewis sold 33 dozen eggs to Nelson's Supermarket in Ferriday, hopped in a car, and made the 330-mile pilgrimage from the family farm to Sam Phillips' Memphis Recording Service.

Jerry Lee was raised with a fine comprehension of the dangers of hellfire. His family was staunchly religious, grounded in the Pentecostal Assemblies of God. His cousin Jimmy Swaggart would follow the righteous path—most of the time.

With visions of saintly music as accompaniment to church services, Jerry Lee's parents had mortgaged their farm to buy him a piano when he was just 8. Little did they know.

Beyond gospel music and hymns, Jerry Lee was influenced by the radio and his piano-playing older cousin Carl McVoy, who would later play rockabilly as well. Jerry Lee also snuck out with another cousin, Mickey Gilley, to eavesdrop on a black juke joint across the railroad tracks from their home, Haney's Big House. Lewis crafted his own style from all these inspirations, as well as country boogie pianists like recording artists Moon Mullican and Merrill Moore. But the piano would soon get him in trouble.

As a teenager, Jerry studied to follow his parents' wishes for him to become a preacher. He packed his suitcase for the Assemblies of God Southwestern Bible Institute in Waxahachie, Texas, where he preached and played piano for services. One Sunday, he added a bit of boogie to the hymn "My God Is Real." It was the wrong audience. After just three months of bible college, he was expelled.

With nothing now holding him back, Jerry Lee devoted himself to the piano, playing in bands at roadhouse dances around the area. Hearing Elvis, he sold those eggs and set out for Memphis.

Jerry Lee Lewis' "Great Balls of Fire" was released on November 3, 1957. Working up a sweat on "his pumping piano," Lewis' version of the Otis Blackwell and Jack Hammer tune reached #2 on the *Billboard* pop charts, #3 on the R&B charts, #1 on the country charts, and #1 on the British pop charts.

Sam Phillips was away on vacation when Jerry Lee arrived to audition. But engineer Jack Clement made sure the demos got a listen. Two months later, Phillips called Jerry Lee back, and he cut "Crazy Arms" in November 1957, which sold an estimated 300,000 copies locally.

For the next six months, Jerry Lee served as a Sun studio musician. With "his Pumping Piano," as he was listed on sides, he played on Carl Perkins' "Your True Love" and "Matchbox" as well as Billy Riley's "Red Hot" and "Flyin' Saucers Rock & Roll." Lewis also became part of Riley's band, the Little Green Men.

In March 1957, Jerry Lee's second single was released, "It'll Be Me"/"Whole Lotta Shakin' Going On." With his cousin J. W. Brown on bass, Jimmy Van Eaton on drums, and Roland Janes on guitar, they recorded "Whole Lotta Shakin'" in one take—Jerry Lee claiming he didn't even know the tape machine was running. By autumn, one million copies had sold.

Throughout his life, Jerry Lee himself would ricochet between the righteous and the wrong, his rockabilly masterpieces such as "Whole Lotta Shakin'," "Great Balls of Fire," and "Breathless" were joyous—and perhaps possessed—denials of God's message. Just as Jerry Lee perched precariously on the unstable edge of his piano stool when he performed, he too saw himself teetering on the edge of damnation. And when he'd kick that stool out from under himself to rock into a solo, it was as if the pits below had opened wide.

Sam Phillips saw Jerry Lee as his next big star after he sold Elvis' contract to RCA Victor. In truth, Sam had two stars on the verge of breaking—Jerry Lee and Billy Riley—and due to the fortunes of being a small independent record label with limited promotional capital, he had to choose between them. Phillips halted the release of Riley's "Red Hot," which he swore could also have been a hit. But Jerry Lee proved himself the right horse to bet on. At least at the start of the race.

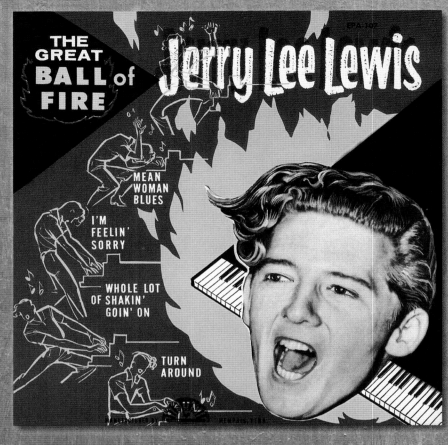

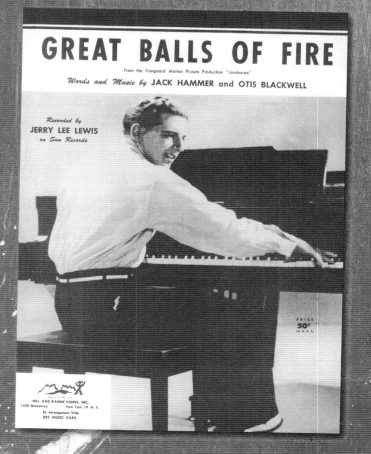

Jerry Lee was on the verge of bringing his rockabilly to England when everything went wrong. Louisiana social mores butted heads with the Old World's sense of propriety as news broke that he was traveling with his child bride—his 14-year-old first cousin, Myra Gale Brown—and that the marriage was polygamous: he was not yet legally divorced from his previous wife. Jerry Lee was crucifed by the press and fans alike.

Jerry Lee toiled in the wilderness for years thereafter. Elvis, Carl Perkins, Roy Orbison, and Johnny Cash all made the leap from Sun to the big time. But no one would have Jerry Lee, and so he was forced to stay with Phillips' label. And like many another rockabilly, he too strayed to country and gospel.

While he would resurrect his career several times, he would never quite regain the glories of his early hits.

Concert poster, Evergreen Ballroom, Olympia, Washington, July 28, 1958. *Pete Howard/Poster Central*

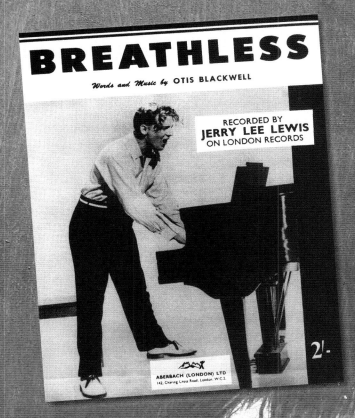

"Breathless" was Jerry Lee Lewis' follow-up to "Great Balls of Fire," released in February 1958. *John Ritchie Collection*

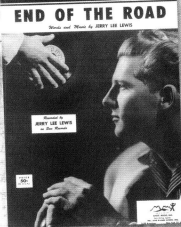

67

"High School Confidential"

JERRY LEE LEWIS

"Fools Like Me"

A Product of the SUN RECORD CO.

No. 296

Jerry Lee Lewis kicked off the 1958 crime drama film *High School Confidential* playing his title track. This rare Sun EP of "High School Confidential" was released the same year.

HIGH SCHOOL CONFIDENTIAL

WORDS AND MUSIC BY JERRY LEE LEWIS AND RON HARGROVE

SEE
JERRY LEE LEWIS
SING THE TITLE SONG IN
"HIGH SCHOOL CONFIDENTIAL"
An ALBERT ZUGSMITH Production
An M G M Release

Penron
Music Publications

HILL AND RANGE SONGS, INC.

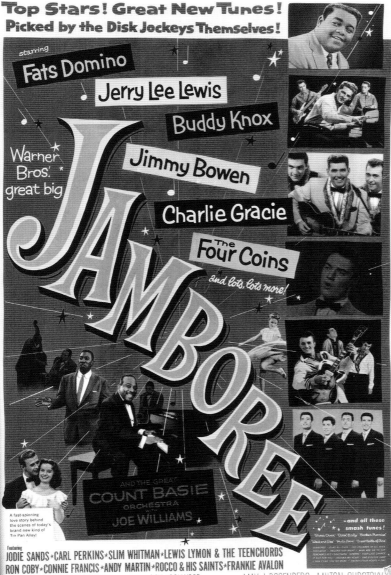

Top Stars! Great New Tunes!
Picked by the Disk Jockeys Themselves!

starring
Fats Domino
Jerry Lee Lewis
Buddy Knox
Jimmy Bowen
Charlie Gracie
The Four Coins
and lots, lots more!

Warner Bros.' great big

JAMBOREE

AND THE GREAT
COUNT BASIE
ORCHESTRA
with JOE WILLIAMS

A fast-spinning love story behind the scenes of today's brand new kind of Tin Pan Alley!

—and all these smash tunes!

Featuring
JODIE SANDS ★ CARL PERKINS ★ SLIM WHITMAN ★ LEWIS LYMON & THE TEENCHORDS
RON COBY ★ CONNIE FRANCIS ★ ANDY MARTIN ★ ROCCO & HIS SAINTS ★ FRANKIE AVALON
SCREEN PLAY BY LEONARD KANTOR DIRECTED BY ROY LOCKWOOD PRODUCED BY MAX J. ROSENBERG & MILTON SUBOTSKY

Jerry Lee Lewis

Jamboree included Jerry Lee Lewis along with rockabillies Charlie Gracie, Jimmy Bowen, and Buddy Knox—to say nothing of Count Basie and Fats Domino.

DECEMBER 4, 1956 was a day that would live in fame. During a Sun Studios recording session for Carl Perkins, other Sun stars stopped by, including Elvis, Johnny Cash, and Jerry Lee Lewis. They gathered around the piano and played a variety of gospel and traditional tunes. Sam Phillips rolled tape as they harmonized, then called the local paper for some publicity.

Memphis Press–Scimitar entertainment editor Robert Johnson rushed over to the studio, accompanied by United Press International writer Leo Soroca and a photographer. In the next day's paper, Johnson dubbed the group the "Million Dollar Quartet."

Sun Records' release of the famed Million Dollar Quartet session—which came after at least some of the cuts had been released on bootleg records in Europe.

"I never had a better time than yesterday afternoon when I dropped in at Sam Phillips' Sun Record bedlam on Union at Marshall. It was what you might call a barrel-house of fun. Carl Perkins was in a recording session . . . Johnny Cash dropped in. Jerry Lee Lewis was there, too, and then Elvis stopped by."

— Robert Johnson, "Million Dollar Quartet," *Memphis Press–Scimitar*, December 5, 1956

ELVIS' BRILLIANCE ECLIPSED MANY ANOTHER ROCKABILLY. BUT *THAT DIDN'T STOP THEM FROM REACHING FOR THE STARS.*

All across the South, other young men and women saw Elvis perform, heard him on the *Louisiana Hayride*, or spun his records on their home players. They told themselves that they too could do it. And learning that a tiny label in Memphis named Sun Records had gambled on Elvis, they hurried, guitar in hand, to Sam Phillips for an audition.

Amazingly, Phillips gave most of them a listen. Many he sent back home to their farms or jobs as gas station attendants. Some he told to hone their craft in Saturday-night juke joints, then come on back and he'd listen again.

But he also recorded many, releasing singles on them with the magic sunrays beaming from the center.

SOME SONGS FELL FLAT. OTHERS HAD THAT SPARK AND BECAME ROCKABILLY CLASSICS.

Sonny Burgess cradles his early guitar of choice—a golden ES-295.
Michael Ochs Archives/Getty Images

MALCOLM YELVINGTON

Born Covington, Tennessee, on September 14, 1918; died February 21, 2001

MALCOLM YELVINGTON was one of the country-music old guard when Elvis' rockabilly broke. Yet rather than be outraged by this new rhythm, Yelvington jumped on the proverbial bandwagon. He recorded a number of singles for Sun that rocked with a downhome beat.

Complete with pedal steel guitar, Malcolm Yelvington and his Star Rhythm Boys straddle the thin line between country and rockabilly, circa 1954. The band's single "Drinkin' Wine Spo-Dee-O-Dee"/"Just Rollin' Along" was Sun's first single after Elvis' two debut discs, arriving on November 10, 1954. *Randy McNutt*

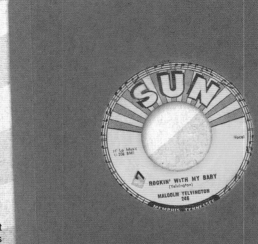

Malcolm Yelvington's "Rockin' With My Baby" was just one of his true rocking tunes. The Sun single was released on August 3, 1956.

EDWIN BRUCE WAS JUST SIXTEEN when he showed up at Sun Studios with fifteen dollars in hand to cut a personal demo. He recorded his own composition "Rock Boppin' Baby," a sublime bit of rockabilly. Bruce told historian Sheree Homer, "We started doing the demo, and the guy running the boards said, 'Hang on a minute,' and went down the hall to Mr. Sam's office and said, 'Come out here and hear this kid.'" Phillips signed him on the spot.

Sun Records promotional photo of Edwin Bruce proudly holding his Gibson ES-175 circa 1956. Bruce was just sixteen at the time—and looks it. Many years later, he became famous for penning the outlaw country anthem, "Mammas Don't Let Your Babies Grow Up to Be Cowboys." It was a long way from Sun Records, but the spirit was much the same.

"Rock Boppin' Baby" on Sun 276 was a stylish rockabilly tune, bouncing between deep-voiced moody verses and rocking choruses, jumpstarted by a stoptime interlude. The single was released on August 15, 1957.

Knox Music, Inc.
BMI
Vocal
U-263

ROCK BOPPIN' BABY
(Edwin Bruce)
EDWIN BRUCE
276
MEMPHIS, TENNESSEE

SUN RECORDS

A PRODUCT OF SUN RECORD CO., INC., MEMPHIS, TENNESSEE

Don't Let Your Babies Grow Up to Be Rockabillies

EDWIN BRUCE

Born Humphreys County, Mississippi, on February 7, 1933; died January 30, 1980

WARREN SMITH BOASTED the purest country voice Sam Phillips said he had ever heard. And despite waxing some of the finest and most quintessential Sun rockabilly sides, Smith was in truth a country ballad singer through and through. In fact, in his most famous rockabilly song, he proclaimed this rocking music foreign and exotic, to say the least.

Smith's five Sun singles were glorious rockers, including "Rock and Roll Ruby" released in April 1956; "So Long I'm Gone"/"Miss Froggie" from April 1957; and the furiously frantic "Got Love If You Want It" from December 1957.

But the song that Smith will forever be associated with is his "Ubangi Stomp," released on Sun #250 in September 1956. Smith sang that he learned his unique beat in Africa:

> Well, I rocked over Italy and I rocked
>   over Spain
> I rocked in Memphis, it was all the
>   same.
> 'Til I rocked to Africa and rolled off
>   the ship,
> And seen them natives do an odd-
>   looking skip.
> Parted the weeds and looked over
>   the swamp,
> And I seen them cats doing the
>   Ubangi Stomp.

Smith put the lesson to good use. He headlined shows all over the South, becoming a true regional star.

With the demise of rockabilly at the end of the 1950s, Smith returned to country and established his name—and likely, a more profitable career—with his pure country voice.

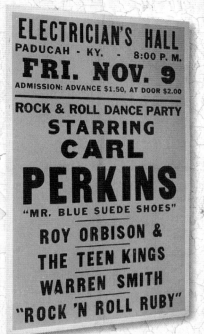

Concert poster, Electrician's Hall, Paducah, Kentucky, November 9, 1956. *Pete Howard/Poster Central*

Warren Smith's "Rock 'n' Roll Ruby" was released in April 1956. The song laid the groundwork for the rocking cliché of a girl who just can't stop dancing. According to rockabilly legend, the song was either written by Johnny Cash or penned by George "Thumper" Jones and sold to Cash for a measly $40. It would go on to be a #1 hit on regional charts, outselling early hits by Elvis, Cash, and Carl Perkins.

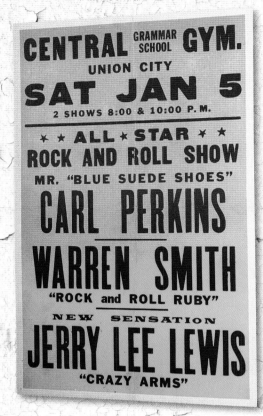

Concert poster, Central Grammar School Gym, Union City, Tennessee, January 5, 1956.
Pete Howard/Poster Central

Concert poster, Dickson Theatre, Dickson, Tennessee, May 7, 1958.
Pete Howard/Poster Central

Warren Smith's "Ubangi Stomp" was one of the great rockabilly classics. It was also a classic of silliness, telling of discovering the rockabilly beat in Africa, promoted by an African chief who spoke like a Hollywood Indian. Released on September 24, 1956, it was backed with the classic ballad "Black Jack David," which originated in 18th century England. Talk about a combination.

"Miss Froggie" was Warren Smith's ode to his woman "shaped just like a frog." Released on April 15, 1957, it was probably the end of that relationship.

Born Pocahontas, Arkansas, on October 5, 1933; died August 2, 2009

By Randy McNutt

Billy Riley could have been one of Sun's other stars, following Elvis and Carl Perkins—or so Riley himself swore to his dying day. Following up his regional smash "Flyin' Saucers Rock & Roll" with "Red Hot," Riley believed he was poised for the big time. But Sam Phillips only had the cash to promote one artist at a time, and Riley remembered him having to choose between promoting "Red Hot" or Jerry Lee Lewis' "Whole Lotta Shakin' Going On." Phillips opted to back Lewis. *Michael Ochs Archives/ Getty Images*

BILLY RILEY

IN 1954, **WHEN BILLY LEE RILEY** was twenty-one, he heard Elvis Presley's "Good Rockin' Tonight." Something stirred deep inside: Riley's foot thumped to Presley's blend of country and the blues. Even the logo on the Sun Records 45-rpm single captivated Riley. He decided to follow it to its source—Memphis.

He liked Presley's new beat sound because it reminded him of the kind of music he had been making back home in Arkansas. He didn't even know how to describe it.

Some newspapers started calling the music "rockabilly" because it sounded like a merger of hillbilly and rhythm and blues. Throughout the South, rural white boys had grown up hearing the blues sung by African-American field hands. The boys borrowed black rhythms, added a country feel, and put their own stamp of personality on the new sound. Guys like Elvis, Carl Perkins, and Jerry Lee Lewis—all Sun revolutionaries—individually pursued the emerging rockabilly sound.

Riley, a native of Pocahontas, Arkansas, came to Memphis because Sun was one of a few companies that would record the new music. Sun had made Presley a regional star; new performers believed the company might do the same for them. The only trouble was, Sun founder Sam Phillips was limited in financial, promotional, and recording resources. He could accommodate only a select few acts, and, of those, he could afford to promote even fewer.

"I guess I wasn't included," Riley said with a laugh, years later.

"But I tell you, my band *was* the Sun sound. We played on a whole lot of those Sun sessions after Sam sold Elvis' contract to RCA." Thirty years on, Riley told Associated Press reporter Joe Edwards: "We've never gotten credit for that, but it's a fact. I was doing what Elvis was doing before Elvis did it: mixing blues and hillbilly, putting a laidback, funky beat to hillbilly music."

Some thought rockabilly so outlandish, so otherworldly that it must have come from outer space. In the midst of the 1950s fear of Martian invaders, it was no surprise that this invasion from the deep South should be blamed on little green men. Witness Ray Scott's "Flyin' Saucers Rock & Roll" as recorded by Billy Riley at Sun on January 30, 1957: "The little green men taught me how to do the bop . . ." The song was such a success that Riley's band—including stellar guitarist Roland Janes, bassist Marvin Pepper, superlative drummer J. M. Van Eaton, and at times, Jerry Lee Lewis on piano—became the Little Green Men in person, marauding towns across Tennessee, Mississippi, Arkansas, and beyond with their music.

"People ask me how I ever came up with the idea to write a song like "Flyin' Saucers Rock & Roll." I tell them this: I saw one of those things. Near Indianapolis in '54, I saw something shaped like a big cigar. It was visible to others, too. That's when the flying saucer and UFO thing was in the news a lot, so I sat down and wrote a song about flying saucers and rock and roll. Now I didn't do it right away and I didn't write about exactly what I saw. I talked about little green men in the song, and, of course, I didn't see any of *those* fellas."

—Ray Scott, interview by Randy McNutt, 1987

Unlike many thin-voiced country and rockabilly vocalists, Riley boomed with a raspy voice that could be described as rockabilly soul. "Billy was simply a great entertainer," said Carl McVoy, who hired Riley and his band to back him. "He had one of the tightest bands around."

In those days, Riley was extroverted, on and off the stage. While performing across the South in 1956, he built a reputation in smalltown clubs and rural roadhouses. His performances—and antics—became legendary among club patrons. So when Jack Clement heard him, he wanted to produce a record for him. Clement, one among the earliest American independent producers, recorded Riley's single "Trouble Bound," backed with "Rock With Me Baby." Clement leased the master to Phillips for his Sun label. Unfortunately, competition for national radio airplay had already grown more competitive in the last two years since Elvis' debut in 1954. Even Riley's label mates became regional competitors. A month earlier, Sun had brought out "I Walk The Line" by Johnny Cash, and that same May, Perkins—the "Blue Suede Shoes" star—introduced his "Boppin' The Blues."

Like Sun's Sonny Burgess, Charlie Feathers, and Barbara Pittman, Billy Lee Riley was just another local performer on the nationally known independent. But that didn't stop him from pursuing a hit. In January 1957, he recorded another single, "Flyin' Saucers Rock & Roll," backed with "I Want You Baby." This time, the credit line on the record read: Billy Riley and the Little Green Men. His band turned Southern audiences on their heads.

Session player Roland Janes, who played with Riley, recalled: "The name Little Green Men came about because of the title of Billy Lee's flying saucer record. I mentioned that this would be a good name, and Sam Phillips agreed, and so it happened. I played guitar in the group. In fact, it was a trio for quite a while—guitar, bass, drums. Our band was so good due to our desire to be creative and to having a certain amount of creative talent in each of us. We also strived to be different. I consider Riley to be one of the greatest talents of that era, both musically [on record] and on stage. He would be classified as an Indian on the warpath; he had a lot of energy and charm. He was very, very good."

Reference to "little green men" came from a reported UFO landing in Kentucky a few years earlier where witnesses described the occupants as being "little green men." The incident was one of many widely reported UFO flaps that occurred across the world in the late 1940s and 1950s.

But there was more, something different about Riley's music, something enthusiastic, and frenzied. His music was explosive, unchecked, rebellious, and hard-edged. He forged it in Memphis bars in the mid- to late 1950s, when he was hired as a Sun session player. It was Riley who played bass on Lewis' "Great Balls of Fire" as well as on other Sun releases. He also played drums, guitar, and other instruments. But he didn't make his name from behind the scenes of the record business. He made it as a performer—well, at least to those who remember him today.

Again, Riley's record didn't hit nationally. It came at rockabilly's most turbulent peak. In September 1957, he followed with another rocking single, "Red Hot," backed with "Pearly Lee." Despite its regional popularity, the record failed to gain a foothold on the national charts.

A disappointed Riley retreated to the clubs around Memphis, experimenting with rockabilly and taking it to the next level—dancing rock 'n' roll.

He said today's fans have some misconceptions about his career. For example, he said, it was Sun singer Billy "The Kid" Emerson—and not Riley, as some people believe—who wrote "Red Hot," and rockabilly singer Ray Scott who wrote "Flyin' Saucers." Riley added, "Many people think I wrote both of those songs. Sometimes people write and say things that happened, and they know they're not the truth. If somebody says something about me that's bad, I don't care. Long as it's right."

In the region where Tennessee meets Mississippi and Arkansas, Riley continued to attract a dedicated club following. He looked like he could be a rockabilly star—trim and muscular, with slick black hair. He wore a sly smile, a fitting look for what fellow Sun vocalist Malcolm Yelvington called "a wild young man." As Yelvington said of Riley: "He played bass, drums, guitar, harmonica—about anything. Billy was a nice guy, but one with an I-don't-care attitude . . . carefree. But he was a solid musician."

Riley hired singer Dickey Lee as a second vocalist for the Little Green Men. "I recall that he used to do a lot of instrumental stuff," Lee said. "His band just rocked. Those guys were fantastic pickers, and they lost the mold when they made Riley. He was a wild man on stage. He had the greatest rock band that ever came out of Memphis, but he was overshadowed by Jerry Lee Lewis and some of the other artists who got more publicity at Sun. Billy Lee, well, he was your authentic rock 'n' roller."

Riley's creativity and talent helped him land a job as a session player for Phillips. One day, when Jerry Lee Lewis had reservations about recording a song with possible hellfire connotations, Phillips launched into a philosophical discourse on religion with the young singer-pianist. Riley listened to both sides of the discussion, then said, "Let's cut it, man . . ." His impatience spilled over into his music. He was the template for today's rockers, complete with a penchant for hard drinking and rocking. The story goes that he once got drunk and dumped wine all over Phillips' recording equipment.

For a time Riley quit backing Sun's stars; he later returned. He recorded other Sun records,

none of which made much money. "We had respect for each other," he later said of Phillips, "but we never did get along too well . . . He knew I had the band that could work with anybody, and he needed us."

Disgusted with his stalled recording career, Riley finally left Memphis for Los Angeles in 1961, as rockabilly was declining in popularity in Memphis and America. He soon found work as a session player in California. But he continued to make his own records. When the Beatles hit in the early 1960s, Riley recorded a harmonica album for Mercury called *Billy Lee Riley . . . Harmonica . . . Beatlemania.* The back cover features candid photographs of Riley smoking a cigarette and laughing in the studio, and blowing a harmonica while holding two others.

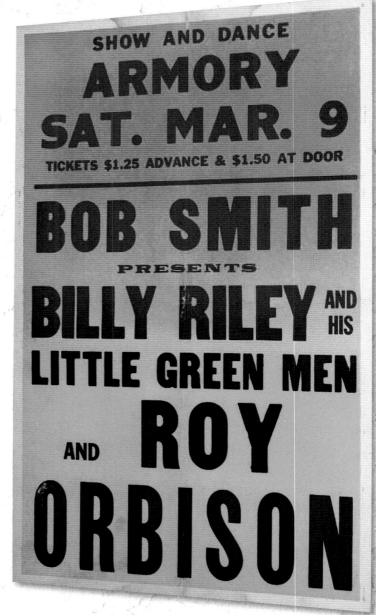

Concert poster, Armory, n.p., March 9, circa 1956.
Pete Howard/Poster Central

Years passed. Rock 'n' roll changed. Only Riley remained the same—a soulful rockabilly picker. He returned home and recorded for some Memphis record companies, but little happened. Then in 1973 Chips Moman called. The hot Memphis pop and soul producer offered Riley a recording contract, which Riley saw as a vindication of his ability. Moman didn't use second-rate talent.

At the time, Riley was living in Arkansas again, working as a contractor doing painting and interior decorating jobs. "I was just an old rock 'n' roller from Memphis—half hillbilly and half rock 'n' roll," he said with a laugh. "I just couldn't relate to heavy metal."

Moman's new CBS-distributed label, Entrance Records, released Riley's single, a Tony Joe White song called "I Got A Thing About You Baby." It stayed on *Billboard's* chart two weeks, peaking at number 93. "We had big hopes for that one," Riley said, "but it just didn't happen. What can I say?"

In 1979, he was invited to perform at a Memphis music festival. Thirty thousand people heard him sing. He was asked for three encores. He wanted more.

Encouraged, he decided to move to Nashville, where he made some records on his own. He traveled to Europe to play for appreciative crowds. He even started writing a book about his rockabilly days.

"The thing that I did was contribute," he said. "I didn't get credit for it."

Billy Lee Riley died in 2009.

May he forever rock and roll.

Billy Riley and His Little Green Men in action. The band essentially became Sun Studios' house band and appeared on numerous recordings from 1956 through 1959. *Ebet Roberts/Redferns/Getty Images*

Born Newport, Arkansas, on May 28, 1931

By Craig Morrison

Sonny Burgess and the Pacers tear up the stage in 1955: The band was widely reputed to have the best rock 'n' roll show anywhere at the time. From left, pianist Kern Kennedy, Burgess, drummer Russ Smith, Jack Nance, Joe Lewis, and Johnny Ray Hubbard. *Michael Ochs Archives/Getty Images*

SONNY BURGESS WAS BORN IN 1931 near Newport, Arkansas. He and his band, the Pacers—Joe Lewis (guitar), John Ray Hubbard (bass), Kern Kennedy (piano), Jack Nance (trumpet), and Russ Smith (drums)—made great rockabilly records for Sun starting in 1956. His powerful voice, strong guitar playing, leadership abilities, and solid, affable personality have made him a legend and a major presence on the international rockabilly scene.

SONNY BURGESS: We opened for Elvis in 1955. Elvis suggested that we go to see Sam Phillips. So in the latter part of '55, we went to Memphis. Sam said, "Add a couple more pieces and come back." We had the typical four-piece band. So we picked up Jack Nance, a trumpet player.

Joe Lewis came up with the name. He flew airplanes and there was a Piper Cub airplane named the Pacer. We wound up with Sonny Burgess and the Pacers. We were playing six nights a week back then. Joe was only 17, still going to high school, playing football. He was making more money than his teachers, playing music. We played the Silver Moon and a lot of other places. One job was in Louisville, Kentucky, in a country club, a debutante's ball: $5,000 for 30 minutes in 1956. That's a lot of money. Then we drove back to Memphis and did the Rainbow Terrace Room for a high school dance.

We had the best show band you've ever seen. It was like a three-ring circus. At the end of the show we'd jump off the stage, no matter how high, with our instruments, still playing. Four of us would jump off: me and Johnny Ray, Jack, and Joe. Russ and Kern would stay up and keep the rhythm going. We opened for Marty Robbins, Ray Price, and Maddox

SUN RECORDS

Brothers and Rose one time in Little Rock at Robson Auditorium. We jumped off that damn stage and we didn't look and we jumped into the orchestra pit, about 10 foot down! Johnny Ray's bass came all to pieces. The bass was not electrified back then. I had a 50 foot guitar cord and later Joe had a 50 foot electric bass cord. We had them made. You get out there in the audience. Jack was playing the trumpet so he didn't have anything to worry about.

We'd go through the records, the 78s, at the radio station. I found Smiley Lewis's "One Night of Sin" and the other side is "Going Home." Our manager was the assistant manager at the radio station, and we'd practice there. The only two songs we ever practiced on when we went to Sun to record were "Red Headed Woman" and "We Want to Boogie." When you hear the record it sounded like we never practiced at all! "Going Home" had a good feel to it and we'd get to singing and we'd jump off the stage and roll around. John Ray would lay down on the bass, Joe would straddle him. Jack would stand up on the back of him playing the trumpet, and I'd grab the neck and pull it around the dance floor. We destroyed that bass two or three times. Or we'd fall all over, roll on our back and kick our feet up, still playing. Now if I fell on my back I couldn't get up!

The bug was one of our big deals. We got the audience to participate. When Roy Orbison played the Moon, he had the original Teen Kings, and they did the bug dance: the big bass player and the little rhythm, and Roy and the mandolin player. And the drummer kept playing. I said, "I like that." We had all of our guys do it except Kern, the piano player; he always kept the rhythm going. Russ could get up off the drums and do a little bit but normally it was the front four that did that. Johnny Ray or I would reach down and act like we're picking a bug up off the floor. We'd look around at the guys and throw it on one of them. He'd start scratchin' all over, tryin' to catch that bug, and jumpin', doing whatever he wanted to do. Then he'd catch it finally and throw it on

another guy. After we got through all of us then we'd throw it on somebody in the crowd and they'd start. It was a great gimmick.

When we went to Sun and recorded "Red Headed Woman" and "We Wanna Boogie," our first two, we actually recorded "One Night of Sin." When Elvis did these four shows and we opened for him, we were doing it. It was our most popular song. The women loved that song. It had suggestive lyrics. Elvis heard it and decided he would record it, which he did. It turned into "One Night With You" because they couldn't get "One Night of Sin" played.

CM: He actually recorded both versions.

SB: That's right. He copied us to a T on the original version too: same way, same guitar, everything. He heard it live; I don't guess he ever heard the recording.

I first saw Elvis—just him and Scotty and Bill—at Porky's Rooftop [in Newport] in early '55. He didn't have much of a crowd to start with. He just had "That's All Right Mama" but I'd never heard nothing like it. Scotty on that guitar created some unheard-of sounds, like Jerry Lee on the piano. Elvis was nothing vulgar, he just felt the music. Hey man, this is different. And this is good." He did three hours maybe four. In clubs back then you couldn't get away with one hour. The people from Europe didn't believe that. We had some boys come over here a few years ago to see Larry Donn and he booked them in Bob King's. Larry and I said, "We've got to do four hours." They'd already blown their repertoire in one hour. We never done the same song twice, memorized everything. We could play most anything.

Porky's Rooftop was on top of his drive-in restaurant. Front Street wasn't clubs but joints. Every lady showed up there to see Elvis: all of a sudden it's full of women. And I seen him at the Moon, he filled it with Wanda Jackson and Bud Deckelman. She had a white dress with all the fringes, the shimmy, the first time I'd ever seen one. Man she looked good. Of course Elvis was after her. The next time he was back at the Moon again, and then we went to Bob King's in December of '55, right before he went with RCA Victor. By then he had added D.J. Fontana.

I also went to Bono [Arkansas] to see him, the first time I ever seen Johnny Cash. Johnny had just come out with a record and he was opening for him in the Bono gym. It was Johnny, Luther, and Marshall; they were under the goal there. They wouldn't let the audience dance, because it's a gym floor and they didn't want 'em scratching it up. They stood up in the stands on either side where you watched the basketball. That's how sock hops started: make them take off their shoes. Then Elvis came on.

We went to Memphis to see him a couple of times. We saw him with Hank Thompson when Hank had a 10 piece band, three fiddlers. It was really good. The star was Carl Smith, good-looking guy. Elvis was the second artist out. Carl Perkins was the first; first time I ever seen Carl. Carl

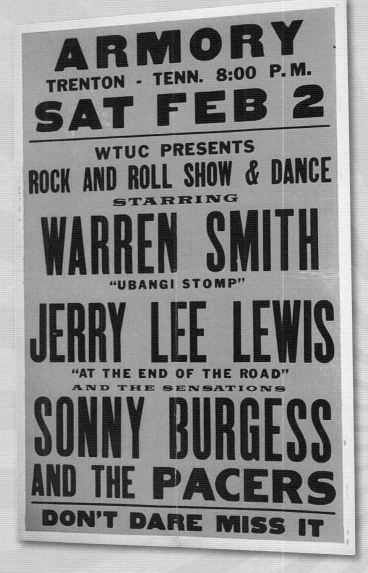

ARMORY
TRENTON - TENN. 8:00 P. M.
SAT FEB 2
WTUC PRESENTS
ROCK AND ROLL SHOW & DANCE
STARRING
WARREN SMITH
"UBANGI STOMP"
JERRY LEE LEWIS
"AT THE END OF THE ROAD"
AND THE SENSATIONS
SONNY BURGESS
AND THE PACERS
DON'T DARE MISS IT

sounded more like a black artist than anybody outside the blacks that Sun ever had, his guitar playing, singing. The last time I seen Elvis was in Memphis when he was in the army, and he was still a real nice guy. I don't know what he was later on. I never went to Vegas or anywhere where he was at.

CM: Did seeing Elvis perform cause you to change anything?

SB: Yeah, you wanted to be like that. Everybody in the world tried to play like Scotty on the guitar, and nobody ever captured that sound he had. Everybody tried to sing like Elvis. He could really sing back then. Sun caught him better than anything he ever done at RCA. RCA never caught him as good as he was. At Bob King's in 1955, he did "Only You" and it had just come out. He had to do it three times that night, and he never recorded the song, but he could flat sing it. Then he said, "Here's a new song that's just come out, it's got great lyrics: wop bop a lop, a lop bam boom, tutti-frutti."

We saw Jerry Lee first in '56 in Helena, at the Catholic Club—the Catholic Church has a little hall there. Bob Neal had a package show and he said, "I want him to play on the show, he's got a record coming out." It was the Ray Price song, "Crazy Arms," his first big hit. He had J.W., his father-in-law—he wasn't yet at that time—with him on rhythm guitar, and that was all: piano and rhythm guitar. J.W. played bass later. I said, "They need drums. Russ, go out there." Russ Smith played with him and later on, when the Pacers broke up in early 1957, he hired Russ to play drums. We'd never heard nothin' like that. Nobody had. He was playing entirely different and could really sing too. Every piano player in the world copies him. He ought to be honored simply on that reason alone.

Jerry Lee's secret was his left hand. He had the best, strongest left hand. He could keep that rhythm going and do all this stuff with his other hand, which the other guys can't do. He put on a good show. He got wild. He tried to take his clothes off in Memphis one day on a Sunday. Got on stage and started taking his clothes off, and they come out and carried him off. Back then he made all of his shows. He's a good guy. I don't know the reason why he doesn't show up when he's supposed to. He's probably got problems, who knows? But he was different. Perkins was a little different. Cash come along with that tick tick tick and that deep voice: perfect. If he'd had just a regular country band, I don't believe Cash would have made it. If Elvis hadn't had Scotty and Bill at that time, I don't think he would ever have got to RCA. It was simply they created that sound.

CM: Part of it was Sam Phillips. How was it to work with Sam?

SB: Sam had that slapback echo which he added to everything. Sam was alright! He just turned the tape machine on, let it run. You'd do what you wanted to do and he'd say, "Well, let's try it again."

CM: How would you like to be remembered?

SB: "He had a good time, he got to see a lot of people and do a lot of things because he recorded for Sun Records." That's the only reason we're all still around. That was the top of the heap back then. All we wanted was to get that 45 out on Sun. It didn't matter if it sold or not.

CM: We always hear about the red hair and clothes. Was that because of the song or had you seen somebody do that before?

SB: No, I always liked red. Red and black are my favorite colors. Elvis was pink and black. Perkins had the blue suede shoes. I got a pair of red suede shoes. I had red socks and a red suit. We had red tux jackets, and I had the pants that went with them. The band had black pants and red tux jackets. I cut my hair fairly short then, kind of a half burr cut. I was reading about a guy named Shell Scotty, a detective in pulp magazines, and he had white hair with black eyebrows. I thought that would be really cool, different. So me and my wife, Joann, decided to bleach my hair white. We were heading out to California that week to join the tour with Cash, in '57 or '58. We put bleach on my hair and it turned orangey-red. Not bright red but orangey-red. It lasted till it grew out.

One of the best bands I ever heard and one of the best showmen I've ever seen was Ronnie Hawkins. He wasn't a great singer but he could put on a show. He'd do anything. He'd keep you laughing. He always had great bands. They played like he wanted them to. We'd run out to the Moon to hear him, we'd run home, practice for a week. We never could get that sound, but he'd make us practice. I said, "how do you do it?" He said, "In the first place, get real good musicians. We practice eight hours a day for two or three weeks before we go out to play." When he hit that stage it was marvelous. He had that moonwalk like Michael Jackson: the Camel Walk; it looks like he's walking but he's standing in place. Got it off some black guy he told me. Then he wrote "Odessa," about a hooker in West Helena, Arkansas. But he was character. We first met him in Fayetteville; he was going to school there. We were doing a fraternity dance and we thought we was hot and they kept saying, "Hey, we've got this boy out here, he can sing." So we got him up and all he'd done was Carl Perkins and Roy Orbison songs. He was good back then but he got a lot better later on. He tried to play guitar; he couldn't play a lick.

Orbison travelled a lot with us from '57 through '59. His band quit him so he was with us. Somewhere on tour, Orbison said—he had that squeaky voice—"Did you ever hear of Ronnie Hawkins? We played there, them kids wanted to hear him sing. He did every one of my songs before I got on stage." Roy Orbison was a character too, he was funny. He travelled 50,000 miles with us for three years, never volunteered to buy a nickel's worth of gas. In Kansas City, Missouri, we got a room for the four of us with two beds, the cheapest we could get, and Orbison goes and gets a cot to bring in with us. We were walking on beds. Elvis kept $100 hidden in his billfold, to have something to get home on.

It was the best time in the world, because everything was new. Everybody was coming out with something that was a little different than what everybody else had. A lot of the music today I like but you don't know who's doing them. They've got no style. They all sound just alike.

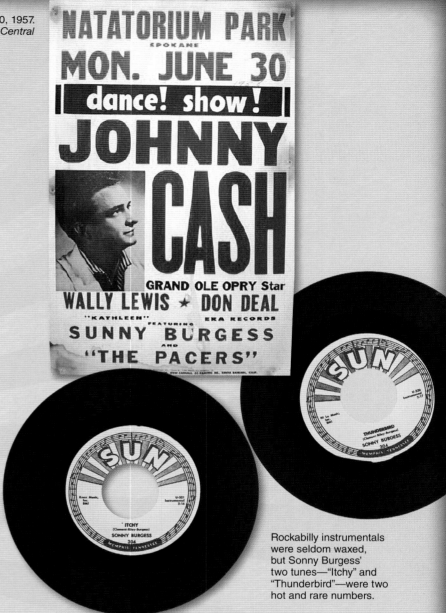

Concert poster, Natatorium Park, Spokane, Washington, June 30, 1957.
Pete Howard/Poster Central

Rockabilly instrumentals were seldom waxed, but Sonny Burgess' two tunes—"Itchy" and "Thunderbird"—were two hot and rare numbers.

"The young singer leaped high into the air and screamed and the crowd of rhythm-hungry teenagers screamed back, for this was the signal that Sonny Burgess and the Pacers were fixing to really start rockin'. At some time during every performance the entire band is very apt to plunge out into the middle of the crowd and perform all sorts of gymnastics from human pyramids to Indian dances. During these unscheduled exhibitions the music tends to become faster and faster until both the Pacers and the audience are almost to the point of exhaustion. Then and only then will they return to the stage to conclude the number. Some of the trips into the crowd have been known to last as long as thirty minutes without stopping."

—Sam Boyce, Arkansas booking agent, 1956

Born Myrtle, Mississippi, on June 12, 1932; died August 29, 1998

By Robert Gordon

Charlie Feathers and His Musical Warriors—Jody Chastain, left, and Jerry Huffman—were one of the tightest rockabilly and country bands in Memphis. *Michael Ochs Archives/Getty Images*

flowered shirt, the brightest ornamentation is the pouch of Red Man chewing tobacco poking through the top of his chest pocket. Despite the fact that it's August, his Christmas lights are still up, the sign of a man thinking about both the past and of things to come.

"Rockabilly is the beginning of the end of music," the genre's greatest enthusiast pronounces. "It is the *onliest*. It'll be the last, there's no more after rockabilly."

It's a grand statement with an elusive meaning, but the subject is getting Feathers worked up like an evangelist in a gin joint. He has to pause, partly to gather his thoughts and partly because he's had a lung removed recently (that's why he chews instead of smokes his 'bacca) and he's not supposed to get palpitated. But words frustrate Feathers, because they limit him.

"It's-just-no-more-music," he says, his hands punctuating the rhythm of the sentence to drive home the point to his congregation of one. "Rockabilly comes from cotton patch blues and bluegrass music. Ain't nothing else exciting left, you see. I seen some guys the other day on the television. They're sickening to me. I watch them boys with the big hats on, *unh-uhmmm*. The world ain't gonna move backwards!"

Some would say Charlie himself needs to study this last statement. His rockabilly cohorts found success when they moved to rock 'n' roll (Elvis, Jerry Lee, Carl Perkins), country (Johnny Cash) and the sappiest pop ("The last band Elvis had was dime a dozen. Get 'em anywhere, he was just singing because he already had it made. The dad gum rockabilly made him."). Charlie stayed with the dad gum stuff, working new ideas into the old genre: He has just released his first ever major-label record, part of the first installment in the distinguished American Explorers Series and includes an updated version of his "I Forgot to Remember to Forget," which became one side of Elvis' first major hit.

THE REBEL INN IS ON HIGHWAY 78, once a major thoroughfare linking Mississippi cotton land to the delta's big city of Memphis. The old motel's neon sign no longer functions properly, and the parking lot these days is more of a teen hangout than a place for weary motorists. James Earl Ray is said to have slept in the Rebel Inn the night before he shot Martin Luther King.

Conspiracy has long haunted Charlie Feathers, who lives on a dead end street behind the motel. The rockabilly great never really made it, never became the star that might seem natural for a friend and inspiration to Elvis Presley. Feathers' modest house is not very different from any other on the block, but is worlds away from the stature of Graceland, the mansion of the rock 'n' roll King.

Beneath a shade tree in his front yard, Charlie is seated in a black rocker. Wearing a faded

It is more than 35 years since Elvis Presley released his first rockabilly record. "Blue Moon of Kentucky" was a fusion of blues and bluegrass, and Charlie Feathers feels he's never received proper credit—for bringing the song to Elvis, for coaching him on his vocals, for helping fuse the genres. He was hanging out at Sun before Elvis or any of the other hillbilly cats came along, talking shop with Sun founder Sam Phillips and trying to tune his being to the music both men heard in their heads. Feathers demoed material for the label, and wrote songs, including "Gone, Gone, Gone," and "Get With It."

Feathers speaks conspiratorially when discussing why fame has eluded him. Sam Phillips passed on his "Tongue-Tied Jill," so Charlie took it across town to Meteor and had a minor hit. "Sam said he was going to hurt me, and he did," says Charlie. "He said that because I left after Elvis left. He could see hisself going out of business."

The reasoning seems far-fetched; Sun still had Johnny Cash and Carl Perkins on its roster. But Charlie is ablaze, his face all the redder against a full head of white hair and thick white sideburns. He accuses Phillips of withholding his best material. "Sam's-got-the-main-cut," he says about songs recorded 35 years ago, believing they'd be hits today if enough people could hear them.

For the first time in decades, as many people as desire can hear his new album. *Charlie Feathers* is a slam-bang rockabilly record, pairing him with former Sun session men. It's got its feet in the past and its head in the present. "We Can't Seem To Remember To Forget" mourns the passing of rockabilly, Feathers singing "That time it slipped away/And that's something we don't want to forget." The irony is that Charlie wanted to record it with his son's band, giving it a more modern punch.

Feathers' voice is itself like a band. The hiccups, yips and other vocal accents punctuate his lines like guitar fills, adding depth and excitement. He keeps your attention by switching from a growl to a whisper. ("That's your rockabilly when you slow it down, lower it. The dynamics! Music is made to make you sit up, so damn much stuff going on.") His oddest vocals are on "Uh Huh Honey"—he begins in a voice thick and deep like cypress swamp water, then takes flight with Ralph Armstrong's piano solo and breaks the treetops like ducks escaping the hunter.

But Feathers is not all gimmicks. For the verses to Hank Williams' "(I Don't Care) If Tomorrow Never Comes," Charlie contrasts the weary tone of a downhearted, abandoned man against a tender but propulsive rhythm section (Stan Kesler, a regular Sun bassist, and J. M. Van Eaton, Jerry Lee Lewis' drummer); at the chorus, he gives the song a twist, looking on his loss as a freedom and singing like a new man. Chris Isaak's guitarist could take a few lessons from Roland Janes' swampy vibrato.

Feathers is the first to admit—to insist—that *Charlie Feathers* is not a pure rockabilly album. "Rockabilly ain't got room for drums," he says. "That train song, 'Pardon Me Mister,' me and my son Bubba run through it down there and it was so outstanding with just the rhythm and the electric guitar. They put the drum on it and killed it." All songs deserve such lovely deaths.

Beneath the tree in his front yard, Charlie has turned the rocker so as not to spit tobacco juice on his guest. He is still talking about the possibilities in rockabilly, illustrating it with a dream project of recording an album of ten different versions of "Roll Over Beethoven." "They say on [*Charlie Feathers* liner notes] I won't do a song twice the same way. Yes I will, if they say that's the way they want it. I'll do it another way if they don't say nothing. I could cut 'Roll Over Beethoven' ten different ways with ten different voices. I can mess around with a song, man."

"He's so far into music that he is, in my opinion, a genius," says Ben Vaughn, who produced the new album. "Like we think of jazz greats: Sun Ra, or Mingus or Monk. No one expects an abstract thinker to come out of rockabilly. But that's exactly what Charlie is. He's never given up on rockabilly and he continually redefines it in his mind."

Feathers remains a devoted apostle of Elvis Presley's, despite his contentions of unrequited appreciation. Challengers to the throne are met with disdain. "Elvis sang so damn hard man. People think of the Beatles and all that—*ohh-hhnnn*. Any mama that washes dishes in the kitchen could sing the same way the Beatles did. 'La la la.' It's not singing from down here [the stomach]. They could stand there and sing 30 days and 30 nights, and never hurt theyselves."

Charlie pauses, and when he continues, his voice is lower, softer, as if someone might overhear. He told Ben Vaughn that Elvis was half-black, and he tells me, "The truth never came

Rockabilly survivor: Charlie Feathers at home, weeks before his death in 1998. *Trey Harrison*

> "Rockabilly is different. Nothin' can touch it, man; and it don't take a big band to do it . . . a lead man and a good acoustic rhythm and a big slap bass. Can't beat it, man! The simpler, the better."

> —Charlie Feathers

out about Elvis. I don't believe Vernon was his daddy. He kicked Vernon out of the house the minute his momma died. Elvis wasn't black-headed, you know that. He had albino hair, yellow as a baby duck. He'd play a show, the minute the show would end, he'd run to the bathroom, wet his hair down with water. If it started drying, it'd kick up like a little yellow baby duck. That's the truth. And his nose was down just like that, flat. I think he done something to his nose later on. I don't want to say too much about it."

Elvis died, but Charlie Feathers has seen rockabilly rise from the grave. "Craziest damn thing I ever seen is this music business. You don't think nobody cares, and yet you meet people from all over the damn world, they come here and they care and they know. I don't understand it man, I do not understand it. I got a song that Dean Martin could sing and it would be a smash hit. I got one right now that Jerry Lee—I went out there and give it to him. He never listened to it, he never heard that son of a bitch. In two weeks time I guarantee that he would have a #1 hit in the nation. . . ."

Beads of sweat have formed on Feathers' forehead, whether from the afternoon sun or the heat of the conversation. Rosemary Feathers, Charlie's wife, has served us sweet tea and the ice is now melted in the glasses. A bird dog in the neighborhood is baying and it sounds like a car alarm. "I'll always write songs," says Charlie. "I'll be laying in there and I know damn well I'm asleep, but a whole damn song will go through my mind." Charlie's dream world is rockabilly heaven, where the ideas remain fresh, even when rooted in the past. In this other world, rockabilly is king and Elvis lives behind the Rebel Inn. "I don't understand why I can't quit. There's got to be another world beyond this one, man. I open my eyes, by the time I get up, damn, somehow or another it'll slip away from me."

Charlie Feathers was disappointed with his lack of success at Sun, where Sam Phillips saw him as purely a country singer. So, Feathers tried cross-town rival Meteor. He told Phillips he was only cutting a demo and would be back, but Meteor released "Tongue-Tied Jill" on #5032. The song was a phenomenal rockabilly single—as well as a bizarre one. It hailed Jill for her speech impediments, including backwoods diction and stuttering. But true love seemed to have won out.

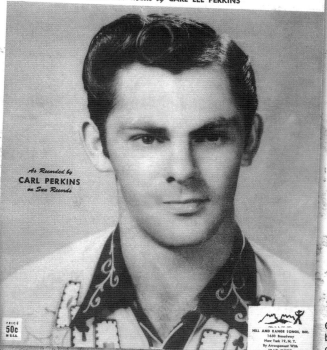

Charlie Feathers didn't write "Blue Suede Shoes," of course, but a rare misprinted sheet music edition featured him on the cover instead of Carl Perkins. *John Ritchie Collection*

Like Edwin Bruce's "Rock Boppin' Baby" and Gene Vincent's "Be-Bop-A-Lula," Charlie Feathers' "Can't Hardly Stand It" on King was a moody masterpiece. With reverb-sodden guitar and Feather's echoing voice complete with his trademark hiccups, he pleads for his woman to be faithful. It was a scary song of barely concealed violence.

CHARLIE FEATHERS: "A lot of folks talk about the early days, but not many [of them] were really around then. But I *know* what I'm talkin' about, man, 'cause I was *there*. Memphis, '54, '55. Hey, Carl Perkins used my band when he come to Memphis. I cut before he did. I worked on a lot of the Sun Records artists' records as an arranger and player. I started out as a kid who liked Bill Monroe. He was my favorite. I *love* bluegrass. My first instrument was a mandolin. I tried to play like Bill Monroe. A lot of bluegrass music is done fast. Back years ago, people had an upright bass and a fiddle around the house. They'd start poppin' that ole bass. All they done down here, see, was that poppin'. The cat-gut strings had a unique sound. Gives you plenty of bottom. Sounds great. Then somebody put that cotton-patch blues with bluegrass and created rockabilly. Guys slipped away and picked. Dee-dee-dee-dee-dee. Most people music I ever heard in my life. But what really made those early rockabilly records was slap-back, man. I don't like gimmicky things done with the voice, drenched in echo. No way. Now you listen to those early records. As far as I'm concerned, man, Elvis died in '55. It was unbelievable that sound he got earlier, on 'Mystery Train' and those other records. Slappin' bass. Slap-back. No drums. What a sound! Right off the floor and onto the record. What a presence! Those records sound so 'out front.' They really explode. Yeah, man."

Interview by Randy McNutt
Memphis, Tennessee, June 1987

"Wild Wild Party" on Memphis was Charlie Feathers at his rocking finest. With vocal acrobatics over an R&B-laced guitar line, it was pure exuberance. As Feathers sang, "It was a wild, wild party and now I know we were lucky to be alive."

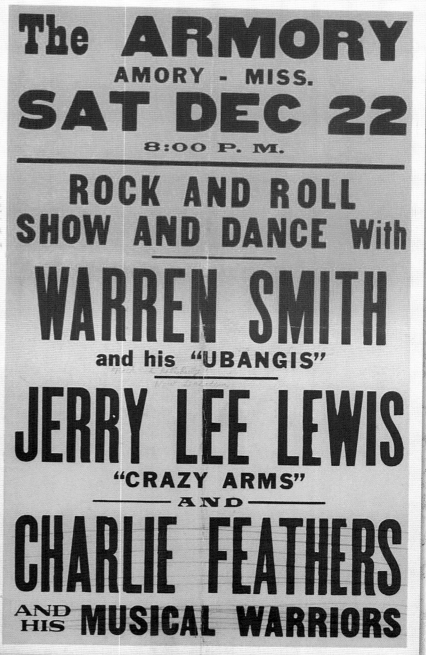

Concert poster, Armory, Amory, Mississippi, December 22, 1956. *Pete Howard/Poster Central*

Born Melbar, Kentucky, on October 31, 1934; died November 29, 1979

LIKE MANY ANOTHER ROCKABILLY, Ray Smith began as a country musician, emulating the likes of Gene Autry and Tex Ritter. Inspired by Elvis, in 1956 he formed his band, Ray Smith and the Rock 'n' Roll Boys and played across the country.

The consummate rockabilly: Ray Smith complete with sequined western jacket and Martin guitar. *Michael Ochs Archives/Getty Images*

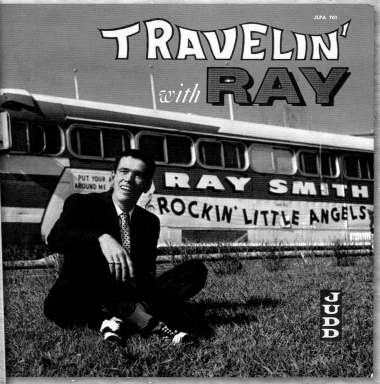

Ray Smith's album *Travelin' With Ray Smith* on Judd Records (here in reissue form) was one of the few period rockabilly LPs.

Rare DJ promo white-label copy of Ray Smith's "Travlin' Salesman" on Sun 372. The single was released on November 21, 1961. Rockabilly was largely history, but Smith rocked on.

Displeased with his lack of success at Sun, Ray Smith moved to Jud Phillips' Judd Records and "Rockin' Little Angel." Released on January 10, 1960, it peaked at #22 on *Billboard*'s Hot 100.

AT JUST AGE SIXTEEN, Carl Mann hit the big time with his rockabilly-tinged recording of "Mona Lisa," released on Sam Phillips' Phillips International label. This earned him the distinction of being Sun's youngest artist to sell a million records.

Publicity photo of sixteen-year-old Carl Mann issued upon release of his Phillips International hit, "Mona Lisa."

CARL MANN
Phillips International Records

Carl Mann was just fifteen when he recorded his first single, "Gonna Rock and Roll Tonight"/"Rockin' Love" in 1957 for the near-forgotten Jaxon Records label. Sam Phillips soon signed him to Sun.

Carl Mann's version of Nat King Cole's "Mona Lisa" became a rockabilly hit on Phillips International, peaking at #24 on the Black singles chart and #25 on the Billboard Hot 100 in 1959.

Gonna Rock and Roll Tonight

CARL MANN

CHAPTER 4

THE STORY OF ELVIS' FIRST ROCK 'N' ROLL SESSION HAS BECOME LEGEND,

taking on near-biblical import. It's a modern-day creation myth at which rockabilly emerged, fully formed.

Yet other rockabilly musicians recall the music being in the air at the time and state that if it hadn't been Elvis, it would have been someone else. The time was right. There were decades of rollicking country boogie, honky tonk, western swing—not to mention blues and R&B—in the air, nearing a flashpoint, all ready to ignite into rock 'n' roll.

In retrospect it seems impossible that it could have been anyone but Elvis. And yet there were many other bands across the South playing hot-rodded country music, blues, and R&B. Some became famous, such as Buddy Holly. Others remained regional favorites, riding the wave of their local hit song while it lasted, then returning to their regular jobs down on the farm or pumping fuel and washing windshields at the corner gas station.

With swank tuxes and stylish ties, the Rock 'n' Roll Trio looked little like their true selves as Tennessee brawlers-turned-rowdy-rockabillies. Still, the grins here certainly had a devilish twinge to them. From left, lead guitarist Paul Burlison, rhythm guitarist and singer Johnny Burnette, and bassist–singer Dorsey Burnette. *Michael Ochs Archives/Getty Images*

THE ROCK 'N' ROLL TRIO was rockabilly at its finest. The group was rough and tough, fast and furious; they exploded onto the scene, cut a handful of classic records, and were gone as quickly as they arrived. The trio never had a chance to sell out or change its tune, and thus remains 100% pure, undiluted and distilled rockabilly.

The band formed in Memphis as the Rhythm Rangers as early as 1951. It included the Burnette brothers, Dorsey (born Memphis, Tennessee, on December 28, 1932; died August 19, 1979) and Johnny (born Memphis, Tennessee, on March 25, 1934; died August 14, 1964). They were joined by lead guitarman Paul Burlison (born Brownsville, Tennessee, on February 4, 1929; died September 27, 2003). Together, they shared a love of music and fighting. Using juke joints and roadhouses as a practice spot for both interests, the Burnettes eventually graduated to become Golden Gloves boxing champions.

When they weren't brawling, they were playing music. The trio performed on Memphis' KWEM radio and at hillbilly roadhouses on the outskirts of Memphis, playing country, bluegrass, and downhome blues—all with a fighter's swagger. They lived nearby a contemporary of theirs, young Elvis Presley, who was enthralled by their singing and picking but reportedly scared off by their love of duking it out with most anybody available.

The details of trio's first recording session are clouded by time. It took place in the mid 1950s at the Von Theater in Booneville, Mississippi. The threesome was rounded out by steel guitarist Al Vescovo (and sometimes, fiddler Tommy Seeley). The Von label was likely run with the theater's owner Sam Thomas. The session funded by Bill Bond (father of upcoming rockabilly Eddie Bond) who sought to manage the band, or radio DJ and fellow performer Buddy Bain. Either way, their first single was released in 1955 and featured Johnny's rockabilly-flavored "You're Undecided" backed by "Go Mule Go." But the green-labeled Von 1006 was not even a regional hit, selling fewer than 200 copies.

Legend has it that the trio auditioned for Sam Phillips, who famously turned them away, saying they sounded too much like their friend Elvis. Dorsey remembered, "We took Sam Phillips some songs and he turned 'em down, but they weren't very good anyway." Johnny later told TV Radio Mirror that they auditioned "Go Mule Go" for Sun Records but were chased back onto the street when the fiddler's bridge broke. Yet Burlison didn't remember auditioning for Phillips and said the incident of the broken fiddle bridge took place during the Von session. If they didn't audition for Sun, it would be surprising—the only budding young rockabillies in Memphis not to. No Sun audition tapes have ever surfaced, although Phillips often recorded over old sessions to reuse expensive tape.

The trio joined local country legend Doc McQueen in his Swing Band in 1954, which had a regular gig at the infamous Hideaway Club in nearby Middleton, Tennessee. Along with playing in the larger band, the Rhythm Rangers also performed during intermissions. Still, they all needed to supplement their music pay. Johnny held odd jobs, hawking appliances door to door as Johnny Cash also did, hustling as a repo man and debt collector; he also served as a deckhand on Mississippi River barges. Both Burlison and Dorsey worked at Memphis' Crown Electric Company, where Elvis was driving a delivery truck.

The Rock 'n' Roll Trio at New York City's Pythian Temple during the band's May 7, 1956, recording session for Coral Records. Even in this photo, the bandmates seem to have a hard time keeping still. *Michael Ochs Archives/Getty Images*

The Rock 'n' Roll Trio first single on Coral Records was the sublime rockabilly classic "Tear It Up," released on May 26, 1956. The song lived up to its title.

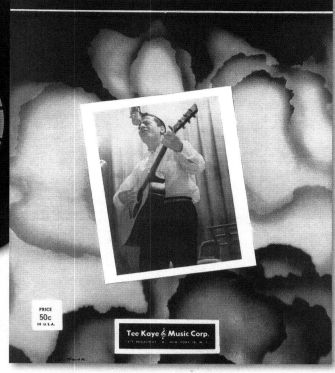

Recorded by JOHNNY BURNETTE and THE ROCK 'N ROLL TRIO on CORAL Records

TEAR IT UP
Words and Music by JOHNNY BURNETTE, DORSEY BURNETTE and PAUL BURLISON

PRICE 50c
IN U.S.A.

Tee Kaye Music Corp.

In February or March 1956, Burlison and Dorsey were laid off, so the trio decided it was time to try to strike it big. They decided to drive to New York City to play music and get electrician jobs via the union there. They stopped off briefly to telephone Doc McQueen and say they wouldn't be playing in the band that weekend. McQueen told them, "Oh well, if y'all make it big, let me know."

Driving though a blizzard, they arrived at last in New York, where they got rooms at a YMCA. Paul and Dorsey found jobs as electricians while Johnny worked in the garment district. They also sought an outlet for their music. They tried out for Bert Parks' *Stop The Music* show but were turned down. Hearing word of Ted Mack's nationally syndicated *Original Amateur Hour* television show, they joined the cast of hopefuls for the Wednesday night auditions. With Elvis recently signed to RCA–Victor, "the Rock and Roll Boys from Memphis," as they became known, were viewed by the show's producers as possible stars. They won three straight appearances in April and May 1956, garnering them a slot on the finalists' tour in September 1956.

Henry Jerome, a bandleader at the Hotel Edison, saw the trio on TV, and offered to manage their future. He got Johnny a daytime job as an elevator operator at the Edison and moved the trio into the hotel from the YMCA. He then got them a contract with Decca's Coral Records division. Burlison later said they made a mistake by signing so quickly with Coral: "Capitol Records was after us, ABC Paramount, Chess, and Decca. I wanted to go to Capitol, but [Jerome] said it didn't matter: a hit record would make us rich."

Jerome now sought to polish up the band's name. Johnny recommended "The Burnette Brothers," to which Burlison joked they should be called "The Burlison Brothers." They compromised on the somewhat generic, but perfectly descriptive "Rock 'n' Roll Trio."

On May 7, 1956, Coral's A&R director Bob Thiele led the trio to the Pythian Temple in New York City for their first recording session. The old studio was legend: Bill Haley and His Comets had cut "Rock Around The Clock" here. A grand, barn-like building with great natural echo, it was ideal for rockabilly.

The trio was booked to be backed by the 32-piece Dick Jacobs Orchestra and they recorded a first song, George Motola's suave "Shattered Dreams." The track came out sounding like a Broadway tune at its worst. Jerome and

Thiele then turned the session over to just the trio. The orchestra was sidelined, although they were paid union scale of $41.25 each to sit and watch. Orchestra drummer Eddie Gray sat in with the band (and studio sheets indicate famed session guitarist George Barnes may also have played with them). The trio cut four more tracks that were pure, unadulterated rockabilly.

Coral released a first single on the trio in May 1956, featuring "Tear It Up" backed with their old Von cut "You're Undecided." They then headed out on the road in Dorsey's '55 Ford, making appearances on *Steve Allen's Tonight Show*, Dick Clark's *American Bandstand*, and Perry Como's *Kraft Music Hall*. The first Coral single was a strong seller in Boston and Baltimore, but failed to make the national charts.

In July 1956, the Rock 'n' Roll Trio was back in the studio. Coral sent them this time to Owen Bradley's famed Quonset Hut studio in Nashville, where the band was filled out by members of Bradley's A-Team of session musicians, including bassist Bob Moore, big-band drummer Farris Coursey, and guitarist Grady Martin. Bradley himself added piano to several tracks.

The four-day session was incredibly fruitful, resulting in several singles and the tracks that would fill out the band's famous LP. In August 1956, Coral released a second single on the trio: "Midnight Train"/"Oh, Baby Babe." It was followed in October 1956 by a third single, "The Train Kept A-Rollin'"/"Honey Hush." During summer 1956, they toured with Carl Perkins and Gene Vincent as part of the Ted Mack Touring Show and appeared at the finale of the *Original Amateur Hour* at Madison Square Garden. Jerome also signed them with the General Artist Corporation, which booked them at state fairs and on package tours.

After the trio added drummer Tony Austin to better duplicate their Nashville-session singles, Jerome began billing the group as "Johnny Burnette and Rock 'n' Roll Trio." Putting Johnny in the spotlight added to the factitious and fight-prone relationship between the brothers. Dorsey had sung lead on several songs, such as "Sweet Love On My Mind" and "Blues Stay Away From Me." Finally, following an autumn 1956 show at Niagara Falls that ended in a brawl between the brothers, Dorsey quit. It was the beginning of the end.

Johnny and Burlison quickly hired bassist Johnny Black, Bill Black's brother. Dorsey, meanwhile, launched his own Dorsey Burnette and the Rock 'n' Roll Trio, which set off on a Southern tour.

By 1957, the trio had basically split apart. Johnny recorded a session on March 22, 1957, with Grady Martin on guitar. Coral released yet another single in December featuring "If You Want It Enough"/"Rock Billy Boogie" from the July 1956 sessions. Yet the band here was listed as simply "Johnny Burnette."

By Fall 1957, the trio was no more. Johnny and Dorsey both were pursuing solo careers, although they'd join forces occasionally, at least once including Burlison.

In all, the Rock 'n' Roll Trio truly lasted just one year, but the music they made remains.

Like his younger brother, Dorsey Burnette was also a boxer. He was also an electrician—as was Paul Burlison. Both worked at Memphis' Crown Electric Company, where a young Elvis was a delivery truck driver.

Concert poster, Armory, Amory, Mississippi, October 11, 1956.
Pete Howard/Poster Central

Johnny Burnette was pure energy. He worked odd jobs, from loan repo to Mississippi River bargeman as well as Golden Gloves boxer—all while trying to make it as a rock 'n' roller. Here he's pictured in a later Liberty Records promotional shot.

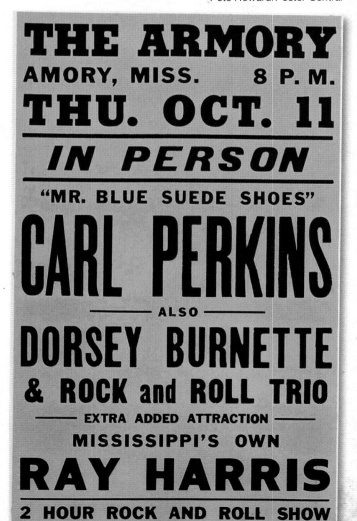

The Rock 'n' Roll Trio liked train songs. "Lonesome Train," released on January 5, 1957, was hard-charging rockabilly.

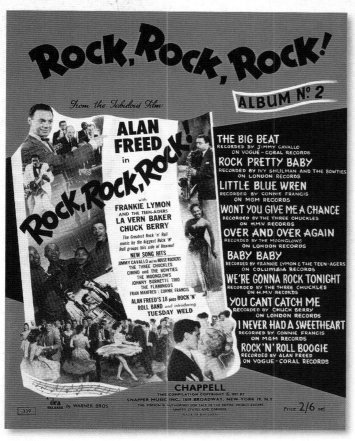

Songbook from the film *Rock, Rock, Rock!* featuring the Rock 'n' Roll Trio minus Dorsey Burnette. The elder brother quit the band weeks before filming due to never-ending disagreements with Johnny. As a replacement, the band hired Johnny Black—Elvis' bassist Bill Black's brother.

Rare Coral soundtrack single from *Rock, Rock, Rock!* for the Rock 'n' Roll Trio's "The Train Kept A-Rollin.'"

The Rock 'n' Roll Trio's famous eponymous debut LP was released on Coral Records in December 1956. Collecting prime cuts from several sessions, it remains perhaps the greatest rockabilly LP of all time.

Rock, Rock, Rock! soundtrack.

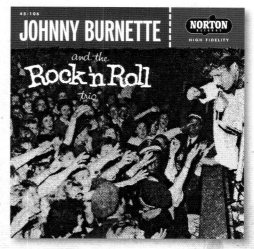

Live recording of the Rock 'n' Roll Trio from the Paramount Theatre in Brooklyn in 1956, released on Norton Records.

PAUL BURLISON

Born Brownsville, Tennessee, on February 4, 1929; died September 27, 2003

By Craig Morrison

THE ROCK 'N' ROLL TRIO WAS Johnny Burnette (1934–1964) on vocals and acoustic guitar, Dorsey Burnette (1932–1979) on vocals and upright bass, and Paul Burlison (1929–2003) on electric guitar. They began playing together in 1951 and their recordings from 1956 are rockabilly gems. When they toured, they added drummer Tony Austin. And when Dorsey quit, he was replaced by Johnny Black, the brother of Bill Black who played with Elvis.

I met Paul in 1982 at his home in Walls, Mississippi. He was welcoming and friendly and happy to reminisce, lighthearted, with an easy laugh that bubbled up frequently, the tempo of his speech accelerating when he got excited telling a good story. We talked for hours, about his first guitar instruction from a black neighbor when he was 10, his years of playing on the radio, starting in 1949, with Shelby Follin, Howlin' Wolf, the Doc McQueen band (which included the Burnette Brothers), and much more. While talking about his influences and guitar style, we passed his guitar back and forth, playing for each other.

Burlison's career had many of the steps that other rockabillies went through: music at home, meeting other musicians in the community, working in a trade (Burlison was an electrician), joining bands, playing on the radio, recording for an independent label, performing on television, getting signed to a manager and a major label, touring, appearing in a film (Alan Freed's *Rock! Rock! Rock!*), few if any hit records, personnel changes and the break up of the band (the Burnette brothers went to California and wrote songs for Ricky Nelson and had individual hits), and retirement from music, eventually to return via the rockabilly revival. Two years before the interview, Paul had made a tribute album called *Johnny Burnette's Rock and Roll Trio and their Rockin' Friends From Memphis*, and the next year the reunited Trio (Paul, Tony, Johnny Black, plus Rocky Burnette, the son of Johnny Burnette) performed in England.

PAUL BURLISON: We was playing in Doc McQueen's band when we went to New York City [in early 1956]. I should have told him, but we made up our minds to go at the last minute. We won the *Ted Mack Amateur Hour* [television program] three times and that gave us a lot of exposure. Ted Mack kept calling us "the rock and roll boys from Memphis." I think the first time I heard anybody call it "rockabilly" was Alan Freed, then we started calling it rockabilly, 'cause we was trying to play rock music with a hillbilly flavor.

Coral Records didn't know nothing about rockabilly. They had a 32-piece band when we did "Tear It Up" at the Pythian Temple, biggest recording studio in New York City, where Bill Haley cut "Rock Around the Clock." The orchestra leader said, "Okay, boys, tell us what to do and we'll do it." We said, "We don't know what to tell you. We just play what we feel like playing." We dismissed everybody but their drummer, Eddie Grady. He was playing with brushes and I couldn't hear him. I turned the guitar down a bit, and he played a little harder. I said, "Don't play good—just play loud!" He said, "Come on, I'm going to bust the head on my drums if I play louder." He put the drums aside and got his plastic suitcases, beatin' on his suitcases on "Tear It Up" and "You're Undecided."

After we got it, they wouldn't even play it back. Then we went out on the road. We didn't hear it until after we got back to New York and the record was already out. We told Henry [Jerome, their manager], "We don't like that sound." It was too tinny, too shrill, and too much treble on the guitar. Up there, you just run over it four or five times, 'cause they didn't know what to look for. And so much distraction with reporters asking questions and girls walking around with coffee, tea, and doughnuts. You can tell I had a frustrated look on my face when I was putting that cigarette

After the Rock 'n' Roll Trio, Paul Burlison returned to his wife and family and work as an electrician. He ventured back into music in his later years, performing with the Sun Rhythm Section as well as his own band, sometimes featuring Johnny Burnette's son, Rocky, and Dorsey's son, Billy. *Ebet Roberts/Redferns*

out [in a famous photo] and I wasn't getting what I wanted. They wouldn't let us get relaxed.

Can you see the difference when we went to Nashville, how I toned it down? Owen Bradley played it back to you. When we were there, I felt more at home and the studio was smaller, a back room like we'd been playing in. He let us get real relaxed. It was closed sessions, they closed doors and let nobody come in except a few friends; our manager was there. We hung around for a couple hours and got comfortable, and he said, "Let's try something." So we did, and he played it back to us, "Well how does this sound?" We'd tell him what we wanted, a little deeper or more treble. If we liked it, we just said, "That sounds good." He let us do it.

Coral Records let us pick our own material. We picked the songs from the heart, what we liked and said this is the way we want to do it. We had the authority to do this. They didn't care, so we had the whole run of the thing. We were playing what we liked, we didn't have a producer picking songs for us, telling us what to do. We went around to the record stores in Nashville and picked out one or two a day and worked on them that night and did them the next day.

CM: How did you come up with that technique of playing notes two octaves apart? Did you do that with your thumb and middle finger?

PB: Yeah, or sometimes these two fingers [thumb and index]. One day we was in Philadelphia, Pennsylvania, playing with the Four Aces and some others. They'd book six, eight groups on one show. I was walking down the hallway to go on stage and the strap on top of my amplifier broke and the thing hit the floor. I was sitting in the dressing room, messing around with the guitar doing like that, it was fuzzy with the tube pulled down.

CM: Was that the first time you did that technique?

PB: Yeah, in the dressing room with the tube loose. Johnny was playing an E chord and I was playing in a G position but I'd take my fingers off and play in octaves. He wasn't singing "The Train Kept A-Rollin'," it was another song, and I got to doing *doom diddle doom daddle doom daddle*. We started grinning at each other, then we got off on something else. When we got to Nashville, I told Owen Bradley about it at the Barn, where we cut the stuff, and he said, "Let me hear it." So I started doing it and he said, "Well, let's do it." Every time I wanted that sound—I just left the cover off the amplifier after that—I just reached down and wiggled the tube and hit the strings and it would sound real fuzzy.

Carl Perkins had just recorded "Blue Suede Shoes" when we was on *The Ted Mack Show*. There wasn't many like that out at that time: Bill Haley, Elvis. Gene Vincent came on the scene a few months after we did, with "Be-Bop-A-Lula." Buddy Holly wasn't even on Coral, he was on Decca. We was on Coral before he was. I never did meet him.

We had a lot of good times on the road; we used to laugh and cut up. I had a lot of fun with the Perkins brothers. We knew them real well: Carl, J. B., and Clayton. We chummed around together because we was so close to home. They was from Jackson, Tennessee, and we was from Memphis. Tony, our drummer, was from Jackson, knew 'em real good, kin to 'em.

CM: Many people think that your band did some of the finest rockabilly music ever made. I do.

PB: I appreciate that. It makes me feel good to know we did contribute a little bit. It wasn't all done in vain, people did like what we were doing. But there was a lot of good ones around. The first five records of Elvis was the best rockabilly he ever did, the best rockabilly you'll ever hear anywhere. The stuff on RCA was good and it sold millions, but those five records: that moves me right today. We had our own sound. We weren't copying Elvis, Vincent, Holly. We weren't copying anybody. . . .

When you have the big hits and everything—I didn't go through that and maybe I'm glad I didn't in the long run, because if we'd have had a big hit I probably would have stuck with it. It could have been a completely different life. I've lived a good life. I've enjoyed my children, been fishing with them, weekends we camped out. Those trophies over there, my kids won every one. To me that's like gold records, they mean just as much, 'cause I was right there with them. A lot of friends that stayed on the road for 20, 25 years never got to see their children grow up, they was gone. You weigh the good against the bad and see if it's really worth it, if you want to pay the price.

I was married. I had four children at the time when I quit. I had two children when I went first to New York. Johnny had two and Dorsey had two. I married in 1950. Same woman. And Dorsey was married to the same woman and Johnny was married to the same woman as long as they lived. They stood by us, sure did, and our wives were good friends. We all lived in the same neighborhood, close together.

I didn't study music; I play by ear—but I practiced hard and played an awful lot. I put a lot of hours in the guitar playing when I was growing up. I had been playing music for a long time and it was hard, like living in two different worlds, to go right back and get your knuckles skinned up and run an electric drill all day long, and been lying around hotels all day and playing music at night, riding a car and eating at good places. Then you come home and put on your old work clothes and go back to boring holes in houses and pullin' wire through it. I'm struggling and Johnny comes out with "Dreamin'" and "You're Sixteen" and here I had a five-year contract, notarized, and I was getting a third and just signed all my rights away a few months before. You can imagine how I was feeling.

You spend that much time on the road, you get a certain amount of glory and money but you're not getting a lot. It was taking most of the money that we made to live. We couldn't stay in a low rated hotel. We'd always try to stay in the same hotel as the people we was playing shows with, and wear decent uniforms and clothes and drive a good car, and it just about took everything that we made at that time. I enjoy talking about it now because I don't depend on it for a living.

GRADY MARTIN

Who Played: Lead, Guitar on the Famed Johnny Burnette and the Rock 'n' Roll Trio Recordings?

Born Chapel Hill, Tennessee, on January 17, 1929; died December 3, 2001

By Vince Gordon and Peter Dijkema

Grady Martin picks his trademark Paul Bigsby guitar.

Martin with his trademark fat tone that appeared on numerous rockabilly recordings.

Without a doubt, Burlison played on the May 7, 1956, trio recordings at the Pythian Temple, New York. That session spawned two classic rockabilly tracks—"Tear It Up" and a ripoff of Elvis Presley's "Baby Let's Play House" titled "Oh Baby Babe." The playing on that session is a typical single-string, blues-influenced Esquire/Telecaster sound, which I happen to love! However, it's a far cry from the sophisticated jazzy stuff found on the Quonset Hut recordings. The classy chord playing on "Please Don't Leave Me," for instance, is a completely different approach to lead guitar playing than that on "Tear It Up," which was recorded only three months earlier.

So why didn't Paul Burlison play lead on the trio's first major recording sessions?

Actually, at the Quonset Hut it was the rule rather than the exception that band musicians were replaced by studio musicians and only the singer was allowed to participate. I purposely use the term "allowed," because that is definitely the impression you get when reading about the policy at Owen Bradley's studio. This was a highly professional studio and they were set on making hit records, not satisfying the egos of sidemen.

At the Quonset Hut, the studio musicians used to replace band musicians were nicknamed "the A Team." The ones most frequently used to back rockabilly acts included Grady Martin on guitar, bassist Bob Moore, drummer Buddy Harman, and Boots Randolph on saxophone.

FOR YEARS, IT NEVER STRUCK ME that anyone but Paul Burlison could be playing the brilliant lead guitar on the classic Rock 'n' Roll Trio songs recorded at Owen Bradley's Quonset Hut studio in Nashville on July 2–5, 1956. I used to tell people who asked me rockabilly gear questions, that the only one I ever heard who got a fat and full sound out of a Fender Esquire or Telecaster was Paul Burlison.

Today, I believe the mystery is solved: It wasn't Paul Burlison playing a Fender Esquire at all. Instead, it was studio musician Grady

When Johnny Carroll came in to record at the Quonset Hut, he was told he couldn't use his own musicians and Martin, Moore, and Harman took over. After Buddy Holly had cut some unsuccessful records, he was also forced to use the A Team for his last session for Decca. It resulted, among other things, in a brilliant version of "Rock Around With Ollie Vee" with E. R. "Dutch" McMillin on sax. Even Sonny Curtis, who wrote the song and played lead on the first version, thought the "A Team version" was better.

As none of the Rock 'n' Roll Trio members or Martin are still with us, I had the luck of tracking down bassist Bob Moore. He confirmed that Grady Martin played lead guitar for Johnny Burnette and the Rock 'n' Roll Trio and that he, himself played bass on the July 4, 1956, and March 22, 1957, sessions. Moore said he most likely played his 1947 top-of-the-line Kay Swingmaster upright bass with gut strings.

Still, most people who agree that Martin played lead guitar on many of the July sessions also believe that it was in fact Burlison who played lead guitar on "The Train Kept A-Rollin'" and "Honey Hush." Many rock historians have singled out "The Train Kept A-Rollin'" as the first rock 'n' roll recording ever with a heavily distorted electric guitar.

Burlison used to tell a famous story about how he got the distorted guitar sound on these recordings: One day, he dropped his small Fender Deluxe amp and when he played through it, the sound was distorted. Burlison, being an electrician by trade—he actually worked at Crown Electric in Memphis where Elvis Presley drove the delivery truck—found that a tube had come loose and was acting as a rheostat, thus creating distortion. Apparently he was able to re-create that effect in the studio by pulling the tube loose. This is his explanation of how the distorted guitar sound on "The Train Kept A-Rollin'" and "Honey Hush" came about. Burlison also stated that he'd not been able to re-create that distortion later, because it could only be done on a Fender Deluxe and he didn't have his anymore.

While this may be partly or even completely true, something just doesn't add up . . .

"Honey Hush" and "The Train Kept A-Rollin'" are not as distorted as you might think: If you listen closely, you can hear that only the low E string is distorted. On both songs you hear pretty clean treble strings along with the distorted bass string. The distortion from a worn-out power tube is different from what you hear on these records. With a worn tube, every single tone is distorted, sounding a bit like a fuzz pedal: think of "Satisfaction" by the Rolling Stones. How can pulling one tube loose only mess with one string or frequency?

If you can get a 6V6 tube to act like a rheostat with a Fender Deluxe, it should also work with any other amp and any other tube. The key should be the bad contact between tube and socket.

When thinking about how the distortion/fuzz was created, I was looking for a method that would result in what you hear on the record: Only the bass E string is really distorted; the other strings have normal distortion for a '50s tube amp (some of the blues recorded at Sun was considerably more distorted, than the treble strings on these two songs). The low E string is a whole lot louder than the other strings; sometimes the high E string almost disappears in the background, for instance. And, especially on "Honey Hush," you frequently hear a strange "clang" noise together with notes played on the low E string—and sometimes, you only hear the "clang" where there obviously should have been a played note on the bass E.

I realized that all these things had little to do with the amp, but a lot to do with the pickup on the guitar. The explanation is simple: First, you set your amp to have what would qualify as normal distortion for the time period, but with a lot of bass. Then you take a screwdriver and raise the pole piece on the pickup under the bass E string—and only on that one. Raise it as much as possible without making the string unplayable, and there's your "The Train Kept A-Rollin'"/"Honey Hush" distortion.

So who played the solos then?

Given Burlison's unlikely explanations about the whole event, I don't see how he could have played the solos. Apart from that, the technical level is too high for his playing. For one thing, the timing on "Tear It Up" and "Oh Baby Babe" leaves a lot to be desired, whereas the timing on "The Train Kept A-Rollin'" and "Honey Hush" is dead-on groovy, which is the typical trademark of a session musician. The choice of notes is very similar to "Rock Billy Boogie" and the other Nashville tracks and have nothing to do with what Burlison played in New York. It was Grady Martin. I have no doubt about it.

There's also no doubt in my mind that Paul Burlison *wanted* to play the lead on all the recordings, as he played with the band live. There's no reason to think it was his decision not to play. After the records were released, Johnny Burnette and the Rock 'n' Roll Trio were promoted as if Burlison had played the lead guitar. Again, this was not his decision and something he might just have got caught up in, like so many other band musicians have been, before and after him.

Studio musician Grady Martin had worked really hard to get so good; I've heard it said that he played up to ten hours a day. Burlison was an electrician by trade. Of course, he couldn't compete with that. He did his best as you can hear on the Pythian Temple sessions and his intentions were honest, I'm sure. Burlison went on the road with Johnny Burnette and the Rock 'n' Roll Trio and played his heart out to promote the albums. This essay is only about getting some facts straight. Nothing else.

Paul Burlison (1929–2003) was a great guitarist and he definitely deserves his place in rock 'n' roll history. But Grady Martin (1929–2001) was a *brilliant* guitarist and he should be credited for some of the best rockabilly guitar work ever, simply because he did it.

Born Lubbock, Texas, on September 7, 1936; died February 3, 1959

By Greil Marcus

Buddy Holly and his Crickets—bassist Joe Mauldin and drummer Jerry Allison—appear on the BBC-TV program *Off the Record* in 1958.
John Rodgers/Redferns/Getty Images

BUDDY HOLLY WALKED into the room sideways. In terms of pure power he can't stand up to those with whom he's most often linked as a pioneer of rock 'n' roll: Elvis Presley, Little Richard, and Chuck Berry. He recorded nothing as immediately overwhelming—nothing that so forced an absolute confrontation between performer and listener—as "Hound Dog," "Tutti Frutti," or "Johnny B. Goode." The most musically extreme record of Holly's time was Little Richard's "Ready Teddy": Elvis can't keep up with Little Richard's version, but Holly, despite guitar playing that almost changes the sound of the song entirely, can't keep up with Elvis.

Buddy Holly shied away from the violence implicit in rock 'n' roll as it first made itself known, and from the hellfire emotionalism on the surface of the music. He was a rockabilly original, but unlike Gene Vincent—or Carl Perkins, Jerry Lee Lewis, or Sun label wildmen like Billy Lee Riley and Sonny Burgess, who after the release of his "Red Headed Woman" dyed his hair red and bought a red suit and a red Cadillac—Holly looked for space in the noise. He built his music around silences, pauses, a catch in the throat, a wink.

"That'll Be the Day" may be a very hard-nosed record, but its intensity is eased by its brightness—by the way it courts the prettiness that took over later Holly tunes like "Everyday," or even "Oh Boy" or "Rave On." "Hound Dog" aims for the monolithic, and falls short; "That'll Be the Day" is all pluralism, fully realized. The singer is acting out his role in a dozen accents; like Rod Stewart combing his hair a thousand ways in "Every Picture Tells a Story," he's talking to the mirror, rehearsing what he's going to say, writing it down. He's saying it on the phone while the phone's still ringing at the other end, going over how perfectly he said what he meant to say after he's said it, savoring the memory. Holly is reaching for Elvis's roughness, but even as he does so he communicates doubt that he can carry it off—or that anyone should.

And that's why "That'll Be the Day" is a more convincing record than "Hound Dog"—as Bobby Vee put it, thinking back to first hearing the record on the radio in Fargo, North Dakota, in 1957, when he was 14-year-old Bob Veline: "To me it was the most original, fresh, unique record I ever heard—and I was right, it was."

Holly could be utterly sure of his self-doubt; Elvis couldn't be as sure of his arrogance, and so he muffles it with a self-mocking laugh. In that part of himself that was addressing "Hound Dog" to the world at large, to the world that mocked him, you can hear Elvis meaning every word of "Hound Dog"; in the part of himself that was addressing the woman in the song, he's just kidding. Buddy wasn't kidding on "That'll Be the Day." Holly's performance is tougher—just as "Well . . . All Right," a 1958 single with no orchestration other than acoustic guitar, bass, and fluttered cymbals, is tougher still.

Holly's most frightening sincerity was cut with playfulness, a risk-free sense of fun, and an embrace of adolescent or even babyish innocence that was likely as calculated as his famous hiccups. Without that innocence and playfulness, his sincerity could have led him to take himself so seriously that today his music might sound hopelessly overblown; without his sincerity, many of his songs would now sound moronic. Instead he so often struck a perfect balance.

"Anarchy had moved in," Nik Cohn wrote of the '50s in *Awopbopaloobop Alopbamboom*—the first good book on rock 'n' roll, the book Cohn first called *Pop from the Beginning*. "For thirty years you couldn't possibly make it unless you were white, sleek, nicely spoken, and phony to your toenails—suddenly now you could be black, purple, moronic, delinquent, diseased, or almost anything on earth, and you could still clean up." What Buddy Holly was saying, what he was acting out, was that you could also be ordinary.

A photograph was taken in Lubbock, Texas, in 1955, on the occasion of Elvis Presley's second visit to Buddy Holly's hometown. In this picture, Elvis, surrounded by teenage girls and boys and children, looks bigger than anyone else: taller, wider, taking up more psychic space. Even with a dumb, open-mouthed look on his face, you can feel his glow.

On Presley's far left, just peeking into the frame, is an 18-year-old Buddy Holly, the only male figure (among 30-odd people in the picture) wearing glasses, somewhere between geek and nerd, looking curious. You would never pick him out of this crowd—or would you? No, probably not: there's no aura around his body, no portent in his posture, not even any obvious desire in his eyes. Just that curiosity: but even as he pokes his head forward for a closer look, he holds his body back. His curiosity is a form of hesitation, a drama of doubt. That quality of doubt is what gives the Buddy Holly in this picture the interest he has—and the longer you look at the picture, the less stable it appears to be. Who can identify with who? Who would want to identify with the nobody? But who can really identify with the god—and in this black and white photo, no matter what the expression on his face, it's plain a god is in the room. Elvis Presley and Buddy Holly, sharing the same time and space—they're both magnets, Elvis the black hole, Holly merely earthly gravity.

It was Buddy Holly's embodiment of ordinariness that allowed him to leave behind not only a body of songs, but a personality—as his contemporaries Elvis, Chuck Berry, Little Richard, and Jerry Lee Lewis did, and Carl Perkins, Danny and the Juniors, Larry Williams, Fats Domino, the Monotones, Arlene Smith, or Clyde McPhatter did not.

The personality was that of the guy you passed in the hall in your high school every day. He might be cool; he might be square. He might be the guy who slammed your locker shut every time you opened it, but the guy who did it as a laugh, as a version of a pat on the back, a "Hey, man." He might be the guy who got his own locker slammed shut in his own face, and not in fun. Whoever he was, he was familiar. He was not strange; he was not different; he did not speak in unknown tongues, or commune with secret spirits.

"That'll Be the Day" was written by Buddy Holly and drummer Jerry Allison. It was recorded by the band on February 25, 1957, at Norman Petty's famed Clovis, New Mexico, studio—one of the great rockabilly-producing studios after Sun and the Nashville Quonset Hut. The tune was later one of the first demoed by the Quarrymen in far-away Liverpool, a skiffle group that later changed its name in honor of the Crickets to become the Beatles.

Except that he did. "Well . . . All Right" is not just a good song, or a great recording; with a quietness that is also a form of loudness, the drum sticks moving over the cymbals like wind on water, the feel of death in the lack of any physical weight to the sound, the sense of a threat in every promise, "Well . . . All Right" is also the casting of a spell, but no one ever seemed less like a sorcerer than Buddy Holly.

"An obvious loser," Nik Cohn said. "He was the patron saint of all the thousands of no-talent kids who ever tried to make a million dollars. He was founder of a noble tradition." What Cohn is describing is how the gawky, wide-eyed Buddy Holly who Gary Busey summoned up for *The Buddy Holly Story* in 1978—someone who looks as if he's about to fall down every time he does that Buddy Holly move where he folds up his knees like a folding chair—is as believable as the cool, confident, hipster Buddy Holly that Marshall Crenshaw plays at the end of *La Bamba* in 1987, performing "Crying, Waiting, Hoping" on that last stage in Clear Lake, Iowa, then waving Ritchie Valens onto the plane: "Come on—the sky belongs to the stars."

If Holly looked like an ordinary teenager, on the radio he came across as one. His presence on stage, on the airwaves, seemed more accidental than willful. From his first professional recordings, the mostly muffled numbers cut in Nashville in 1956, to the Clovis, New Mexico, sessions produced by Norman Petty in 1957, on through the soulful solo demos he made in New York in late 1958 and into the next year, the most glamorous element of Holly's career was the plane crash that ended it—on February 3, 1959, leaving his 22-year-old body in an Iowa cornfield along with those of 17-year-old Ritchie Valens and 29-year-old J. P. Richardson, the Big Bopper.

Concert poster, Forum, Wichita, Kansas, November 2, 1957.

So Buddy Holly entered history differently from other rock 'n' roll heroes—and, somehow, his ordinariness has carried over into the way in which one might encounter people whose lives brushed his. Some years ago, on a panel in New Orleans, David Adler, author of *The Life and Cuisine of Elvis Presley*, shocked me and everyone else in the room with the story of how, during his research in Tupelo, Mississippi, he met a woman who was in the Presleys' one-room house when Elvis Presley was born—and he believed her because of the way she described how the shoebox containing the still-born body of Elvis's twin Jesse Garon was resting on the kitchen table.

A gasp went up. We were in the presence of someone who had been in the presence of someone who had been present when an event took place that ultimately would change the world—and leave all of us present in that world different than we would have otherwise been if this event had not taken place.

But nothing like that feeling attaches itself to the story I heard when, without asking, I found myself listening to a woman tell how, missing Buddy Holly's last concert as a 12-year-old because no one she knew was vulgar enough to go with her, she asked a friend to drive her to the site of the crash before the morning light was up, and how men with stretchers were still there when she arrived. Or listening to a woman who lives down the street from me in Berkeley describe how, as a girl, she witnessed the collision of two planes over Pacoima Junior High School, Ritchie Valens's alma mater, in 1957, a disaster that killed three students and that, at least until he climbed onto that Cessna at the little airport in Mason City, Iowa, left Ritchie Valens determined to stay out of the air if he could. Or listening in an Italian restaurant in New York in 1995 when, as if he'd never told the story before, Dion DiMucci quietly went through the details of the life-threatening conditions he and everyone else endured while traveling the upper Midwest on ruined buses for the Winter Dance Party tour in January and February 1959, and why he nevertheless gave up his seat on the plane that night. Or listening in San Francisco in 1970, as Bobby Vee told the story of how, when the news of the plane crash reached Fargo Senior High School the next morning, with everyone geared up for the show that evening, just over the state line in Moorhead, Minnesota, Bob Veline and his high school band, which lacked a name and had not yet played a single show, answered the call of the local promoter and, after rushing out to buy matching angora sweaters and 25-cent ties, and naming themselves the Shadows, took the stage that night along with those who were left.

Thus did he begin to tell his own part of the greater rock 'n' roll story: a story that—as Bob became one of various post-Holly Bobbys, made over on the terms of Holly's anybodyness, with anything that made this particular anybody unique air-brushed out—took the form of such first-rate teen-angst classics as "Take Good Care of My Baby," "It Might as Well Rain Until September," "The Night Has a Thousand Eyes," and, in 1962, as a shameless tribute, or an honest thank you, *Bobby Vee Meets The Crickets*. The plane crash gave Bob Veline his big break; as he saw it, it also gave him a legacy to honor, a mission to fulfill.

Because of the way Buddy Holly died—cut off in the bloom of youth, with his whole life ahead of him, chartering a plane because his clothes were filthy from the bus and he wanted to look good on stage, because he wanted to sleep for a few hours in a warm bed, and do a good show—he immediately became a mythic figure. A queer mythic figure: a mythic figure you could imagine talking to. One you could imagine listening to what you had to say.

But that sense of ordinariness in Buddy Holly is also ridiculous. It's ridiculous that a full-length biography—Philip Norman's 1996 *Rave On*—could be written about someone who never reached the age of 23, written without padding, without discographical pedanticism, quotidian minutiae, a potted social history of the 1950s, banal or for that matter profound musings on the emergence of the American teenager, rock 'n' roll, modern youth culture, or the meaning of the Alamo. And it's ridiculous that anyone could have left behind a body of work as rich as that Buddy Holly set down between the beginning 1957 and the end of 1958. But in that body of work is a story that can be told again and again without it ever being settled.

Some of the songs are obvious, despite a charm that isn't: "Everyday," "It Doesn't Matter Anymore," "Raining in My Heart," "It's So Easy," "Heartbeat." "Even the obvious beaters, things like 'Rave On' or 'Oh Boy,'" Nik Cohn wrote, "were Neapolitan flowerpots after 'Tutti Frutti.'" Cohn is right. But more of what Holly did is unlikely before it is anything else.

You could start with "Not Fade Away," probably the oddest Buddy Holly record of all. On paper, it's nothing but an under-orchestrated Bo Diddley imitation. But as you hear it, no matter how many times you've heard it, it sounds nearly impossible. You can't date it by its sound, its style, the apparent recording technology. But while this is the Crickets, with Jerry Allison playing drums—or a cardboard box—Joe Mauldin bass, and Holly guitar, as they did on the leaping "That'll Be the Day," "Not Fade Away" is all stop-time, every build-up cut off and brought up short, the whole song starting up again, like the car it drops into the rhythm like a new dance step: "My love bigger than a Cadillac." With verbs evaporating out of the lyric, the thing feels less like any kind of pop song than a folk song, and less like the Rolling Stones's 1964 wailing-down-the-highway version, their first American single, than the Beatles's "Love Me Do," their first single anywhere, from 1962, which the late Ralph J. Gleason, music columnist for the *San Francisco Chronicle*, would refer to as "that Liverpool folk song," confusing some readers, like me, into wondering if perhaps it actually was.

With the hesitations in the beat, in the vocal, the recording is not easy to listen to, because it does not really make sense. It is absurd in the most wonderful way. Always, when people have talked about the 1920s and 1930s recordings Harry Smith brought together for his 1952 *Anthology of American Folk Music*—the likes of William and Versey Smith's "When That Great Ship Went Down," Dock Boggs's "Country Blues," or the Memphis Jug Band's "K. C. Moan"—they've found themselves drawn to the same phrase. "The music sounds as if it came out of the ground," they say, and that's exactly what "Not Fade Away" sounds like, which is to say that it also sounds more like flying saucer rock 'n' roll than Billy Lee Riley's "Flyin' Saucers Rock & Roll."

Then there is "Peggy Sue," from 1957, and the 1958 home recording of "Peggy Sue Got Married." Here is where the ordinariness of the singer creates a unique kind of intimacy with the listener—even though the quiet, troubled, happy man in "Peggy Sue Got Married" is hardly the hard, even avenging man in "Peggy Sue," a man who refuses to explain himself and demands that you believe him anyway.

This man rides the coldness of the music, as cold in "Peggy Sue" as the music in "Peggy Sue Got Married" is warm: the battering, monochromatic tomtom rumble from Jerry Allison that opens "Peggy Sue," named for Allison's girlfriend (when the song was written: the next year she was his wife, and 11 years later his ex-wife); the bass strum behind that; the instrument beneath both you can barely register. No leaps, no grand gestures, just a push head-down into the wind the song itself is making, and then that harsh, cruel guitar solo, emerging as inevitably as any in the music, and also a shock. The song is unexplainable, at least by me—but not by Jonathan Cott, writing the Buddy Holly chapter in *The Rolling Stone Illustrated History of Rock & Roll* in 1975.

"The women of '50s rock 'n' roll, about whom songs were written and to whom they were addressed," Cott says, "were as interchangeable as hurricanes or spring showers, Party Doll ornaments of the song. But with Peggy Sue, Buddy Holly created the first rock and roll folk heroine (Chuck Berry's Johnny B. Goode is her male counterpart). And yet it is difficult to say how he did it. Unlike the 'Sad-Eyed Lady of the Lowlands'—whom Bob Dylan fills in as he invents and discovers her—Peggy Sue is hardly there at all. Most '50s singers let it be known that they liked the way their women walked and talked; sometimes they even let on as to the color of their sweethearts' eyes and hair.

"But Buddy Holly didn't even give you this much information. Instead, he colluded with his listeners, suggesting that they imagine and create Peggy Sue for him."

Buddy Holly's "Not Fade Away" was based on an African "hambone" or "juba" beat as translated by Bo Diddley and played by drummer Jerry Allison on a cardboard box. The song was recorded by the Crickets in Norman Petty's studio on May 27, 1957. With Holly's simple-yet-stinging guitar work and the near-mystical lyrics, it was an otherworldly pop-rockabilly classic.

Cott notes that Holly would later intensify this complicit relationship in "Peggy Sue Got Married," beseeching both his listeners and himself to keep secret what they both know to be true, as if by its revelation the rumor "heard from a friend" will irrevocably become fact. Holly cannot sing "You're the one," but "She's the one." Ultimately Peggy Sue, Holly's own creation, is as much of a mystery to him as anyone else. "He has become one of his own listeners," writes Cott, "as Peggy Sue vanishes, like Humbert Humbert's Lolita, into the mythology of American Romance."

Buddy Holly "suggested" that his listeners "imagine and create Peggy Sue for him," Cott says. The idea sounds so far-fetched, and yet in "Peggy Sue Got Married" it's literal: "I don't say / That it's true / I'll just leave that up to you."

And there are, finally, the remainder of Buddy Holly's last recordings, the solo pieces with guitar, acoustic or electric, that he taped in his and his wife Maria Elena's apartment in Greenwich Village in 1958—though the word *finally* seems wrong, because these are also the recordings that are most suggestive of the music Holly had yet to make, and the life he had yet to live. There is a version of Mickey and Sylvia's "Love Is Strange" that is more than anything strange—strangely abstract, so much so that the strings added after Holly's death let you imagine the singer resisting them in advance. Even odder, and far more affecting, is a reworking

Concert poster, Auditorium Theater, Rochester, Minnesota, January 19, 1957.

"Peggy Sue" started life as "Cindy Lou," named for Buddy Holly's niece. Penned by Holly and Jerry Allison, the title was soon changed to "Peggy Sue" in honor of Allison's girlfriend—and future wife—Peggy Sue Gerron. The tune hit the top ten on both American and British charts.

"It's So Easy" sheet music.

Buddy Holly's debut LP, *The "Chirpin'" Crickets*, released on November 27, 1957.

Concert poster, Cincinnati Gardens, Cincinnati, Ohio, April 14, 1958.

of Mickey and Sylvia's "Dearest," a composition that, written with Bo Diddley, is quiet, graceful, most of all a whisper—and, here, pure Holly, taken very slowly, as if the feeling the song calls up is so transporting that it would be a crime to let the song end. There is "Learning the Game," sung with tremendous confidence, the singer moving right into the music, riding the clipped guitar strum, no hesitation, no lingering—no speed, but no pauses, either. He never raises the tone, never increases the pressure.

And there is "Crying, Waiting, Hoping," overdubbed twice after Holly's death—in New York in 1959, leaving Holly kicking up the traces of his fate, and in Clovis in 1963 with the Fireballs, where there is no doubt that Holly has been in the ground for years. In the initial recasting, you can feel the seriousness of the composition, the great weight Holly gives the title words as the song opens. The melody is almost too sweet to bear. At the end, Holly repeats the title words again, isolating them from the rest of the music, as if they are a manifesto, a flag he's unfurling: "Crying—Waiting—Hoping"—the end.

It is this music that allows anyone to picture Buddy Holly in the years to come: to imagine his style deepening, his range increasing, his music taking shapes no one, not Holly, not his fans, could have predicted. When he died, Holly had plans for his own production company, publishing firm, management company, record label, all under the name Prism; the business cards were printed. He saw himself recording with Ray Charles, or making a gospel album with Mahalia Jackson. He was spending time in Village jazz clubs and coffeehouses, at the Village Vanguard, the Blue Note, the Bitter End, Café Bizarre; he'd registered at the Actor's Studio. But his career was slipping in late 1958. He and the Crickets had split up. The money he'd made, a fortune, was sitting in a bank in Clovis, New Mexico, and sitting on that money was producer and publisher Norman Petty, forcing Buddy Holly to live on loans from his wife's aunt. If you can see Buddy Holly as an entrepreneur in the music business, president of Prism Music, you can also see him, a year or two down the line, as a contract songwriter, side-by-side with Carole King, Gerry Goffin, Cynthia Weil, Barry Mann, Ellie Greenwich, and Jeff Barry at Don Kirshner's Brill Building adjunct: Buddy Holly, like everyone else, writing songs for Bobby Vee.

But if you can see Holly in his cubicle in Aldon Music, you can also see him sitting in the audience at Folk City or the Gaslight—perhaps there to see the Texas folk singer Carolyn Hester, whom he'd backed on guitar in Norman Petty's studio in Clovis in 1958 on his own "Take Your Time" and other tunes, none of them released—but this night also watching Bob Dylan (who would himself back Hester on harmonica in 1961 for her third album, on Columbia, on "Come Back Baby," which Dylan would teach her) getting up out of the audience to sing "Handsome Molly" or "No More Auction Block."

And you can see Dylan back in the crowd a few minutes later, watching as Holly, whom Dylan would have noticed the minute he walked in, himself stood up to play "Not Fade Away," stamping his foot for the beat, or "Well . . . All Right," Dylan watching the smile on Holly's face for the "Well all right so I'm going steady / It's all right when people say / That those foolish kids can't be ready / For the love that comes their way" lines, Holly daring the hip crowd to laugh at "going steady" and no one daring to laugh, everyone frozen by the way Holly lets "the love that comes their way" drift into the smoke of its own air.

It's certain that in 1962 Bob Dylan would not have forgotten, as he would declare in 1998, when he accepted the Grammy for Album of the Year for *Time Out of Mind*, that on January 31, 1959, he was present in the Duluth Armory for Buddy Holly's third-to-last performance, and that, as he sat in the audience, as he told the nation and the world, "Buddy Holly looked right at me"—meaning that, on that night, Buddy Holly had passed on the secret of rock 'n' roll, of all music, of life itself, one avatar to another: a secret which, as of that night at the Grammys, Bob Dylan was plainly unready to pass on in turn.

Buddy Holly

exclusively on

The famous promotional photo of Buddy Holly, complete with trademark glasses, drape suit coat, and snapping fingers.

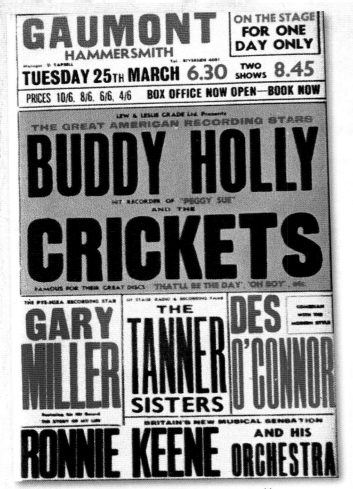

Concert poster, Gaumont Theatre, Hammersmith, England, March 25, 1958.

"HE WAS THE PATRON SAINT OF ALL THE THOUSANDS OF NO-TALENT KIDS WHO EVER TRIED TO MAKE A MILLION DOLLARS. HE WAS FOUNDER OF A NOBLE TRADITION."

—NIK COHN, AWOPBOPALOOBOP ALOPBAMBOOM, 1968

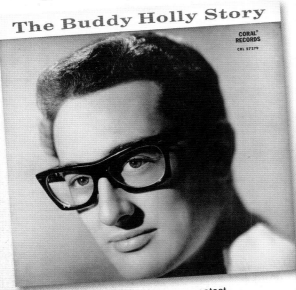

Posthumous *The Buddy Holly Story* greatest hits LP from Coral.

Concert poster from the final tour, Kato Ballroom, Mankato, Minnesota, January 25, 1959.

Born Lubbock, Texas, on September 7, 1936; died February 3, 1959

JOHNNY HORTON WAS THE ORIGINAL honky-tonk man. Following the legacy of Hank Williams, he added a rockabilly rhythm and wrote odes celebrating the honky-tonk life. He later married Williams' widow, Billie Jean, before also dying a tragic death at an early age.

Johnny Horton's great earliest hits were part country, part rockabilly. He achieved national recognition with his country-pop crossover saga songs, such as 1959's "The Battle of New Orleans," which won the 1960 Grammy Award for Best Country & Western Recording. From then on, rockabilly was no longer part of his show. *Michael Ochs Archives/Getty Images*

Johnny Horton's "Honky Tonk Man" was recorded on January 11, 1956, at Owen Bradley's famous Nashville Quonset Hut studio and featured Grady Martin's glorious twanging guitar.

THUMPER JONES A.K.A. GEORGE JONES

Ode to 'White Lightnin''

Born Saratoga, Texas, on September 12, 1931

ONE OF COUNTRY MUSIC'S greatest voices, George Jones also dabbled with rockabilly, but suitably masked as "Thumper Jones." His handful of rockabilly sides included the rollicking "White Lightnin'," which became his first #1 country hit, in 1959.

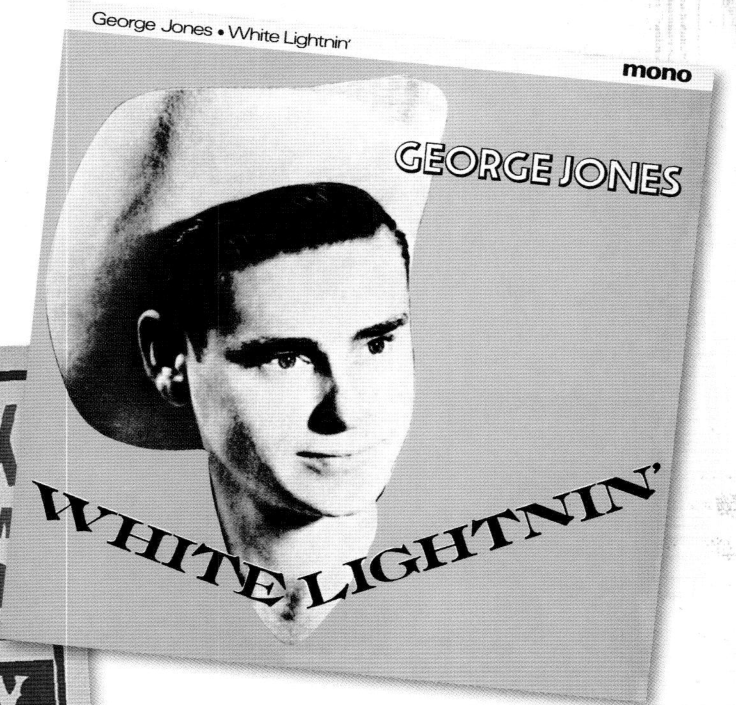

George Jones • White Lightnin'
mono
GEORGE JONES
WHITE LIGHTNIN'

George Jones hid his country career behind the moniker Thumper Jones when playing rockabilly. His rowdy rock 'n' roll was collected on White Lightnin' issued by England's Ace Records.

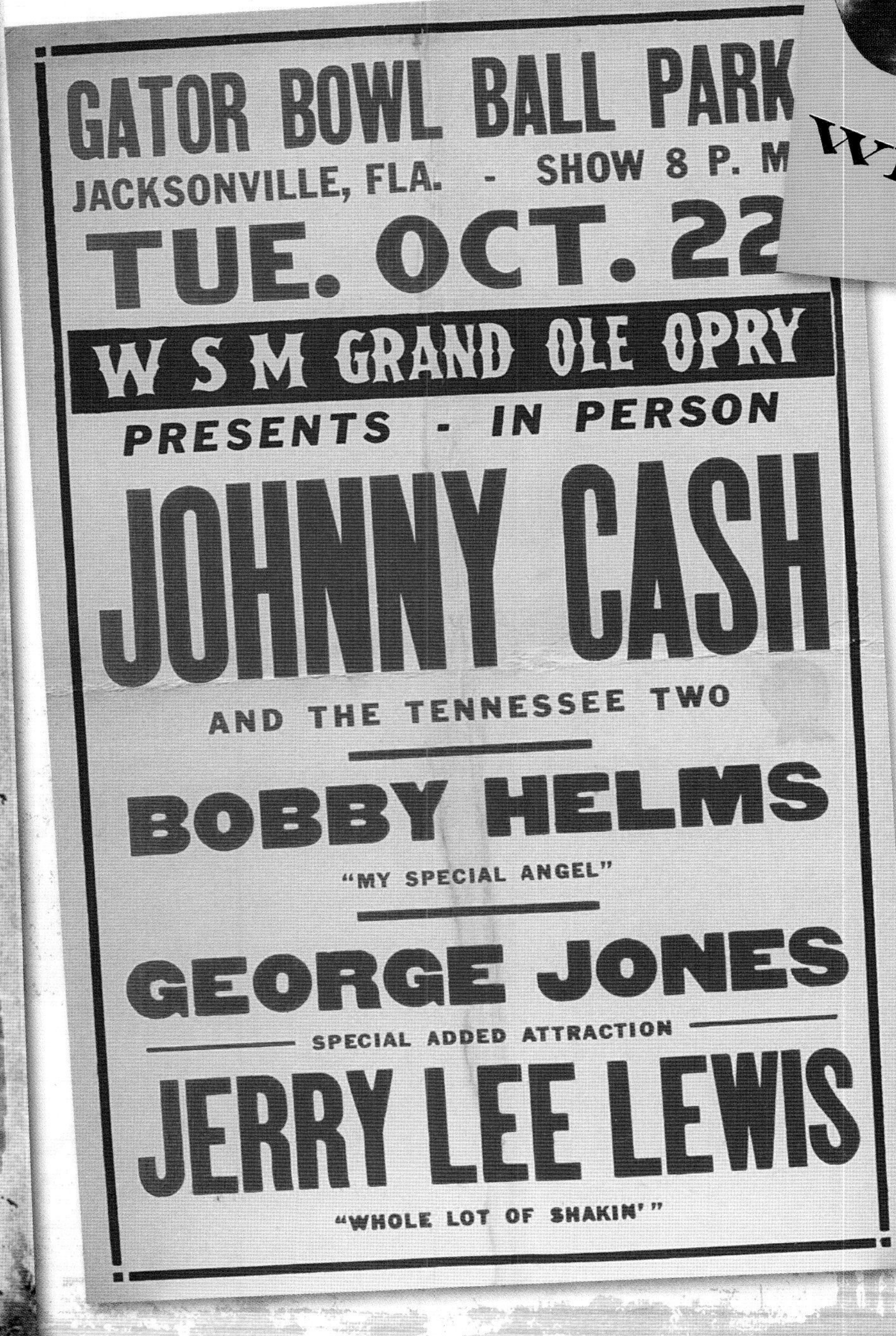

GATOR BOWL BALL PARK
JACKSONVILLE, FLA. - SHOW 8 P. M
TUE. OCT. 22
W S M GRAND OLE OPRY
PRESENTS - IN PERSON
JOHNNY CASH
AND THE TENNESSEE TWO
BOBBY HELMS
"MY SPECIAL ANGEL"
GEORGE JONES
SPECIAL ADDED ATTRACTION
JERRY LEE LEWIS
"WHOLE LOT OF SHAKIN'"

Concert poster, Gator Bowl Ball Park, Jacksonville, Florida, October 22, 1958.
Pete Howard/Poster Central

Born Maud, Oklahoma, on October 20, 1937

By Craig Morrison

Wanda Jackson records at a Capitol Records studio.
Michael Ochs Archives/Getty Images

WANDA JACKSON WAS BORN October 20, 1937, in Maud, Oklahoma, and recorded country music before she did rockabilly. The interview took place in a Montreal hotel on October 2, 2004, before her concert that night. I had already profiled her in *Go Cat Go! Rockabilly Music and Its Makers*, but this was the first time we met. Her husband, Wendell Goodman, who is also her manager, helped arrange the interview. That month they were celebrating their 43rd wedding anniversary. They have a son and a daughter. During the interview, Jackson was filmed by Mike Wafer, and some of the questions were supplied by Patricia Chica. These two soon finished their film *Rockabilly 514*, about the Montreal rockabilly subculture; I had the honor of being the film's narrator. The concert promoter, Nathalie Lavergne, was one of the film's main characters whom the filmmakers followed over the course of a year. Her concert series, called the Rockabilly Jam, evolved into Montreal's Red, Hot, and Blue Weekender. In 2009, Jackson was inducted into the Rock and Roll Hall of Fame as an Early Influence.

CRAIG MORRISON: What originally attracted you to rockabilly?
WANDA JACKSON: Elvis! (laughing) They came along at the same time. Elvis and rockabilly music are all wrapped up together. The others came along in rapid succession: Carl Perkins and Jerry Lee Lewis and then me. I jumped in and tried my hand at it.
CM: Was Elvis's rockabilly the first you heard?
WJ: Yes. In 1955 when I graduated from high school I was ready to go on tour. My dad quit his job so he could travel

Wanda Jackson's first LP, *Day Dreamin'*, on Capitol Records, released in 1958.

Agency promotional brochure for Wanda Jackson and other country stars, circa 1957.

with me and help me, and [me] being an only child he could do that. My mother worked so it was okay. The first person I worked with was Elvis Presley, and at that point I'd never heard of him. I just thought "that's a very funny name." It was very Southern: "Elvis." But when I met him—we met first at a radio station the first day of our tour—I was really awed. There was such a charisma around him that everyone felt. You couldn't deny the charisma, so I was looking forward to seeing what he did on stage. My dad and I were backstage. I had been on [stage] of course; Elvis was closing [the show]. I was doing something and didn't get out there right when he started, and we heard all this screaming. My dad said "Wanda, maybe there's a fire!" I came out of the dressing room looking around, "what in the world?" And it's the audience! This blew us away. We'd never seen anything like that. Rockabilly/ rock and roll hit me really hard; I said, "boy, this is great!"

CM: Tell me about your dad, Tom.

WJ: He was a fiddle player and guitar player and he sang. But it was in the days of the Depression, so after he met my mother and they were married—then shortly I came along—he couldn't continue in his music. The first thing to go when times are hard is entertainment.

CM: You must have had a lot of music at home. Did your father show you how to play guitar?

WJ: Oh yeah. When I was about six he bought me a little guitar. I can still see it today—I have a photo of it—it had the Uncle Sam hat on it because it was wartime. He put it in my hands and eventually I could reach around it and he started teaching me chords.

CM: What were the first songs he showed you or that you knew how to play?

WJ: Jimmie Rodgers' songs—he loved Jimmie Rodgers and he had a whole collection of those big old 78 records. Now I have them and they're wonderful—and fiddle breakdowns and I would accompany him, and the songs that were currently popular. I have a hand-written songbook that

I treasure. My mother wrote out all the words to the Bob Wills songs, Spade Cooley, Tex Williams, all these people and their hits, and I still remember most of them. I'd love to do an album of the '40s country things.

CM: I saw you perform at Viva Las Vegas in 2001. There's a famous picture of you on this poster.

WJ: That's one of the first dresses that I designed and my mother made me.

CM: That was a good team.

WJ: I know it. My career was a family affair. Dad acted as my manager and traveled with me. Mother held down a job and made all my clothes and answered fan mail for me.

CM: Now your husband is your manager too so it's still a family affair.

WJ: Now he does it all. I think I must be pretty needy! (laughing)

CM: We all need a lot, don't we?

WJ: Some of us just need more. (we laugh)

CM: When I saw you perform, I was delighted that you did a Jimmie Rodgers song, the "Blue Yodel No. 6 (She Left Me This Mornin')."

WJ: That was my favorite.

CM: And Hank Williams' version of "Lovesick Blues."

WJ: Country music and rockabilly are like first cousins, and I've found that if they like "Mean Mean Man" and "Hot Dog! That Made Him Mad," they'll love "Blue Yodel No. 6" and "Lovesick Blues." If I'm at Viva Las Vegas I do more of the rock things, and if I'm at a country festival then I'll do a little bit more of the country. I always do both.

CM: What was so special about rockabilly music in the '50s?

WJ: It was so fresh and new, it turned the music industry upside down. A lot of country artists really suffered, because all of a sudden radio stations that were playing country records stopped, and became all rock and roll stations. Country music had to take a back seat to it for many years. I was one of the fortunate ones that could continue doing both. There was a few others: Marty Robbins had some hits in the early '60s or late '50s with some of his. There was a few of us.

CM: When you sing I hear a lot of Marty Robbins' phrasing. Were you a fan?

WJ: I was a fan of his. I always enjoyed working with Marty Robbins. He was just so different. He was like Elvis in the respect that you didn't ever know what they were going to do next. If they were in the building you wanted to be there, that's where it was going to happen. Marty was such a great talent.

CM: What did it feel to be a young rockabilly performer in the '50s?

WJ: Well I was a young performer. I graduated from high school when I was 17 and I didn't start to do rock and roll/ rockabilly until '56, so that would have made me 18. I was a teenager still. The mind set was different in the '50s. My dad traveled with me, certainly to help me, but for my reputation's sake. A woman's reputation was very important and we had to keep that intact. There would be six stars and all the bands, but there would be one girl always and if I was that girl, I got all kinds of respect and I was always grateful for that. If I walked into the room, the language changed, everything.

CM: A lot of the earlier female country singers had trouble unless they were part of a family band or they were singing with their brother.

WJ: Some of that trouble was brought on by the girls themselves. They would put themselves in situations that I wasn't willing to do.

CM: You had a good upbringing.

WJ: A Christian upbringing.

CM: You've said that your roots in country music provided longevity in your career, but I know that your return to the church in 1971 has also been a foundation. I think of three aspects: the family, the country music root of which rockabilly is part of, and the religion. You've had a beautiful, long career and it's still going fantastically well. You've got such a foundation to rest on and the support of your husband now.

WJ: Yes, I've lived a charmed life. God is so good to give me all these people that have helped me. They've never tried to take away from me, they were all for me. You can't ask for more than that. Who would have ever thought at my age now, to be considered the queen of rock and roll or rockabilly, maybe being inducted into the Rock and Roll Hall of Fame and all these beautiful young people that esteem me and know all of my songs, I'm just flabbergasted. I'm having the time of my life now.

CM: We're delighted for you too and for us because we get to share it. Were there other people that you particularly enjoyed working with?

WJ: Oh yeah, you always have favorites that you have a little more rapport with. A lot of country artists: Sonny James was good friend of mine, Red Foley of course. Hank Thompson was so instrumental in my career and became my mentor. I loved traveling with him. He was interesting and a very intelligent person. He flew his own plane and he'd let me fly it with him when my dad would let me. I learned so much from Hank; I always loved just to be in his presence. I met him at an impressionable age. I was 15 when Hank Thompson heard my radio show and called me and invited me to come sing with his band. He was my very favorite singer, so I just couldn't believe that he's calling me asking me to sing with him. That was just the beginning of a wonderful friendship and a great relationship. Hank went on to help me get my first and my second recording contract. I've never been a real assertive person and my dad wasn't either and so sometimes I wonder, if Hank hadn't taken it upon himself to help me get those record contracts, would I have pushed and pushed until I got it? I don't know, but he did it for me. Hank, to this day, is such a professional. I got to learn stage mannerisms and things you do and don't do on stage, and off. He highly respects his audience.

Elvis did too. I would watch him and I learned a lot from Elvis: the respect of his audience and not to take yourself so seriously. Because I'm kind of a serious person. I don't want to be but it's just my nature. When something would happen on stage, he just had a ball and he would play and kid with his audiences. If you've seen me perform, you see me doing that, I picked that up and incorporated it. That's the type of person I wanted to be. I was like a sponge, soaking up everything. Nothing got past me, I was right there either taking notes or mentally remembering these things. They've been valuable tools for me.

CM: I saw you do that in Las Vegas, when you talked about the songs that you wrote for Vince Gill and Randy Travis. Then you said, "Oh, I'm just stringing you along..."

WJ: I'd say, "Gotcha!" If somebody's got on a hat, I'll take it off and turn it sideways, or pull it down over their head, or take it off and put it on myself.

CM: How has rockabilly changed since the '50s?

WJ: Rockabilly hasn't, because it's frozen. It's crystallized I think. The mutations of it are still going on. The new artists are capturing the same thing that we did. They work very hard to get the same sound, the feel, so therefore it doesn't ever change. I can listen to Kim Lenz or Marti Brom and say, "Golly, that could have been released in the '50s." There's a tribute album just released, called *Hard-Headed Woman: A Celebration of Wanda Jackson* with 21 artists, and they captured the sound real well. Some of them did their own thing, but it's still not the new with all the bells and whistles. It's just pure, good recording, good music.

CM: How did you like that album? Was your reaction "What are they doing to my songs?"

WJ: I loved it. Well, no that was interesting to me. My husband

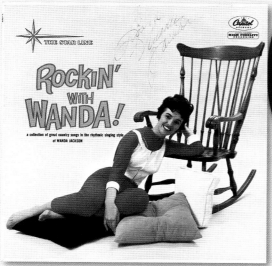
Autographed copy of Wanda Jackson's second LP, *Rockin' With Wanda!*, released in 1960 on Capitol.

Elvis recorded "Let's Have A Party" in 1958, but it was Wanda Jackson's version of the song, released in 1959, that became a Top 40 pop hit.

would say, "They're taking a lot of liberties there aren't they?" I said, "Well, certainly, they're artists. They have the freedom to do that."

I love the way the girls put their own feeling in them. I had never heard the songs like that. So it's good.

CM: On some of the songs that you recorded that were originally done by men you changed the gender. There's a new verse in "Riot in Cell Block #9" about all the girls in the prison going crazy when the tall and handsome troopers arrive.

WJ: I don't know where I got that, but it was already changed. I didn't do that to that song.

CM: Did you ever meet Janis Martin?

WJ: I still to this day haven't had a chance to meet her. For the most part, I was out there by myself, just shaking and shimmying, screaming and rockin' and rollin'.

CM: But it's not like that now, there's lots of them and they all point to you as a role model. Marti Brom's going strong. There's so many.

WJ: She's so good, yeah. There is and they're so cute. In the '50s, there wasn't any other women except if they were in a band, like a Bob Wills record might have a girl singing a yodel song or something. There wasn't until Kitty Wells came along and she had the cover song ["It Wasn't God Who Made Honky Tonk Angels" in 1952] to Hank Thompson's "Wild Side of Life" and it zoomed up to number one. Then the producers and people with record companies would say, "Oh, maybe we should look at some of these females." That's what happened in my case. I started recording in '54 and strictly country.

CM: You looked up to Kitty Wells.

WJ: Absolutely.

CM: You were a big fan of Rose Maddox, too. Didn't you hear her on the radio when you were living in California?

WJ: Yeah, their records were very popular, Maddox Brothers and Rose. But I would see them in person in different places. Mother and daddy went and took me along. If it was music, daddy always took me. I thought she was just great, so feisty. She wore pretty clothes and sang fast songs. She was definitely a role model for me.

CM: I got to see her once, singing with a bluegrass band at a folk festival.

Wanda Jackson was big in Japan way back when: Her "Fujiyama Mama" single rocked Japanese rockabillies in 1958, hitting #1 on the charts. She subsequently toured Japan in February and March 1959.

WJ: That must have been interesting. I finally got to meet her.

CM: Do you think rockabilly is going strong now?

WJ: Rockabilly is still going strong. I don't know as far as record sales, but there's a lot of venues and a lot of bands, because we have so many of these festivals and they're adding to them all the time. I go a lot to Europe.

CM: I have the album, *Rock 'n' Roll Your Blues Away*, the Swedish one [from 1984], that got you back into recording rockabilly. Now you're able to be true to yourself in your shows where you do country, rockabilly, and gospel, and you get to do your mission from the stage. You found a way to integrate all of that. You're up there like a radiant light shining and you can see the audience positively affected by that. Whether they get the message of the ministry or whether they just feel the happiness in the music, it's wonderful.

WJ: They know by what I'm saying, hopefully, that this has been a *real* experience for me. It's not something where I'm going to throw in a gospel song and hope somebody likes it. I even thank them for allowing me to sing and to tell my story briefly, but to tell them what Christ has done for me. I do appreciate it, they wouldn't have to.

CM: It made such a change for you.

WJ: It does for anybody.

CM: Could you tell me about Billy Gray?

WJ: My first Decca release was with Billy Gray, called "You Can't Have My Love," and I think it got up in the top ten in Billboard's country charts. He was the bandleader for Hank Thompson, and Hank, having a publishing company, would get songs. He wrote mostly everything that he recorded, but other people would send him songs and they found this duet. I think the song helped me get the contract. Naturally, Gray and I were real good pals.

CM: I love it in that song when you sing "I'm not the gal to shine your shoes," because that's the Wanda Jackson personality: strong.

WJ: That's my reputation anyway.

"Mean Mean Man" sheet music. *John Ritchie Collection*

"Not even twenty years old, Wanda Jackson sounded like she could fry eggs on her mons veneris. And that, more than anything, was the problem . . . the public was simply not prepared to accept a young lady who looked and sang as Wanda Jackson did."

—Nick Tosches,
Unsung Heroes of Rock 'n' Roll, 1984

Promotional photo of Wanda Jackson and Her Party Timers, circa 1965.

WANDA JACKSON and HER PARTY TIMERS

JIM HALSEY ARTIST MANAGEMENT Agency

Capitol RECORDS

Wanda Jackson's 2009 album *I Remember Elvis* featured glorious guitarwork by Danny B. Harvey.

Teamed up with Jack White, Wanda Jackson cut stellar versions of Amy Winehouse's "You Know I'm No Good" and Johnny Kidd and the Pirates' "Shakin' All Over." Released as a single in 2010 on White's Third Man Records, they were some of Jackson's best tunes ever.

Born near Mobile, Alabama, on January 30, 1938; died September 4, 1983

The Phantom's rare 1960 Dot Records EP featured "Love Me" and "Whisper Your Love" as recorded two years earlier.

CALL HIM PAT BOONE'S alter ego. The Lone Ranger of rockabilly. The Kiss of Hillbilly Bop.

The slick moniker and eye mask of the Phantom were gimmicks, sure, but the style was perfectly in keeping with the brash arrogance of the music and the starstruck times.

Under that mask was Jerry Lott, a.k.a. Marty Lott. Born in 1938 near Mobile, Alabama, he grew up in rural southern Leaksville, Mississippi, near the Alabama border.

Lott was infected with that new brand of Elvis music and launched a band. He had written a single song, "Whisper Your Love," which was about as mainstream as it comes: a midtempo countrified love song edging into pop balladry.

In summer 1958, Lott's manager, Johnny Blackburn, rented time at Gulf Coast Studios in Mobile, Alabama, to record the tune. The band laid down the track, and was packing to go home and await the call of stardom. "I'd worked three months on the other side of the record," Lott told Derek Glenister of *New Commotion* magazine in 1980. "Somebody said, 'What you gonna put on the flip-side?' I hadn't even thought about it."

Such was the innocence, even naivite of the times. So, Lott and band shot from the hip on a B-side.

"Someone suggested I write something like Elvis 'cause he was just a little on the wane and everybody was beginning to turn against rock 'n' roll. They said, 'See if you spark rock 'n' roll a little bit.' It wasn't any problem at all, and I wrote 'Love Me' in about ten minutes. I put all the fire and fury I could utter into it. Me and Johnny Blackburn worked the controls in the studio, as we didn't want it to sound like a commercial record, that was for sure! I was satisfied with the first take, but everybody said, 'Let's try it one more time.' I didn't yell on the first take, but I yelled on the second, and blew one of the controls off the wall."

"Love Me" kicks off with that rowdy "Yeah!" that sets the pace for a loose-limbed, wild-child romp that's some of the best rockabilly ever. Jerry Lott sang his instant composition and pumped the rhythm guitar; Frank Holmes picked the lead electric guitar, Pete McCord slapped the string bass, Bill Yates tickled the piano, and H. H. Brooks set the drumming heartbeat behind all the mayhem.

"I'm telling ya, it was wild. The drummer lost one of his sticks, the piano player screamed and knocked his stool over, the guitar player's glasses were hanging sideways over his eyes, he looked like he was hypnotized!"

But wild went nowhere without a record deal in 1958. Blackburn sat on the tapes for more than year without locating an interested label. Finally, Lott grabbed his masters and hopped a Greyhound to Hollywood in search of a contract. And it was here that the Phantom's take takes a turn into near-fantasy.

On a whim, Lott trailed pop crooner Pat Boone to church one Sunday and persuaded him to audition his tapes. And amazingly, Boone was tantalized. It was Boone who came up with the promotional gimmicks of the Phantom nickname and the mask, which Lott was required to wear at all times on stage. Boone planned to release the single on his own label, Cooga Mooga—a euphemism for the Holy Father

Himself, as in "the Great Cooga Mooga." But in the end, Lott signed with Boone's management, which struck a deal with Dot Records-, a deep-pocketed subsidiary of Paramount Pictures. So finally in 1960, two years after being recorded, the Phantom's one and only single was released. *Billboard* hailed the single as "A wild vocal which attempts to outdo Presley at the latter's wildest."

Dot Records had no idea what they had in the Phantom. "Love Me" was cataloged alongside other Dot pablum such as Debbie Reynolds and Lawrence Welk. Hollywood was no place for Mississippi rockabilly, and the sole single died a quick, sure death.

"THE PHANTOM"

Marty Lott – "1959"

MEAN MOUNTAIN MUSIC
P. O. Box 04352
MILWAUKEE, WISCONSIN 53204

The Phantom, a.k.a. Marty Lott, armed with his Gibson J-45 in 1959. *Courtesy Norton Records*

Jimmie Logsdon was a country music stalwart, but was happy to try out rockabilly during the Elvis craze. Raised on Hank Williams, he subsequently returned to country.

A Rocket in the Pocket

JIMMY LLOYD, A.K.A. JIMMIE LOGSDON

JIMMY LLOYD: "Vic McAlpin and me wrote 'I Got a Rocket in My Pocket' coming back from the *Louisiana Hayride* in Shreveport one day in 1958. Somewhere between Shreveport and Nashville, Vic—who also managed me—started saying something about the rocket age and rock 'n' roll. Then, somebody—must have been Vic—came up with the title to the song. Of course, we had to tone it down a little. Too risqué. I cut the song for Roulette Records under the name Jimmy Lloyd because I was already recording country music as Jimmy Logsdon. Back then, rock music was not so readily accepted by everybody, you see, and I thought I'd better have the two names. Besides, I was cutting for Decca as a pure country artist. Anyway, 'Rocket' took off to number one in Memphis and the Louisiana area, knocking off Jerry Lee Lewis on his own turf. I think if finally sold all of 50,000 copies. Looking back on the rockabilly thing, though, I'm kind of glad that it didn't happen for me. All I can remember is being on television in Memphis, and having to lip-sync 'Where the Rio Del Rosa Flows,' the record that I had out on Roulette before 'Rocket.' The kids were screaming. I was nervous. I was in pretty good shape then for a guy in his thirties, but all I could think was: What am I *doing* here? Can you imagine me with a hit record as a rocker? They would have had to heel me out as the oldest living rocker. That's one reason why my rockabilly career was rather short. I decided to stay country. What's interesting is that today few people remember my country records, but many people have heard of 'Rocket.' Did you know, for instance, that they used the record in the movie *The Right Stuff*? Yeah, they sure did. That's me singing. Oh, and I'm still waiting for my royalty check, too."

Interview by Randy McNutt
Louisville, Kentucky, November 1986

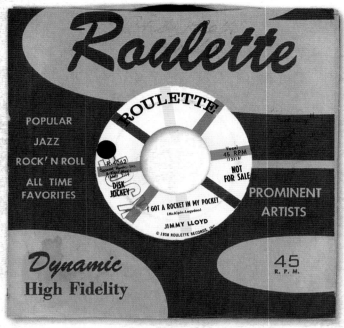

Jimmy Lloyd's "I Got a Rocket in My Pocket" on Roulette.

"I got a rocket in my pocket and the fuse is lit . . .
–Jimmy Lloyd, "I Got a Rocket in My Pocket,"
1958

"Where the Rio De Rosa Flows" was Jimmy Lloyd's rockabilly-tinged homage to San Antonio, Texas.

NEW MEXICO ROCKABILLY Jerry Nixon began life as English lad Gerald Hall James. Caught after a botched bank robbery when he was 17, he was sent to a youth borstal detention center. Freed, he signed on in 1955 as a sailor aboard an American ship setting out from Southhampton for New York harbor. Upon arrival, he claimed he was Jerry James Nixon, a fine upstanding Minnesota boy. He was setting out on a new life.

Travelling across the United States, he wound up in New Mexico by 1956, working in a cardboard-box factory. Here, he heard Elvis on the radio, hearing his own destiny as well. Although he had little musical ability, he talked his way into fronting a working band, the Santa Fe Flames, which became his own Volcanoes.

The band was aptly named: They spewed energy, which covered up for any musical shortcomings. Local studio owner, manager, and businessman Leonard Sanchez invited them to his Quality Records in 1956 to wax several of their originals.

The band toured the Southwest, even opening for Gene Vincent at the Big D Jamboree in Dallas, Texas, in 1958. By 1960, they had cut their rockabilly masterpiece, the rollicking hit "Saturday Midnight Bop."

But all was not well at Q Records. Sanchez assured the boys he was investing his earnings. Unfortunately, he was investing in cockfights and poker games, and Q went under, taking Nixon's musical career with it.

THE Q-RECORDINGS NEW MEXICO '58–'64

JERRY J. NIXON

GENTLEMAN OF ROCK'N'ROLL

MONO

"I never ever thought of myself as a musician! I never thought I was good enough and we had too much fun to take it too seriously. But when I look back on it now, a couple of tracks don't sound at all bad to me . . . with that loud crazy guitar and strong beat . . ."

—Jerry J. Nixon

"Q"

Q-1077-A

45 RPM

SATURDAY MIDNIGHT BOP
(Sanchez, Nixon)

JERRY J. NIXON
and The Volcanoes

Born Joplin, Missouri, on October 24, 1934

By Deke Dickerson

Promotional photo of Glen Glenn sporting a very country cowboy shirt.

IT SEEMS TO BE ETCHED IN STONE that rock 'n' roll was invented in Memphis, Tennessee, one summer night in 1954 by a young truck driver named Elvis Presley. Many would have you believe that Memphis was the only city in America where such a convergence of white and black music could occur, and that young Mr. Presley was a genius of the highest order who created rock 'n' roll singlehandedly from his own design.

Of course, this notion is false. Just as there were dozens of people at the turn of the century working on the invention of the automobile, the real story behind the invention of rock 'n' roll is a convoluted one, filled with more interesting twists and turns than the Mississippi River.

Our story concerns another important city at a important time—Los Angeles, California, in the 1950s—and two energetic young musicians who came of age during this exciting time period: Glenn Troutman, aka Glenn Trout, aka Glen Glenn, and his guitar-playing compatriot, Gary Lambert.

Perhaps nowhere in America was there such a diverse melting of cultures as Los Angeles at mid-century. Hillbillies from the South worked side by side with Mexican immigrants, African-Americans came from the eastern United States for the multitude of factory jobs, and scores of other cultures converged in Southern California as well.

Along with this vast influx of immigrants came some of the finest music from across the country. Dust Bowl migrants such as the Maddox Brothers and Rose brought rowdy hillbilly and country music from their native Alabama to the West Coast; African American performers such as Louis Jordan, Pee Wee Crayton, and Slim Gaillard brought their rhythm and blues and jazz to Central Avenue in Los Angeles; Jewish music impresarios like Jerry Lieber and Mike Stoller produced doo-wop and blues within the black community; and the sounds of Mexico wafted from almost every neighborhood from the San Fernando Valley to San Diego, wherever there were Mexican immigrants.

This was the atmosphere that bred Glenn and his music, and that inspired the guitar playing of Gary Lambert. A richer mixture of musical inspiration could hardly be imagined. While Elvis certainly was the important catalyst in the explosion of rock 'n' roll, the fact is that the seeds had already been planted all across the country, and it was just a matter of time before this new music sprang to life.

Glenn's records rank as some of the finest of the era, and they have stood the test of time as perhaps the best examples of rockabilly to emerge from Los Angeles in the 1950s.

The story of Glen Glenn begins in Joplin, Missouri, where he was born Orin Glenn Troutman on October 24, 1934. Joplin was a small town tucked away in the Ozark Mountains, and country music figured heavily in its heritage (*Grand Ole Opry* member Porter Wagoner was also from the same area, and was in fact Glenn's cousin by marriage).

Orin was soon being called by his middle name, Glenn, to avoid confusion with his father Orin Orville Troutman, and the name stuck. His parents Louise and Orin had a love for country music and encouraged young Glenn in his musical pursuits from an early age. The family radio was often tuned to station KVOO in Tulsa, Oklahoma, where Glenn first heard Bob Wills and the Texas Playboys. Once Glenn heard Wills he was hooked on country music. Eventually he began tuning in to *The Grand Ole Opry* and soaking up influences from Roy Acuff to Little Jimmy Dickens, Red Foley, Ernest Tubb, and many other country stars. From a very young age Glenn tried his own hand at singing, often imitating his country music idols.

Fate intervened in 1948 when the Troutman family loaded up the truck and moved westward to San Dimas, California, located about an hour east of Los Angeles. Like thousands of others from the South, Glenn's family came west for the promise of a better life. Little did the Troutmans know the sorts of opportunities it would open up for the burgeoning musician in their family.

In addition to the country music he knew and loved, Glenn soon found himself listening late at night to a famed Los Angeles disc jockey, Dick "Huggy Boy" Hugg, on a local black radio station that played blues, R&B, and vocal groups. The music he heard would have a profound influence on him.

In 1950 or 1951, Glenn bought a Gibson guitar and then a Martin D-28, and he spent virtually every waking minute teaching himself all the songs he heard on the radio. Eventually he met a kindred spirit in Gary Lambert, a fellow high school student who played hot guitar and was looking for someone to play with.

Gary was from La Verne, a small community just down the road from San Dimas. He had quite a local reputation as a hot picker and impressed nearly everybody who heard him play. His style was half Merle Travis and Chet Atkins thumbpicking, and half Joe Maphis flatpicking, and it was well suited to the material Glenn was interested in at the time. Gary was in a comfortable enough position to afford some of the finest equipment, and this too bolstered his reputation locally. Gary had a regular square-dance gig, and soon Glenn was joining him on rhythm guitar. After the two got together, they were soon rehearsing an act as a duo. All this excitement caught up with Glenn, and he dropped out of high school in the eleventh grade to pursue music full time.

Glenn and Gary began making the rounds as perpetual hangers on. Even though they were too young to get into most shows, they would stand outside and listen to the music, soaking it all in. They would often go to the Riverside Rancho near Griffith Park, where the setup enabled them to stand directly outside the club and hear the music. One of their fondest memories involves guitar legend Joe Maphis, who played the Riverside Rancho every Sunday night. Glenn and Gary would go and listen to him from outside every week, and eventually Joe became so taken with the boys that he would come outside and smoke cigarettes during his break and talk to them, offering advice about how to break into the local country music business.

Joe Maphis was a hugely influential figure in Los Angeles country music history. He and his wife, Rose Lee, had a honky-tonk hit with Joe's composition "Dim Lights, Thick Smoke (and Loud, Loud Music)," but it was his guitar playing that left the biggest mark. He was one of the fastest guitar players who ever lived, and he wore the crown "King of the Strings" for his prowess on any stringed instrument: guitar, banjo, fiddle, mandolin, or bass. Starting in 1954, he was the leader of the house band on the popular *Town Hall Party* television show, where he was seen by everyone from Compton Okies to Beverly Hills elite.

Joe told Glenn and Gary about an amateur contest being held on Sundays at the Rancho by a local disc jockey, the "Squeakin' Deacon" from country station KXLA in Pasadena. Every Sunday they would broadcast a live radio show from within the Riverside Rancho. It was a two-hour show, the first hour being the amateur contest, the second hour featuring big-name stars like Joe Maphis and Merle Travis.

Glenn and Gary went down one Sunday and entered the contest and, to their amazement, won the prize the first time out, singing a version of Joe and Rose Lee Maphis's "Dim Lights, Thick Smoke." The prize was a wristwatch, but the real reward was the encouragement it offered the two youngsters. Glenn recalls not being able to sleep for about a week afterwards, he was so excited.

Glenn and Gary, now billed as the Missouri Mountain Boys (even though Glenn was the only one actually from Missouri), made the rounds to all the Los Angeles–area country music shows. They made sure they were always seen, showing up like clockwork at the *Town Hall Party* in Compton and Cliffie Stone's *Hometown Jamboree* in El Monte. They knew how to sneak backstage at all these venues, and they befriended many of the artists, including Lefty Frizzell, Gene O'Quin, Merle Travis, the Collins Kids, and Johnny Horton. The hundreds of backstage photographs that Glenn began taking at this time are evidence of the sheer number of musicians they were rubbing elbows with.

The pair auditioned for both the *Town Hall Party* and the *Hometown Jamboree*, but they didn't find a regular paying gig until they struck paydirt with the *County Barn Dance* in Baldwin Park, just down the road from El Monte.

The *County Barn Dance* was another fixture on the crowded Saturday night roster of live televised country music shows in Los Angeles. It featured an impressive roster that included Les "Carrot Top" Anderson, Skeets McDonald, the White Brothers (Clarence and Roland White, in their

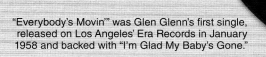

"Everybody's Movin'" was Glen Glenn's first single, released on Los Angeles' Era Records in January 1958 and backed with "I'm Glad My Baby's Gone."

Glen Glenn on stage along with his long-time friend Gary Lambert on lead guitar, here playing a Gretsch solid-body.

pre–Kentucky Colonels and Byrds days), and Gary Lambert's future wife, Jean, who appeared with an act called the Three Country Girls, later renamed the Smith Sisters. The show also had many guest stars each week, and it was here that Glenn and Gary befriended aspiring guitarist Eddie Cochran, who was then half of the Cochran Brothers act. Glenn and Gary appeared regularly on the *County Barn Dance* throughout the years 1954 and 1955, and they became quite well known throughout the local country music community.

Their association with Eddie Cochran became quite close over the next couple of years. In addition to appearances on the *County Barn Dance*, Glenn and Gary did a show with the Cochran Brothers during a short stint living in Northern California in 1956 when the Cochran Brothers were doing the same thing. By all accounts Gary Lambert and Eddie Cochran bonded through their love for Chet Atkins, Merle Travis, and other hot pickers (both bought brand new Gretsch guitars around this time), and in fact Gary recorded quite a few home demos of the two of them playing together, which were collected on the Stomper Time CD *Eddie Cochran and Gary Lambert*. Eddie also loaned out his bass player, Connie "Guybo" Smith, to Glenn and Gary for live shows and recording over the years. Glenn recalls that when Eddie went solo and started

having hits, he started hanging with the rock 'n' roll crowd and they didn't see him around their country music shows any more.

It was during 1954 and 1955 that Glenn first began recording. Most of these recordings were primitive home demos done on Gary Lambert's portable recorder. Other early recordings that have survived are from live television and radio performances that were taped by their close friend Glenn Mueller on his reel-to-reel recorder (off the radio or TV).

Perhaps Glenn's most interesting performance from this time period is "That's All Right (Mama)," recorded live on radio station KXLA in January 1955. According to Glenn, he had not yet heard Elvis Presley's Sun Recording of this song, but he had heard country singer Gene O'Quin perform it on the *Hometown Jamboree* show. It was also around this time that Glenn started trying to incorporate more of the blues and R&B material that he heard on the *Huggy Boy* show into his country music act. Not long after recording "That's All Right (Mama)," Glenn heard Elvis Presley for the first time and soon was performing rock 'n' roll every chance he could get.

Other early performances included rollicking live versions of "Jack and Jill Boogie" and "John Henry," both recorded on KXLA in May 1955. These recordings really demonstrate the concept of hillbillies latching on to boogie woogie and rhythm and blues and forging ahead with this new music known as rock 'n' roll. By the time Glenn made his next recording in January 1956, he was moving even more into the rock 'n' roll direction, cutting his own versions of "Baby, Let's Play House" and "Be-Bop-a-Lula."

Later in 1956, Glenn had an opportunity to go back to Missouri and tour with his cousin Porter Wagoner. Glenn leapt at the chance and soon was making regular appearances on the popular *Ozark Jubilee* show broadcast out of Springfield, Missouri. Porter was supportive of Glenn's forays into rock 'n' roll, and in fact a great version of Glenn singing "Shake, Rattle and Roll" was recorded live at the *Ozark Jubilee* in July of 1956 with Porter's band backing him up (they also did a great version of "There She Goes" for the country listeners).

Glenn toured with Porter to the East Coast and throughout the Midwest, logging lots of great road stories and rubbing elbows with just about everybody in the business. Porter was also trying to get Glenn his own recording contract with UA Records, but he couldn't get a deal because the label thought Glenn was stuck between the country and rock 'n' roll markets. This was undoubtedly true, and in fact Glenn has said himself that he was really a country performer doing rock 'n' roll material. Although Glenn had some great experiences with Porter on the road, California was home, and Glenn got homesick for his family and moved back to San Dimas after only a month or so with Porter's group.

In September 1956, Glenn had his first professional recording session at the Garrison Studio in Long Beach,

California. This was a four-song demo of excellent country material that Glenn paid for himself and intended to shop around for a record deal. Although the material was excellent and featured top-notch talent such as Ralph Mooney on steel guitar, Glenn failed to get a recording contract with any of the labels he played the demos for.

Rejoining the *County Barn Dance* and reuniting with Gary Lambert, the next major figures to emerge in Glenn's career were The Maddox Brothers and Rose, who were to play a large part in the crucial next phase of his career.

The *County Barn Dance* had big guest stars every week, from Ray Price to Faron Young, and the Maddox Brothers and Rose were regulars on the show. During this time period, they were perhaps the most popular act on the West Coast, with their wild stage antics and novelty tunes. Fred Maddox (the de facto leader of the group) was particularly smitten with rock 'n' roll music, and he took an instant liking to Glenn and Gary and their brand of rockabilly.

Fred Maddox suggested to Glenn and Gary that they go check out Elvis Presley when he played in San Diego. The show galvanized the two youngsters and reinforced their opinion that they needed to be playing rock 'n' roll instead of country. When they saw all the hundreds of screaming girls, the choice was obvious which direction they'd be taking. Fred took the boys backstage and they struck up a friendship with Elvis, Scotty, Bill, and D. J. They would visit Elvis once more when he came back to the West Coast and stayed at the Knickerbocker Hotel in Hollywood. In fact, Bill Black would later even play on one of Glenn's demos while visiting with Fred Maddox.

As fate would have it, it was about this time that The Maddox Brothers and Rose were having internal issues, and during a tour to the Pacific Northwest, Rose and Cal Maddox quit the band, leaving Fred in quite a jam. Glenn recalls getting a phone call from Fred Maddox's wife Kitty, asking him to join them when they returned from the tour. Henry Maddox's wife Loretta stepped in to replace Rose as lead vocalist, and Glenn was now in Cal's position as rhythm guitarist and vocalist. Using the name the Maddox Brothers and Retta (short for Loretta), they continued their grueling touring schedule.

This worked out well, as many country acts were now bringing young rock 'n' rollers along on tour as a novelty act. Glenn would play rhythm guitar while the others sang, and he played straight man to Fred Maddox's jokes. Then Fred would bring him to the microphone to do a few Elvis Presley hits of the day.

Glenn toured extensively with the Maddox Brothers and Retta, recalling that they burned up a brand-new 1956 Cadillac in only nine months, with all the miles they put on the car. Eventually the group decided that the lineup with Retta wasn't working out, and Fred decided to quit touring so much and work regularly in Southern California. Fred put Glenn in charge of the house band at the Copa Club in Pomona, which Glenn affectionately termed "Fred Maddox's

Playhouse." This new base of operations brought in a stellar roster of guest stars, and Glenn wound up meeting just about every star that toured through the area, including Johnny Cash and Buck Owens, to name just two. Fred loved to kid around and call Glenn by his new stage name "Glenn Trout the Stinkin' Fisherman," a play on Johnny Horton's nickname "The Singing Fisherman." This was the first time Glenn's name had been changed for the stage, and he stuck with Glenn Trout for a year or two until it was changed yet again to his better-known moniker.

Glenn got back together with Gary Lambert around this time, and they recorded several home demo tunes at Gary's house. A session on May 12, 1957, yielded three excellent performances, including "Don't You Love Me," an original by Glenn, and covers of Mac Curtis's "If I Had Me a Woman" and Sonny Fisher's "Hold Me Baby." Asked about how he knew such unknown (at the time) rockabilly classics, Glenn reports that he and Gary had gotten into the practice of taking the unwanted rockabilly records sent as promos to KXLA, who wouldn't play them, thus discovering many great obscure songs.

Around this time, Fred Maddox also convinced local car dealer Cal Worthington to have Maddox's band on the newly launched television show *Cal's Corral*, which was broadcast live every Sunday afternoon for three hours.

Luckily, Glenn's friend Glenn Mueller archived many of his live appearances on reel-to-reel tape, and they have been reissued in recent years. Several recordings exist from Squeakin' Deacon's show on KXLA with the Maddox band backing Glenn up, including "Baby Let's Play House" and "Be-Bop-a-Lula."

Shortly thereafter, Fred Maddox left *Cal's Corral* over a pay dispute. Apparently Cal Worthington didn't want to pay the bands for playing on his show, even though the musician's union insisted that he pay everybody union scale. Cal then wrote checks to the musicians and instructed them to sign and return the checks to him without cashing them, thus getting around the union requirements. Cal then discovered that Fred Maddox was not only cashing the checks he wasn't supposed to cash, but that he was cashing his entire band's checks and keeping everybody's money!

Glenn remained on the show and the *Cal's Corral* live recordings from late 1957 include the classic rock 'n' roll lineup of Glenn's band, including Gary Lambert back on lead guitar, Connie "Guybo" Smith (on loan from Eddie Cochran's band) on bass, and Joe O'Dell on drums.

It was this lineup that Glenn would finally take into the studio on December 3, 1957, to record his first official rockabilly demo. As with the earlier country session, Glenn paid for it himself, intending to use it to get signed to a record label. Wynn Stewart, a fellow Missourian transplanted to California, had had Glenn appear on his show and had been using Gary Lambert as his guitar player on several dates. Wynn had been after Glenn for some time to get a recording contract and make some records. Glenn told Wynn about his failed country demos, and Wynn lit a fire under Glenn to do a rockabilly demo and shop it around.

Although Wynn would go on to record for Challenge and Capitol and eventually became one of the originators of the Bakersfield sound with such excellent records as "Wishful Thinking" and "It's Such a Pretty World Today," at this stage of the game he was just another country singer gone rockabilly in the hopes of latching on to some of that Presley magic. He had just cut a great rocker for Jackpot Records, "Come On" (which Glenn would later cover on his 1980s comeback record), and he was after Glenn to capitalize on the rockabilly fad while it was still hot.

Glenn brought his band (which included Gary Lambert, "Guybo" Smith, and Joe O'Dell) into the studio. They were augmented by Wynn Stewart on rhythm guitar and Gary's fiancée Jean Smith (soon to be Jean Lambert) and her sister Glenda, along with Beverly Stewart, singing backup. They cut two songs that day: Wally Lewis's "Kathleen" and Stewart's composition "One Cup of Coffee (and a Cigarette)."

Glenn immediately took the acetate dubs and began shopping them around to all the Los Angeles–area labels. One of his first stops was Imperial Records, where Jimmy Haskell asked Glenn to leave one of the dubs for them to consider. What Glenn didn't know was that Haskell was really only interested in the arrangement on "Kathleen," which he borrowed lock, stock, and barrel for his upcoming Ricky Nelson recording of "Poor Little Fool." It was a harsh lesson for Glenn and straight out of the plot of the newly released Presley movie *Jailhouse Rock*. Back in the 1950s, these sorts of things happened on a regular basis.

Glenn had more luck at ERA Records, which was owned by Lou Bidell and Herb Newman. ERA had just enjoyed massive successes in the pop market with Gogi Grant's "The Wayward Wind" and "Suddenly There's a Valley." Bidell and Newman were looking to cross over into the teenage market, and Glenn was exactly what they were looking for: a good-looking young rockabilly kid with some catchy rock 'n' roll songs. They signed Glenn to a contract and a scant six weeks after making his demo, Glenn was at the famed Gold Star Studios in Hollywood recording for ERA. What Bidell and Newman didn't know was that in another twist of fate echoing Elvis Presley's life, Glenn had received his draft notice in the mail, and Gary Lambert had agreed to volunteer at the same time so they could be stationed together.

January 8, 1958, marked the day that Glenn Troutman nee Glenn Trout would forever be known in the music world as Glen Glenn. Newly rechristened by the ERA bigwigs for the teen market, Glen brought his band back to the studio and in one day cut the bulk of the material that his legend rests upon—four of the best rockabilly songs ever committed to tape. "Everybody's Movin'" and "I'm Glad My Baby's Gone" were both written by Glen, and two were by Wynn Stewart: a new recording of "One Cup of Coffee (and a Cigarette)" and another great slow rocker, "Would Ya."

The Glen Glenn sound, as defined by these classic recordings, was fairly unusual. It was rock 'n' roll, but it wasn't wild and it wasn't at a breakneck speed. It had country elements such as Glen's hick-inflected vocals and Gary Lambert's twangy guitar, but had the necessary rockabilly backbeat to make the Presley teenagers go for it. The songs were catchy and described the rockabilly hoodlum lifestyle in a simple way that anyone could latch on to (they definitely played a part in the English teddy-boy popularity of Glen's records in the 1970s). The excellent production by the experienced hands at Gold Star (who were also responsible for Eddie Cochran's hits, Ritchie Valens's "La Bamba," and many others) contributed mightily to the fantastic sound on these records, with perfect slapping bass thumping away at the bottom end and Gary Lambert's great lead guitar loudly mixed into the top end.

Glen's first single, "Everybody's Movin'" backed with "I'm Glad My Baby's Gone," was released as ERA 1061 in late January 1958, less than two weeks after he had recorded it. The song was doing well and could have been a hit, but in a cruel twist of fate Glen and Gary had to report for active duty in the Army just two weeks after the recording session.

When Glen told Bidell and Newman at ERA about his draft notice, Glen was told that they wouldn't have signed him if they had known he wouldn't be around to promote the records. From that point on, ERA didn't sink their full promotional muscle into Glen's releases. It's one of the great rock 'n' roll "What if?" stories, and one wonders whether Glen Glenn would today be a household word if Uncle Sam hadn't come calling.

Nevertheless, ERA still had faith in Glen's talent, and they wanted to record more material. After Glen and Gary's initial eight-week basic training at Ford Ord in Central California, they received a two-week leave. During that time, on April 4, 1958, they returned to Gold Star studios and laid down more legendary tracks: "Blue Jeans and a Boy's Shirt" a songwriting collaboration between Glen and Bobby George, and "Laurie Ann," basically a rewriting of "Kathleen" by Wally Lewis, Ned Miller, and Bonnie Guitar. They did several takes of each song that day, which have seen the light of day in recent years. The band on that session was the same as at the January session, with the added voices of the female backup singers from the earlier Garrison studio session (the Smith Sisters, Jean and Glenda, plus Beverly Stewart).

ERA released Glen's second single in June of 1958—"Laurie Ann" backed with "One Cup of Coffee"—as ERA 1074. Again, the single had serious hit potential, but by this point Glen and Gary were stationed at Scofield Barracks Army Base in Honolulu and couldn't do much to help their careers. It was here that Glenn Troutman received the telegram from ERA Records informing him that his name was now Glen Glenn! Glen recalls hearing his song on the radio and listening helplessly, knowing that he couldn't do anything to promote it back in the states. Further tragedy ensued when Dick Clark tried to get Glen for a personal appearance on American Bandstand to perform "Laurie Ann," but his commanding officer wouldn't let him fly back to the U.S. Although Dick Clark made "Laurie Ann" a Pick of the Week, and it made several local charts, including number two on Los Angeles station KRLA, the record didn't get the push it deserved and once again Glen was robbed of a hit.

During Glen and Gary's tenure in Hawaii they managed to perform quite a bit and befriended local DJ Tom Moffatt, who featured Glen as an opening act for several visiting shows, including one spectacular three-day gig at the Civic Auditorium in Honolulu in July 1958 with the Everly Brothers, the Four Preps, Bobby Day, and Robin Luke. Glen is in great form in the photos that survive from this show, doing all the Presley moves and really setting the crowd on fire.

During their time in Hawaii, Glen and Gary did manage to record another tune at least once. They took some local musicians and went into Webley Edwards's studio in Honolulu to cut the great "Kitty Kat," which had been written for them by their friend Glen Mueller (the same one who had taped the live performances over the years). Although this was one of their best songs and performances, it sat in the can until it was eventually released in the '70s.

ERA Records continued to believe in Glen, even though he was unable to tour and promote his records, and they released his third 45 in early 1959 as ERA 1086: "Blue Jeans and a Boy's Shirt" backed with "Would Ya." The record was a great rockabilly two-sider, but, predictably, it failed to make a dent and has become the hardest to find of all of Glen's ERA records.

In 1959 Lou Bidell and Herb Newman split ERA Records into two labels, with Bidell retaining rights to ERA and Newman striking out with the new Dore label, which was meant to cater to the new pop teen idol market. Newman figured Glen's ticket to stardom might reside in the Bobby Rydell/Bobby Vinton vein, and when Glen took another leave back to the states in February 1959, he returned to the studio.

This time around, Glen was backed by Ernie Freeman's band (which included the legendary

Plas Johnson on saxophone) and two sides were cut: "Suzie Green from Abilene" and "Goofin' Around," and they were released as Dore 523. Neither was written by Glen. Although they weren't bad songs, they didn't suit Glen's style and it was obvious that this wasn't the right direction for him. The 45 was released in late 1959 and, once again, with Glen in the Army and unable to promote it, it sunk without a trace.

Glen and Gary returned to California in early 1960 after their two-year stint in the Army. At first, things seemed to fall back into place, with Glen and Gary making appearances on *Cal's Corral* again and playing gigs for Fred Maddox, but the music industry had changed while they were overseas. Gone was the fire of rockabilly, and the country market in Southern California had been permanently injured by rock 'n' roll's new pop direction. Many of California's country musicians had left for Las Vegas and Reno, where there was still regular work to be found. Others, like Glen Glenn and Gary Lambert, found day jobs and settled into "normal" life.

Glen began working for General Dynamics in 1960, and soon thereafter he met Mary Forrester, who became his wife in 1961. With a regular job and two kids, Glen didn't have as much time for music, but he and Gary continued to perform together at the Palomino Club and other small Southern California honky-tonks throughout the 1960s. Gary went back into his family's construction business and played throughout the decade as a guitarist for just about every local country band in the Inland Empire. He also went on to raise a family with his wife, Jean.

Glen and Gary recorded one more track together for Dore in 1961 at Gold Star studios: "I'll Never Stop Loving You," which was a solid Marty Robbins–type pop-country effort. The session was incomplete, with no final take of the song finished that day. It sat in the can for three years until Glen returned to Gold Star for one last stand in July 1964, laying down the vocal overdub for "I'll Never Stop Loving You" and recording one more tune in order to have enough songs for a new 45 release.

This last session was quite the star-studded affair, with A-list session musicians Jerry Cole on guitar, Carol Kaye on bass, and Ritchie Frost on drums, all of whom appeared on many Los Angeles–produced hit records by (for instance) the Beach Boys, Ricky Nelson, and others. The session yielded the fun novelty tune "I Still Didn't Have the

Sense to Go," which was paired with "I'll Never Stop Loving You" and released as Dore 717 in the fall of 1964. This record turned out to be Glen's last 45. The advent of the Beatles effectively killed Glen's chance at stardom, and apart from a demo recording done at his house ("It's a Sad Thing to See"), this would be the last recording he would make in the original era of rock 'n' roll.

The story doesn't quite end here, however. Although Glen faded into obscurity in America, his records were prized and revered by the burgeoning Teddy Boy 1950s revival scene in England and Europe starting in the late 1960s. With the 1977 album release of *Hollywood Rock and Roll* on England's Chiswick Records, Glen's classic rockabilly sides were rediscovered by a slew of young rockabilly fanatics. "Everybody's Movin'" became a standard in the rockabilly songbook. Ace Records released a best-selling album of alternate takes and live recordings, *The Glen Glenn Story*, that sold incredibly well for an obscure rockabilly artist

such as Glen. After its encouraging sales, Glen and Gary Lambert, his old guitar-playing buddy, went into the studio and recorded a new album, *Everybody's Movin' Again*, for Ace Records, which also sold well.

Glen and Gary began performing again around Los Angeles, backed by young new bands that idolized them. Eventually Glen finally relented to the many offers he had received from Europe and flew overseas to perform at the English Hemsby Festival and other festivals across Europe.

Glen's influence, via the slew of reissue recordings, was quite surprising to him. He discovered that Bruce Springsteen, Tom Petty, and Bob Dylan had all performed "Everybody's Movin'" in their live concerts. Dylan even personally asked Glen to open a Hollywood Palladium show for him, marking a personal high point in a career that had already spanned over forty years.

Glen Glenn and Gary Lambert are still around, playing the occasional show and meeting with visiting fans that love to hear their stories from the past. Glen loves the attention from the young fans who idolize him as one of rockabilly's original architects.

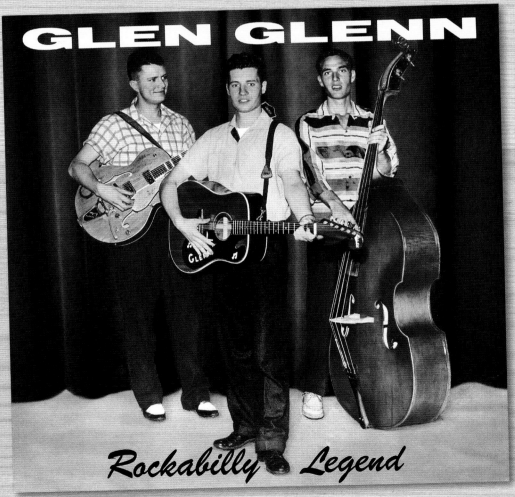

A collection of Glen Glenn's alternate takes and other rarities was released during the revival years.

Born Sutherlin, Virginia, March 27, 1940; died September 3, 2007

MANY FEMALE ROCKABILLIES were tagged as the "Female Elvis," but Janis Martin probably had the clearest rights to the moniker. She recorded the song "My Boy Elvis"—and more importantly, her stage moves were closest to those of Elvis'.

After secretly marrying her boyfriend in 1956 and becoming pregnant, her label, RCA, dropped her in 1958. For all purposes, her musical career was over—until the rockabilly revival of the 1980s.

The EP that outraged Col. Tom Parker: This rare South African RCA–Victor EP gave top billing to Janis Martin over Elvis. The EP was quickly pulled from distribution.

Janis Martin rocks the RCA studio.
Michael Ochs Archives/Getty Images

Janis Martin recounted that she wrote her rockabilly hit "Drugstore Rock And Roll" simply from experience, hanging around and rocking with pals at the local drugstore. The song became a national hit, selling more than 750,000 copies.

"Will You, Willyum" was the A-side to "Drugstore Rock And Roll" and released in 1956.

127

Born Nashville, Arkansas, on January 21, 1938

By Craig Morrison

Pat Cupp cut some rocking rockabilly sides, but due to the media of the day, he was known only in his local Arkansas region.

IN 1956, **PAT CUPP RECORDED** a handful of songs, such as "Long Gone Daddy," "I Guess It's Meant That Way," "Do Me No Wrong," and "Baby Come Back," all cherished in the rockabilly world. Inspired by the first wave of rockabillies, he did shows with Elvis Presley, Carl Perkins, Roy Orbison, Johnny Cash, and others. Following a stint in the Air Force, he carried on in music as a sideline to his career in engineering.

Cupp returned to the world of rockabilly when he performed at the Hemsby festival in England in 1995, to a rapturous reception. He continued to appear at other festivals, but had difficulty with his hearing. I interviewed him, a charming, personable man accompanied by his beloved wife, in 2005 in Green Bay, Wisconsin, following his performance at Rockin' Fest II. He had a new CD at the time—*Pat Cupp* on Wild Hare Records— recorded with a solid band of younger rockabilly musicians and featuring mostly his original songs. His hearing loss became too profound and after a show in France in 2008 he retired, reluctantly, from the stage.

PAT CUPP: I was raised in a very musical family. My mother and dad, my brothers and my sister were all musicians. Back then, in the '40s and early '50s, country music was referred to as hillbilly

music: Hank Williams and all. We didn't know anything about that, because we were in the pop field: Hit Parade and big band music from the radio, Glenn Miller, Artie Shaw.

My mom was a piano player. My dad was a ukulele player. He idolized Ukelele Ike [Cliff Edwards] a popular musician in the '20s and '30s. My dad taught me to play a little four-string ukulele when I was about four or five years old. When I got big enough to get my hands on a guitar then I was able to buy one. I began to play guitar, but the songs I learned were popular songs.

I was born in Nashville, Arkansas, on January 21, 1938, but moved to Magnolia, Arkansas. In Magnolia at 13 years old, I won a talent contest at a horse show. Bob Wills and the Texas Playboys was a western swing outfit. They were traveling all over Texas, Arkansas, doing rodeos and horse shows, a big thing in my part of the country. They would play on a stage in the back of a flat-bed truck out in the middle of a rodeo. A lot of these places promoted talent contests, you had tap dancers, comedians. My mother played the organ background music while the little two-wheel carriages that's got the trotters were racing around the track. My mother played for me, and I sang "I Apologize," some Vic Damone, Frank Sinatra type tunes. It's as far from country as you can get.

I won a six-month radio show on the local station, KVMA. The sponsor was Piggly Wiggly Grocery. I, of course, included my family. The name of the show was *Pat Cupp and Friends*. My dad was my announcer and my mom arranged all the music that would be done by the family. We did the Mills Brothers, Ink Spots, [Perry] Como, Vic Damone, all that, and my theme song was "Me and My Shadow." We recorded the Sunday afternoon program at our house during the week and at night when Dad was home. The show was first recorded on a wire recorder, because this was the equipment that the radio station had at the time. Later, we had to buy a tape recorder when the radio station changed their equipment. The show was a success and extended another six months.

In 1953, when we moved to Texarkana, Arkansas, from Magnolia, I still had no country music in my background. I became friends with a fellow who played football for Texarkana, "Cheesie" Nelson. His name was Carl. He was a country music fan, and mimicked people of the day: Faron Young, Webb Pierce, all those.

One day he came running to my house with a record, a 45, in his hand and he says, "You've got to hear this. This is going to knock your socks off." Not being a country and

western fan, I didn't figure I'd be really interested. I didn't have a record player to play it on. We had to go to another friend's house and he had a small portable record player. We put this Sun recording on and I heard for the first time, "That's All Right Mama" by Elvis. When I heard this song and Presley singing it, I knew instantly it wasn't like anything else I had ever heard, and I had heard a lot of music in my time, even being so young. I immediately liked it.

My mother and I were very close. She was a tremendous musician. I went home and told her, "I have found it! I found the music that I would really like to do. This fellow named Elvis Presley, he's got a unique way of presenting himself and he's a good-looking guy, that's part of it, but it's the music that I'm interested in, it's the rhythm and the voice, he's just got something that really catches you." She said, "We'll have to hear it." So I got the records and let her hear and she said, "If that's what you want to do, then that's what you will do. We'll get you into this." She wanted me to be an entertainer, so did my dad. We went to Jim Lefan, a KOSY radio announcer in Texarkana, who was doing all the promoting and said, "We want to do this, we want to get involved in it." There was nothing else like it. We learned "That's All Right Mama" and the flip side, and as his records began to come we learned everything he did. I played the guitar; Cheesie did the singing. He didn't act like Presley, he just mimicked his voice. I was not singing anything at the time of this music.

We got to see Elvis at the auditorium in Texarkana. The next trip he made he had a fender-bender car wreck between Fauke, Arkansas, and Texarkana and was late for his show. The promoter, Jim Lefan, knew about Cheesie and I doing this little act just for fun and he had an audience full of people getting upset that Elvis hadn't shown up. So he called Cheesie and I at the local drive-in downtown. We went immediately to the auditorium and stepped out on the stage and he sang the Elvis stuff; I played guitar behind him, and kept the crowd. Most of those people knew us, and they screamed and hollered because we was doing it, and then Elvis came in right at the last part. He was really amused at what he saw. We were probably the first Elvis impersonators there ever was! He enjoyed it. He took the show over, naturally, but he did tell us to wait in the wings and at intermission, after the first 30 minutes or so, he took us downstairs in the dressing room and said "Who are you guys? Why are you doing this?" We talked about girls, but mostly music. Then he left and did the rest of the show. This happened a couple of times where we had little meetings with him when he came through Texarkana.

In the meantime Carl Perkins starts coming along. He gets on the Sun label. All this between 1954 and middle 1955. Here's Carl, older than I am. I'm not but 18 and Carl's somewhere around 20 or so, around Elvis's age. But I'm still a young guy, and I'm real excited about this. They all had songs. We didn't have anything to base our stuff on so we said, "Well, we'll write. This is all new, we'll just write what

we think fits in this category." The roots of rock and roll in my book started out with the Elvis approach to rhythm and blues music. Rhythm and blues has been around a long time. But rockabilly was a short-lived music. It happened so fast. Part of it being, when Elvis hit RCA–Victor off of Sun, RCA–Victor had a picture of what they wanted Presley to be. They took him away from the root music and, even though he was unique, they made him more of a commercial entertainer. Carl Perkins stayed in that field and continued but there wasn't very many other guys that were getting into it and getting hit records. Elvis had dominated and nobody came up to his caliber so they couldn't break through. That little short period of rockabilly music coming off of hillbilly into a rock beat was born in 1954 through around late '56. Some people say '57. That eventually spun off to the Beatles and all these other people. From then on the times changed, the approach changed, it got into hard rock in the '70s.

CRAIG MORRISON: In one of your rockabilly recordings, "Baby Come Back," you mention "Blue Suede Shoes," "Heartbreak Hotel," and "Put Your Cat Clothes On." That last one is the title of another Carl Perkins song. He recorded it but it was not released until the '70s. My guess is you heard Perkins play it live.

PC: No, I never heard Carl do that song. When my mother and I wrote this song you're speaking of, "Blue Suede Shoes" was out, "Heartbreak Hotel" was out. The only thing I can come up with—we did shows with Carl—is that Carl heard my song. I do not remember hearing that phrase from him. Maybe he wrote that song after he heard what we did. Anyway "put your cat clothes on and let's go out" was a phrase that you said in that time. I won't take the claim for giving him a song title; I think it was just coincidence that he would write a song later, "Put Your Cat Clothes On," because that was just a popular phrase. I used it in a song and he happened to write one.

Born Gold Mine, Louisiana, on August 22, 1936; died February 13, 2010

Although he hailed from Louisiana, Dale Hawkins became a rockabilly star on Chicago's Chess Records label. Chess saw the success of Sun Records with Elvis and immediately began seeking out its own roster of rock 'n' rollers.

Dale Hawkins' hit "Susie-Q," released in 1957 on the Chess subsidiary, Checker Records. Based on Louisiana guitarist James Burton's rollicking lick, the song reached #27 on the pop chart as well as making it on the R&B chart. According to legend, the term "susie q" referred to an old-time dance step, but Hawkins' turned it into an ode to a rockabilly siren.

DALE HAWKINS: "I had a little band in '57. Played in the clubs around Shreveport, Louisiana. I was just a kid then, working part-time in a record store in town. I was into a lot of blues, and I liked what Scotty Moore was doing on guitar with Elvis. But we sort of had our own sound in Louisiana that came from our heavy blues influence. Our band had the riffs for 'Suzy-Q' for some time, and we kept putting them together until one day I finally said, 'That's it.' It was just sheer *sound*. And, it worked. We went into the studios at KWKH Radio in Shreveport to cut the song. I know that sounds unusual today, but they used to do a lot of recording there. We cut the session one night between midnight and 1 a.m., when the transmitters were changed. We sent the tape to Chess Records in Chicago, and Leonard Chess said he wanted it. After some weeks went by, though, we got tired of waiting for the record to come out. I sent a copy to Jerry Wexler at Atlantic Records, and he put out the word: Chess had better do something or get off the pot. Two weeks later, our record was released. It broke in different parts of the country at different times. We got instant calls. We knew it was a hit after only a week and a half, man. At that time, the independent labels were coming on strong because the big ones weren't into that stuff so heavily yet. And our little record, it just sounded so much like Louisiana. James Burton and I played guitar on the session. The special sound of the guitar came from a reverb thing done in Chicago. The overall sound was our own, though, from our area of the country. Just a little bit of the blues, man."

Interview by Randy McNutt
North Little Rock, Arkansas, December 1986

John Ritchie Collection

Chess released Dale Hawkins' *Oh! Suzy-Q* LP in 1957 based on the success of the single.

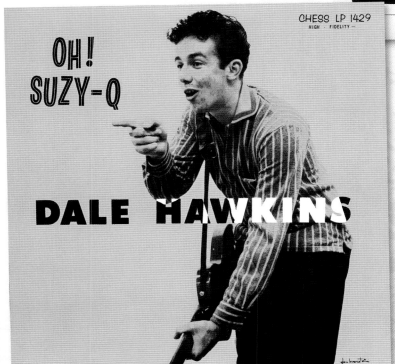

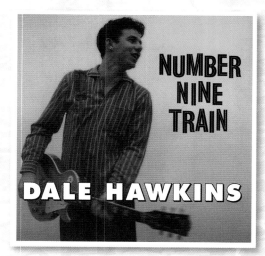

Norton Records released *Daredevil*, an EP of outtakes and rarities from Dale Hawkins, including an alternate take of "Susie-Q."

Born Harlan, Kentucky, on May 24, 1935

RUSTY YORK BEGAN as bluegrass and country musician, before hitting it big in 1959 with his single "Sugaree" on Chicago's Chess label. But his rockabilly phase was short, and he returned to bluegrass music in the 1960s.

Continuing its search for another Elvis, Chess signed up Kentucky rockabilly Rusty York. *Randy McNutt*

BUBBLING INTO THE HOT 100

"BACK IN THE U.S.A."
CHUCK BERRY
chess 1729

"CRACKIN' UP"
BO DIDDLEY
checker 924

OUR ORIGINAL'S THE HIT

"SUGAREE"
RUSTY YORK
chess 1730

HIS SECOND HITS!

"MY LIFE IS A MYSTERY"
b/w
"YOU'RE ON MY MIND"
ROD BERNARD
argo 5338

HOT!

Rusty York cut his rockabilly classic "Sugaree" for Chess in 1959.

RUSTY YORK

Born Pacoima, California, on May 13, 1941;
died February 3, 1959

RICARDO ESTEBAN VALENZUELA REYES—better known as Ritchie Valens—was a Mexican-American rockabilly based in the San Fernando Valley. Like Eddie Cochran, he recorded at Hollywood's Gold Star Studios, but his singles and LPs would be released on the Del-Fi label.

Valens tragically died in the February 3, 1959, plane crash that also killed Buddy Holly and J. P. Richardson, the Big Bopper.

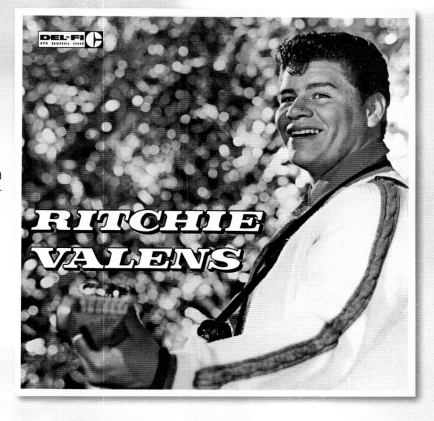

Ritchie Valens' eponymous debut LP was released posthumously in March 1959 on Del-Fi Records.

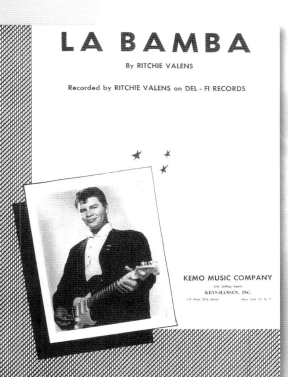

Ritchie Valens' version of the traditional Mexican song "La Bamba" became an American Top 40 hit despite the Spanish-language lyrics. The song is a classic Son Jarocho style from Veracruz and named for a dance. Valens added the rock 'n' roll beat, backed by session musicians, including famed drummer Earl Palmer and bassist Carol Kaye. *John Ritchie Collection*

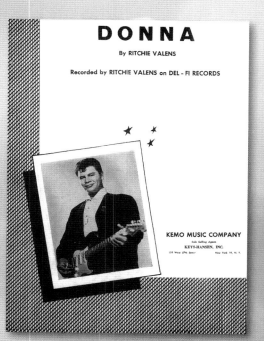

"Donna" was written in tribute of Ritchie Valens' high-school sweetheart, Donna Ludwig. Released in 1958, it reached #2 on the Billboard Hot 100 chart the following year, becoming Valens' highest-charting single. *John Ritchie Collection*

Born Teaneck, New Jersey, on May 8, 1940; died December 31, 1985

IN A BIZARRE TWIST of early reality television, Ricky Nelson played himself in the beloved TV series *The Adventures of Ozzie and Harriet* starting in 1949. As he became a teen, his interest in rock 'n' roll grew. In 1957, he performed on the show, launching a second career as a singer. He counted James Burton as his guitarist and Lorrie Collins of the Collins Kids as his love.

Over his career, Nelson boasted 53 songs on the Billboard Hot 100 between 1957 and 1973, including nineteen top-ten hits.

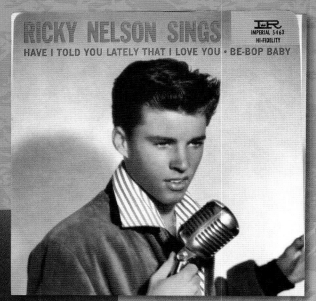

The look: Ricky Nelson was a true teen idol, as captured on the cover of the *Ricky Nelson Sings* Imperial EP.

Ricky Nelson sings to adoring fans alongside guitarist James Burton on stage in 1957. *Ralph Crane/Time Life Pictures/Getty Images*

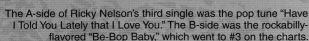

The A-side of Ricky Nelson's third single was the pop tune "Have I Told You Lately that I Love You." The B-side was the rockabilly-flavored "Be-Bop Baby," which went to #3 on the charts.

RICKY NELSON

ERSEL HICKEY

Born Brighton, New York, on June 27, 1934; died July 12, 2004

A PROMOTIONAL PHOTOGRAPH of Ersel Hickey cast him in a quintessential rockabilly pose, complete with golden Gibson ES-295, the right cat clothes and shoes, and a perfect snarl on his face. Yet much of Hickey's music was closer to pop than true hard-nosed rockabilly. His biggest hit, "Bluebirds Over the Mountain," reached #75 on the pop charts.

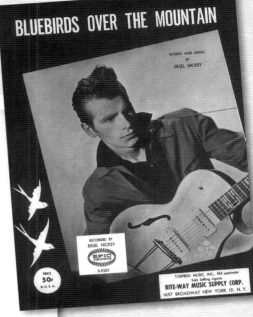

BLUEBIRDS OVER THE MOUNTAIN

WORDS AND MUSIC BY ERSEL HICKEY

RECORDED BY ERSEL HICKEY
EPIC RECORDS
5-9263

PRICE 50¢ IN U.S.A.

TORPEDO MUSIC, INC., Phil Landwehr
Sole Selling Agents
RITE-WAY MUSIC SUPPLY CORP.
1657 BROADWAY NEW YORK 19, N. Y.

After hearing Elvis Presley's "I Don't Care if the Sun Don't Shine" in 1954, Ersel Hickey became a rockabilly devotee. Still, most of Hickey's own songs had a pop flavor instead of a hard-edged rock 'n' roll rhythm. His biggest hit was "Bluebirds Over the Mountain," released in 1957. The tune was later also covered by Ritchie Valens. *John Ritchie Collection*

Bluebirds Over The Mountain

ERSEL HICKEY

EPIC
9263

MGR.
MICHEAL CORDA

ERSEL HICKEY

Pure rockabilly: Ersel Hickey strikes a now-famous pose with his golden Gibson ES-295.
Michael Ochs Archives/Getty Images

Born Godley, Texas, on October 23, 1937; died February 18, 1995

Johnny Carroll strikes a perfect rockabilly pose in a still from the film *Rock, Baby, Rock It*.

"ROCK, BABY, ROCK IT!" Starring KAY WHEELER, JOHNNY CARROLL and DON COATS

JOHNNY CARROLL: "As a kid, I appeared on local radio shows in Cleburne, Texas, and in high school I started singing in bands. Somehow, I blundered my way onto shows with big names. We were doing rhythm and blues and country on the same shows then. Of course, Elvis, bless his heart, he broke the ice for the rest of us. A bunch of us were doing that mixed bag around here in the mid-'50s. Anyway, Ferlin Husky let me do the first fifteen minutes of his show in '56. There was a promoter who then came to ask us to record. We went to Nashville to cut some stuff, but I was a minor then so Decca Records wouldn't let me record. After the band got that settled, our promoter got me in the movie *Rock, Baby, Rock It*. He produced the film. Meanwhile, I had done some shows with Presley, so I knew Scotty Moore and Bill Black. When they left Elvis, they asked me to front a band for them. Bill got me on Sun Records. That didn't lead to much at the time. Rockabilly died in 1960. I stayed out of everything until '75. But it has always been music with me. I've done this for a living. I managed clubs and engineered in recording studios when I wasn't performing. After being out of the performing thing from '60 to '75, though, I sang one night and said, 'Oh, yeah. *That's* what I want to do.' I thought I was over the hill. But

at the age of 49, I find out now that I'm not. In fact, if I had to quit on a high note in my career, it would be in France recently. June '87. The crowd was great. I've teamed up with country singer Judy Lindsey now. We play country in the U.S. and rockabilly in Europe. Rockabilly is so popular over there. The place is a fantasyland for old rockers . . . I cut two versions of 'Wild, Wild Women.' I wrote the song after hearing 'Wild, Wild Young Men.' No plagiarism involved. I told the publishers what I had done, and they said that everything was all right because the songs were so different. Anyway, I cut the first version at Owen Bradley's studio in Nashville around March of '56. For Decca. We cut three singles in two days. The musicians were Harold Bradley, electric rhythm guitar; Owen Bradley, piano; Grady Martin, electric lead guitar; Bob Moore, bass; and Buddy Harman, drums. Now those were some *good* pickers, some of the guys who also played on the Brenda Lee sessions. I was pleased with the sound they gave the record. That first Decca session was the only time I ever used session players on my records. They gave the tracks a pretty good sound, I think. It didn't sound like Presley and mainstream rock 'n' roll. But after thirty years, those records of mine have held up well. They have definition. I used my road band to record "Wild, Wild Women" number two—and the tracks for *Rock, Baby, Rock It*—at Sellars Studios in Dallas, not long after the originals were cut. Decca didn't want us to use their masters in the film, so we re-cut stuff. I think that second recording gave us yet another sound. Both were good. On the Nashville sessions, though, I recorded Johnny Cash's 'Rock 'n' Roll Ruby.' That was my first record released on Decca. Although it sold pretty well—and, incidentally, better than Warren Smith's original— I wasn't all that happy with it because I like Warren's record better. I was kicked in the stomach—well, at least I felt that way—when I first heard Warren's version of the song on Sun. We cut my record from the original Cash demo. Three or four people released the song at the same time. I didn't even know that Warren Smith had recorded it when we cut it. But I soon found out."

Interview by Randy McNutt
Godley, Texas, July and August 1987

The Auditorium
KLAMATH FALLS, OREGON
SAT. NOV. 28th
From 9 p.m to 1 a.m. - Admission Before 9 $1.25 - After 9 $1.50
SHOW AND DANCE **IN PERSON**
★ ★ ★ Warner Brothers Recording Star ★ ★ ★
JOHNNY CARROLL
"Bandstand Doll"   "The Swing"
"Sugar"   "Lost Without You"
★ ALSO ★
The Spinners
Warner Brothers Records
★ "Rag Mop"   "Little Otis"
HAVE FUN, GO DANCING

THE SIZZLING STORY OF HOT ROCK AS YOU HAVE NEVER SEEN IT BEFORE...!

JOHNNY CARROLL, New Decca Sensation "Wild, Wild Women" and "Crazy, Crazy Love"

PREACHER SMITH AND THE DEACONS "Eat Your Heart Out" and "Roogie Doogie"

CELL BLOCK SEVEN Playing Up A Storm "Hot Rock" and "The Saints Come Rockin' In"

See KAY WHEELER, queen of rock n' roll, doing the "Rock n' Bop"

THE FIVE STARS doing the new Calypso hit, "HEY JUANITA"

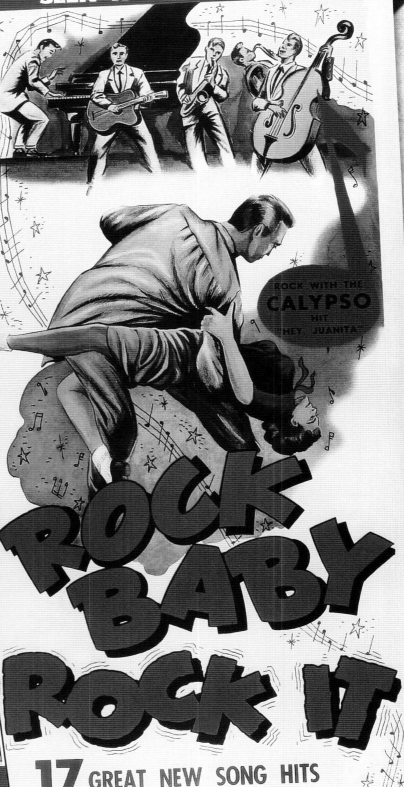

ROCK WITH THE CALYPSO HIT "HEY, JUANITA"

ROCK BABY ROCK IT

17 GREAT NEW SONG HITS

SUNG AND DANCED BY
THE NEWEST ROCK N' ROLL STARS!

A FREEBAR RELEASE ★ PRODUCED BY J. G. TIGER

Rock, Baby, Rock It poster, featuring Johnny Carroll.

Born Happy, Texas, on July 20, 1933;
died February 14, 1999

BUDDY KNOX'S ROCK 'N' ROLL was always closer to the smooth side of pop than to gut-bucket rockabilly. He cut his biggest hit, "Party Doll," at Norman Petty's Clovis, New Mexico, studio, where Buddy Holly also recorded. Released on the Roulette label, it hit #1 on the Cash Box record chart in 1957. The song was later voted one of the Rock and Roll Hall of Fame's 500 Songs that Shaped Rock and Roll.

"Proper dress required." Concert poster, Lakeside Ballroom, Glenwood, Minnesota, July 21, 1959.

Concert poster, circa 1958.

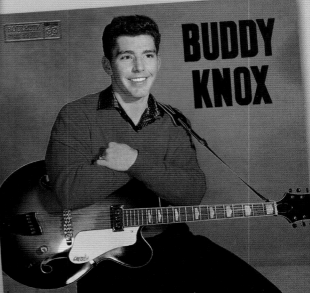

Buddy Knox's eponymous debut LP on Roulette featured his pop-flavored hits "Party Doll" and Hula Love."

Born Santa Rita, New Mexico, on November 30, 1937

JIMMY BOWEN JOINED WITH Buddy Knox and other high school friends in launching the vocal group, the Rhythm Orchids. Bowen's "I'm Stickin' With You" was the flip side of Knox's "Party Doll" single on Roulette and hit #14 on the *Billboard* pop chart itself.

The Rhythm Orchids featured Jimmy Bowen, far left, and Buddy Knox next to him. Much like Elvis' favored Jordanaires, the band was pure harmony, with a pop—rather than rockabilly—edge.

Jimmy Bowen's self-titled debut LP on Murray Hill Records. Bowen sported the rockabilly look, but lacked the hard edge.

By Randy McNutt

KING RECORDS IS REMEMBERED for the rhythm and blues hits of James Brown, Hank Ballard and the Midnighters, and other African-American performers. But King was more than a 1960s soul machine. In the 1940s, it released dozens of seminal hillbilly hits by Cowboy Copas, Grandpa Jones, the Delmore Brothers, and others. Later, King recorded pop and jazz—as well as a surprising number of rockabilly singers who are all but forgotten today.

Texas vocalist Mac Curtis was one of them. "In 1956, the company was looking for the next Elvis," remembered Curtis, whose high school principal once came to his classroom to tell him the label would record him that night in Dallas. "They thought I might be the one. I wasn't."

But Curtis persisted, recording seventeen songs for King and appearing with Alan Freed's rock 'n' roll shows before turning to a dual career in radio and country music.

Unlike Curtis, most King rockabillies slipped into obscurity as soon as their records were released. Their names are ghosts of the record industry's past: Bill Beach, Ronnie Molleen, Joe Penny, Hank Mizell, Delbert Barker, Bob and Lucille, and Fuller Todd, to name only a few. Even Dave Dudley, the future country star, recorded a song for King called "Rock 'n' Roll Nursery Rhyme."

Many of them recorded in King's gothic factory at 1540 Brewster Avenue in Cincinnati, where founder Sydney Nathan operated a studio and pressing plant. His singers often bounced between musical styles. One day they were country, the next rockabilly. Because King recycled vinyl and operated frugally, Nathan could afford to gamble on young talent by pressing 500 to 1,000 records to gauge radio's interest.

When the studio opened in late 1947, hillbilly singers recorded blues songs and blues artists recorded hillbilly songs. (Nathan owned many of the copyrights.) In this austere room, with its one-track recorder, country collided head-on with the blues. By the time King blues shouter Wynonie Harris was hitting with "Good Rocking Tonight" in 1948, King's country acts were recording rhythmic boogie songs that were precursors of rockabilly.

But it was Memphis recording engineer Sam Phillips who in 1954 produced the pioneering rockabilly record "That's All Right" by Elvis Presley on Phillips' independent Sun label. Free to experiment in his own little recording studio, Phillips encouraged the musicians to continue mixing musical genres and to add their own youthful interpretations to the stew. Presley—and other Sun acts—represented rockabilly's rural wing. His tracks were sparse and smooth. Meanwhile, on the east coast, Bill Haley and the Comets—a larger band, with older players—hit with "Dim, Dim The Lights (I Want Some Atmosphere)" on the larger Decca label. Haley's music represented rockabilly's urban, "establishment" wing. His records were fuller—clunky even, relying on traditional combo pieces such as the saxophone. Elvis was all hips and youth and attitude; the older Haley was spit-curled and as confident as a used car salesman.

In Cincinnati, Nathan hardly noticed rockabilly's quick assent. He was too busy earning a living to care. To him, music was a product to be marketed. Who wanted to hear teenage sounds? But once the world discovered Haley, however, Nathan instructed his A&R men and songwriters to jump into the small but growing teenage market then led by Haley. Presley was still known mostly in the South.

In early 1955, King guitarist Louis Innis borrowed a new teenage word recently heard in the movies, and wrote "Daddy-O" with musician Buford Abner and King country singer Charlie Gore. They recorded it in the Haley style, using vocalist Bonnie Lou, one of the label's hit country artists and a regular on Cincinnati's WLWT and its popular show *The Midwestern Hayride*.

Bonnie was no teenager: she had been working as a radio and television staff vocalist for a decade. "I wasn't comfortable singing rock 'n' roll," she explained, "but I did it anyway. When the record hit the top twenty nationally, I asked the station if I could take some time off to tour. Management said no. That hurt; I couldn't promote the record or myself. From there, Mr. Nathan took me to New York to record an album. I always thought that was strange. Everything else had been recorded in Cincinnati."

Meanwhile, King recorded Boyd Bennett and His Rockets, a rockabilly group in the mold of the famous Haley band. Bennett had co-written the song "Seventeen," based on a friend's story about his young daughter, and recorded it for King. The veteran performer, who most recently had worked in television in Louisville, finally had a hit.

"Daddy-O" and "Seventeen" gave King Records two national rockabilly hits from July to November 1955, when King's once-dependable country music—on which the company was founded—had slowed down, and R&B had picked up.

Unfortunately, neither Bonnie Lou nor Boyd Bennett ever came close to repeating the success of their first hits, not even when King teamed Bennett with legendary boogie-woogie pianist Moon Mullican. Bennett's band recorded two more nationally charted singles for King: "My Boy—Flat Top" and

a cover of Carl Perkins' "Blue Suede Shoes" remained on *Billboard*'s chart for ten weeks. Predictably, Bennett's Perkins' cover sounded like urban rockabilly imitating rural.

After Presley joined RCA–Victor and hit with "Heartbreak Hotel" in early 1956, record companies of all sizes searched for Elvis clones. King was in a better position than most independents, having pioneered the pre-rockabilly sound with "fast country" singles a few years earlier. Considering King's talented A&R and songwriting resource pool—a mixed racial group—and its experience, one would expect the label to have turned out some of the nation's most creative rockabilly recordings. But it did not, despite its earlier experiments with hillbilly bop and boogie, and the blues.

King ended 1956—Elvis' peak rockabilly year—with a disappointing track record in rock 'n' roll. But the company celebrated nonetheless, for it released three R&B hits that would foreshadow its future— "Please, Please, Please" by the Flames with James Brown, "Honky Tonk (Parts 1 & 2)" by Bill Doggett, and "Fever" by Little Willie John. "Honky Tonk" also became a huge pop record, outselling the company's two rockabilly hits. The three records influenced singers and musicians and re-established King as a leading R&B label.

From them on, King seemed to pursue rockabilly half-heartedly. Nathan's mature A&R staff was used to writing and recording what they knew—country and R&B. They didn't understand rockabilly or teenage minds.

In retrospect, King's better rockabilly records were those made by the artists who were more closely in touch with their market. But as Charlie Feathers discovered, not every singer had the luxury of bypassing King's A&R staff. Feathers, a former Sun artist, wanted more creative control, but found it difficult to attain because he recorded in Cincinnati. In 1956, he came to King to cut several songs, including "Bottle To The Baby" and "One Hand Loose." He was not impressed. He kept thinking of the studio sound at Sun. "King—and the

Born in Fort Worth, Texas, on January 16, 1939, Wesley Erwin "Mac" Curtis became a regional rockabilly star in the South. His rockabilly lament "You Ain't Treatin' Me Right" was released in 1956 on King Records.

guys in Nashville too—didn't understand what made those Sun recordings great—slapback," he said years later. "They just kept pouring on more echo and wondering why it didn't sound like Elvis."

About this time, a local singer named Bill Beach wrote "Peg Pants" and took it to King guitarist Louis Innis, who thought it sounded too much like country. He made "Peg Pants" as a rockabilly song, using black and white musicians. "The record didn't do anything," Beach said, "but I had a great experience." The single was his last.

In Chicago, Hank Mizell recorded "Jungle Fever" in the mid 1950s. King released it and forgot it. "It took twenty years for a DJ to rediscover a copy of that record—in England, of all places," Mizell recalled in 1989. "He played it and turned it into a hit over there. Imagine my surprise. I recorded a new album in Nashville. I was suddenly in demand."

When Buddy Holly hit with "Peggy Sue" in 1957, a King executive wanted to cover it. A friend called Rusty York and asked, "Can you sing like Buddy Holly?" The Cincinnati country singer said he could, although he hadn't even heard the record. "The engineer put Buddy's version on a turntable and we'd try to play exactly like it," York said. "Syd put it out in two days. It did sell in a few places where Buddy's record wasn't available."

By the 1960s, rockabilly had faded. Yet Nathan still signed an occasional rockabilly. "Orangie" Ray Hubbard— local automobile plant worker by day, nightclub singer by night—might have been the company's last one, with singles such as "Big Cat." He just called himself country.

Hubbard was writing new material when Nathan died in 1968. He sensed that his King recording career died with the big chief, and that rockabilly had already had its brief run.

"It doesn't bother me now, though, 'cause I'm getting too old to worry about that stuff," he said, strumming an acoustic guitar on his porch. "Me, I just keep playing my music whenever I can."

Ray Campi was born in 1934 in Yonkers, New York, but boasted a long, proud rockabilly career in the 1950s as well as during the revival. His biggest hit was "Catapillar" on TNT Records released in 1956. The song was pure energy and rockabilly flash.

THE HISTORY OF ROCKABILLY is largely a story of individual artists and singles that became regional hits, rather than big national stars and a long run of gold records and LPs. Rockabilly was a musical movement limited by the media of the day—the local radio shows, regional tours, small, self-financed independent labels, as well as musicians with day jobs. It was limited by the media of the day, but also made popular on a regional basis thanks to that same handicap.

Born in Nacogdoches, Texas, in 1937, Bob Luman dreamed of the big leagues—baseball, that is. But after he failed in his tryout for the Pittsburgh Pirates, he turned to rock 'n' roll. With James Burton on lead guitar, he made a rousing cameo appearance in the 1957 film *Carnival Rock.*

Born in Gretna, Louisiana, in 1939, Joe Clay's biggest hit was "Ducktail," a fine-rocking anthem to the Elvis-promoted hairstyle. Hal Harris played a tight, screaming lead guitar on the Vik records single.

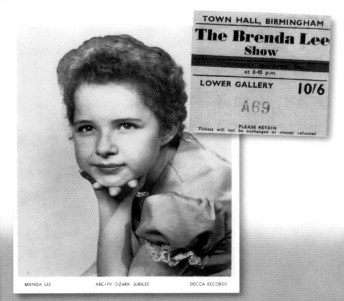

Decca Records sought to cash in on the "Female Elvis" fad with its precocious rockabilly child, Brenda Lee. Born on December 11, 1944, she was named Brenda Mae Tarpley but became "Brenda Lee" on stage at a young age. Her hit "Sweet Nothin's" reached #4 on the pop charts.

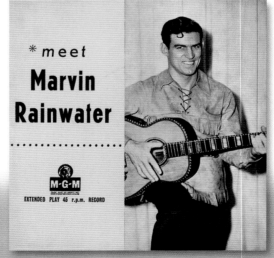

Born in 1925 in Wichita, Kansas, Marvin Rainwater was 25 percent Cherokee and thus often wore Native American garb on stage. Classically trained on piano, he later moved into rockabilly-flavored country, scoring with his 1957 hit "Gonna Find Me A Bluebird."

Born in Detroit, Michigan, in 1938, Johnny Pavlik took the stage name "Powers" and turned to rockabilly. Hearing local legend Jack Scott's version of "Baby She's Gone," he started his own band and later signed to the Detroit label Fortune Records.

Texan star Rudy "Tutti" Grayzell heated up the backroads stages with his version of "Ducktail."

Sid King and the Five Strings were regional Texas stars with western swing–influence rockabilly numbers such as "Drinking Wine Spoli Oli."

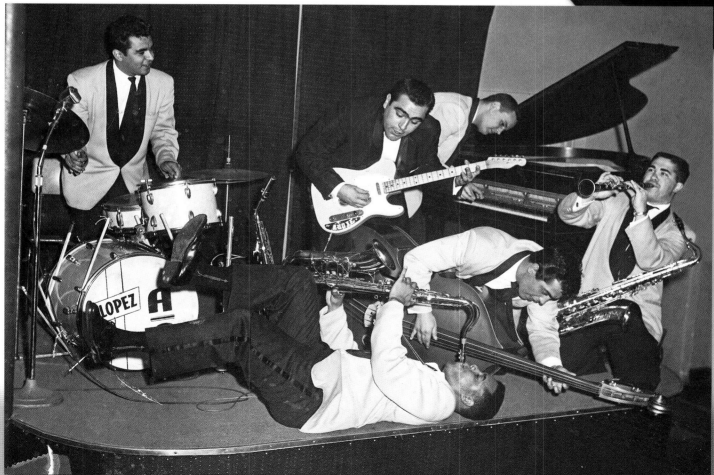

Minnesota rockabilly Augie Garcia was famed for his trademark Bermuda shorts and wild Telecaster sound. He opened for Elvis in 1956 at the St. Paul Auditorium, but his frenzied antics were too much for Col. Tom Parker, who pulled him from the stage, citing a clause in Garcia's contract that barred him from upstaging the headliner. *Buzz Brown/Minnesota Historical Society*

Eddie Bond and the Stompers hit big with a cover of
Sonny Fisher's "Rockin' Daddy" on Mercury.

Louisiana's Rusty and Doug Kershaw became WWVA
Jamboree stars, playing early rock 'n' roll before
switching in later years to fine Cajun music.

Alis Lesley was billed as yet another "Female Elvis"—helped perhaps by
the similarity in names. She appeared on *The Big Show* tour of Australia
in 1957 with Little Richard and Eddie Cochran. Her only hit came with the
1957 single, "He Will Come Back to Me"/"Heartbreak Harry."

A young Ronnie Dawson picks his Fender Stratocaster.
Born August 11 1939 in Dallas, Texas, he scored more rock
'n' roll hits in Great Britain than the United States thanks to
his stinging lead guitar.

The Collins Kids—Lorrie and Larry—were California
stars who hit big with the single "Hot Rod." *Courtesy Bear
Family Records.*

Sheet music for Boyd Bennett and His Rockets' hit "Seventeen," released in 1955.

Joe Bennett and the Sparkletones' hit "Black Slacks" remained on the pop charts for more than four months.

Promotional photo of the Sparkletones at their rockin' best.

Topps personality card featuring Charlie Gracie.

His band still said "country" with the addition of a fiddler and those snazzy cowboy duds, but Ronnie Self was hot-rodded rockabilly all the way. Known as "Mr. Frantic," his stage show was pure electricity. He had the looks and the swagger, but he never truly had the hits. *Michael Ochs Archives/Getty Images*

GENE AND EDDIE

GENE VINCENT AND EDDIE COCHRAN ROARED ONTO THE ROCK 'N' ROLL SCENE FROM OPPOSITE COASTS.

Elvis and the other rockabillies mostly came out of the Deep South, but the spirit spread far as they toured and as Elvis's new tunes were released by RCA–Victor to a wide audience. Now the sound waves reverberated everywhere. Rockabilly had gone national.

From the East Coast, Vincent became Capitol Records' contender to Elvis' crown. He recorded initially in Nashville, but in just his first year on the scene he was cutting tracks in Hollywood.

Cochran, although born in Minnesota, made his mark from Los Angeles' Gold Star Studios on Liberty Records.

In 1960, the duo left the United States to further spread the good word. Touring Great Britain, their music and their style left an indelible mark on rock 'n' roll fans there. It was an image that did not fade away as rockabilly died. Rockabilly continued to burn bright in Europe, sparking a revival years after both Cochran and Vincent's untimely deaths.

Kicking up a fuss: Eddie Cochran performs in Chadron, Nebraska, on October 3, 1959.

GENE VINCENT

Born Norfolk, Virginia, on February 11, 1935; died October 12, 1971

GENE VINCENT   CAPITOL RECORDS   GENERAL ARTISTS CORPORATION
NEW YORK, CHICAGO, BEVERLY HILLS, LONDON, DALLAS

Capitol Records promotional photo of a young Gene Vincent around the time of the release of "Be-Bop-A-Lula" in 1956.

GENE VINCENT WAS FAR FROM being a one-hit wonder, yet his first hit single, "Be-Bop-A-Lula," was so perfect, so cool, so quintessential that it became the single song he was associated with forever after.

Christened Vincent Eugene Craddock, he'd perform under the name Gene Craddock until he struck on rock 'n' roll. He was born in Norfolk, Virginia, which was the South, but hardly the deep South of fertile rockabilly soil. His family later ran a country store in Munden Point, Virginia, near the North Carolina state line, where young Gene listened to and learned country and gospel music, as well as R&B. At age 12, he got his first guitar.

With a father who had fought in the U.S. Navy during World War II and with the Norfolk shipyards calling, Gene dropped out of high school at age 17 and signed on as a sailor. He re-upped in 1955, using his $612 re-enlistment bonus to buy a new Triumph Tiger motorcycle. In July 1955, he suffered a terrible motorcycle accident that shattered his left leg. Doctors sought to amputate, but he refused and the leg was eventually saved. Yet the crash left him with a permanent limp, the need for leg braces at times, and chronic pain

for the rest of his life, which he would seek to drown in painkillers and alcohol. It would also fuel his later legacy as a black-leather-jacketed motorcycle rebel.

Discharged from the Navy due to his injury, he began to play country and rock 'n' roll music around Norfolk. He transposed his name to Gene Vincent, and formed a band called the Blue Caps from a nickname for Navy sailors. His early cadre included bassist "Jumpin'" Jack Neal, drummer Dickie "Be Bop" Harrell, and rhythm guitarman Ervin "Wee Willie" Williams. They soon won a Norfolk talent contest organized by local WCMS radio DJ Bill "Sheriff Tex" Davis. Inspired by the band's theme song, "Be-Bop-A-Lula," Davis took over managing the show.

Vincent had likely written "Be-Bop-A-Lula" in early 1955 while recuperating from his motorcycle crash in the Norfolk naval hospital. He meet fellow sailor Donald Graves there, who reportedly penned the lyrics while Gene wrote the melody. According to rockabilly lore, when Sheriff Tex Davis heard the song, he bought out Graves' rights for $50 and shared copyright with Vincent after signing a music publishing contract with Bill Lowery of The Lowery Group in Atlanta, Georgia. Davis heard a hit in the song.

Davis dialed up a local guitarist he knew, Cliff Gallup, to add some spark to the Blue Caps. Gallup worked days as a maintenance man for the Norfolk County school system, but by night he played with Ricky and the Dixie Serenaders as well as the WCMS house band, the Virginians. He was influenced by Chet Atkins as well as some of the upscale jazzmen. With Gallup on board, Davis organized a demo recording. Knowing that Capitol Records had announced it was seeking an "Elvis" of its own, Davis sent them the demo.

Capitol arranged for Vincent to cut "Be-Bop-A-Lula" at Owen Bradley's "Quonset Hut" studio on 804 16th Avenue South in Nashville on May 4, 1956. Bradley would become famous for the long list of pop country hits recorded at the Quonset Hut, including numerous stellar rockabilly sessions by the Rock 'n' Roll Trio, Janis Martin, and more. He had a revered staff of session musicians known as the A-Team that backed many a star, working behind the scenes and usually without credit in crafting the Nashville—and rockabilly—sound. The A-Team included guitarists Grady Martin and Hank "Sugarfoot" Garland, bassist Bob Moore,

"Be-Bop-A-Lula" was pure sex appeal in its lilting, slow-motion beat and Gene Vincent's breathless profession of love. The song's Lula was reportedly inspired by the children's comic book character Little Lulu, but there any similarities ended. The "be-bop" term came from the hottest jazz going. But the whole phrase was onomatopoeia and pure rock 'n' roll, akin to Little Richard's "Awop-bop-a-loo-mop alop bam boom" from "Tutti Frutti."

and drummer Buddy Harman. Bradley had a standing rule of using the A-Team on Quonset Hut sessions, but hearing the tight sound of Vincent's Blue Caps—especially the astounding guitarwork of Gallup—he left the band to do their stuff. As drummer Harrell remembered, while the song was being cut, he screamed in the background, as he wanted to be sure his family could hear it was truly him on the record.

"Be-Bop-A-Lula" was released by Capitol in June 1956, surprisingly selected by Capitol producer Ken Nelson as a B-side to "Woman Love." But this flip-side single soon became the hit. The song was successful simultaneously on three U.S. charts: it peaked at #7 following a twenty-week ride on the Billboard pop chart; #8 on the R&B chart; and #5 on the country list. In England it reached #16. By April 1957, Capitol boasted that more than 2 million copies had been sold to date.

At the same session as well as four follow-up sessions in June 1956, Vincent and the Blue Caps also cut their classic sides "Race With The Devil," "Bluejean Bop," and "Crazy Legs." But they would never again have a hit like their first one.

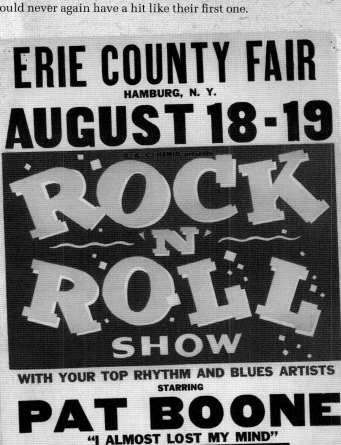

Concert poster, Erie County Fair, Hamburg, New York, August 18–19, 1956.

149

"Crazy Legs" was a typical rockabilly portrait of a young woman who just couldn't stop rocking—an image that would become rock 'n' roll cliché in no time at all. But the song was made classic by Gene Vincent's exuberance and Cliff Gallup's virtuosic guitarwork that upped the ante forever more with its dazzling hammer-ons, pull-offs, and sheer rocking bravado. *John Ritchie Collection*

Gene Vincent's first LP, *Bluejean Bop!*, was released in autumn 1956.

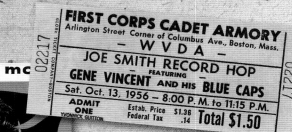

"Race With the Devil" was like a Robert Johnson song hot-rodded into rock 'n' roll. Like Johnson's "Hellhound On My Trail" and several other Delta blues classics, the singer was on the run from the devilish one. But rather than a Faustian pact for the singer's soul, here he was outdoing Satan at his own game—all with Gallup's sizzling guitar lines fueling the race.

John Ritchie Collection

TERP Ballroom
Austin, Minn.

Thursday, Sept. 19

"The Nation's Sensational Group"

GENE VINCENT
& HIS BLUE CAPS

Hear His "Be-Bop-a-Lulu"

For Teen-Agers Only

7:30 to 10:30 p. m.   Adm. 90c per person

As Gene Vincent began touring the United States behind his hits, ace guitarman Cliff Gallup hung up his blue cap. Slightly older than the rest of the band, he was married and preferred to stay at home. He was replaced by Russell Willaford, who performed with the band in the 1956 film *The Girl Can't Help It.*

John Ritchie Collection

"Dance To The Bop" was released by Capitol on October 28, 1957. Gene Vincent and His Blue Caps performed the song on the nationally broadcast *Ed Sullivan Show* weeks later on November 17, 1957. The song spent nine weeks on the charts and peaked at #23 on January 23, 1958, and would be Vincent's last American hit single.

Live EPs from a 1957 Paramount Theatre, New York, concert.

Gene Vincent's second LP was released in summer 1957.

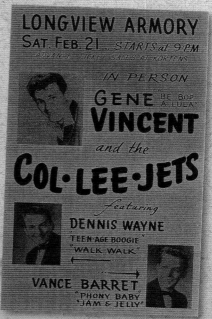

Concert poster, Longview Armory, n.p., February 21. 1957.

Hot Rod Gang was released in Great Britain as *Fury Unleashed*.

CRAZY KIDS...
LIVING TO A FRENZIED BEAT!

FURY UNLEASHED

STARRING
JOHN ASHLEY · JODY FAIR
GENE VINCENT

GENE VINCENT Sings
"DANCE IN THE STREET"
"BABY BLUE" · "LOVELY LORETTA"
"DANCE TO THE BOP"

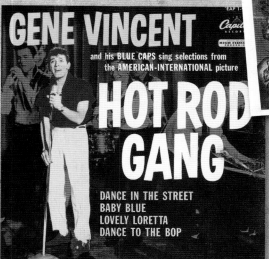

GENE VINCENT
and his BLUE CAPS sing selections from
the AMERICAN-INTERNATIONAL picture
HOT ROD GANG

DANCE IN THE STREET
BABY BLUE
LOVELY LORETTA
DANCE TO THE BOP

CRAZY KIDS...LIVING TO A
WILD ROCK 'N ROLL BEAT!

HOT ROD GANG

GENE VINCENT SINGS
"DANCE IN THE STREET" · "BABY BLUE"
"LOVELY LORETTA" · "DANCE TO THE BOP"

Starring JOHN ASHLEY · JODY FAIR · GENE VINCENT · CHARLES BUDDY ROGERS
Produced by LOU RUSOFF · Directed by LEW LANDERS · Story & Screenplay by LOU RUSOFF · A JAMES H. NICHOLSON and SAMUEL Z. ARKOFF PRODUCTION
An AMERICAN-INTERNATIONAL Picture

Gene Vincent and His Blue Caps appeared in the 1958 teen exploitation flick *Hot Rod Gang*. John Ashley was the film's star and was being promoted as a James Dean who could also sing. Ashley crooned a couple numbers while Vincent looked on, obviously embarrassed for him.

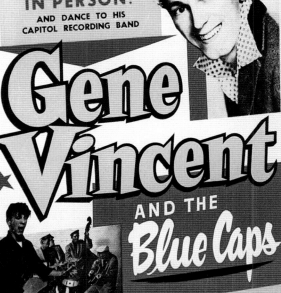

DANCE
MANHATTAN, KANSAS
CITY AUDITORIUM
FRIDAY SEPT. 26
ADMISSION $1.50 Per Person – DANCING 9:00 to 12:00

MR. BE BOP A LU LU
HIMSELF
YOU SAW HIM WITH JAYNE MANSFIELD
in "THE GIRL CAN'T HELP IT"
NOW SEE HIM
IN PERSON!
AND DANCE TO HIS
CAPITOL RECORDING BAND

Gene Vincent
AND THE Blue Caps

GENE VINCENT ROCKS!
AND THE BLUE CAPS ROLL

Gene Vincent Rocks! And the Blue Caps Roll was released in winter 1957.

Concert poster, City Auditorium, Manhattan, Kansas, September 26, 1958. *Pete Howard/Poster Central*

ARMORY
KLAMATH FALLS, OREGON
SAT. Nite FEB. 7th
SHOW and DANCE - FROM 9 to 1 a.m.

In Person . . .
★
GENE
"BE BOP A LULA"
VINCENT
. . . . PLUS . . . . .
CLAYTON WATSON
★ and his Silhouettes ★

Born on June 17, 1930; died October 9, 1988

By Dan Forte

"Galloping" Cliff Gallup—as he was listed on the Blue Caps' first LP—hits a rocking note on his Gretsch Duo Jet in this famous promotional shot from a Gene Vincent recording session.

Albert Lee, and Dave Edmunds, who acknowledged their debt to him in interviews—the latter declaring him "easily the most sophisticated of the rockabilly players" in the September '83 issue of *Guitar Player*.

Gallup's complex, forward-looking leads seemed to jump out of nowhere, and likewise the reclusive Gallup disappeared from the scene after his brief stint with Vincent, returning to his hometown in Norfolk County, Virginia. I didn't know that (or anything else about Gallup) in '83, but one day I read on the back of a Vincent compilation that the band hailed from Chesapeake, Virginia. I picked up the phone and dialed directory assistance.

When I asked for a Cliff or Clifford Gallup in Chesapeake, the operator said, "I have a C. Gallup." I said, "I'll take it" and got the number. (Turns out Gallup's given name was Clifton, incidentally.) I called and a man answered the phone. "I'm looking for Cliff Gallup," I explained. Speaking. "Is this Cliff Gallup the guitar player?" Yes.

Amazingly, the mystery man had been hiding in plain sight. I told him I'd like to interview him for *Guitar Player* magazine—a request that was typically met with enthusiasm. "Well, I'm pretty busy," he said. "If you call back tomorrow, I might be able to talk some." When I did, he frankly sounded irritated—like he was hoping I'd forget. He repeated that he was busy but agreed to do the interview if I called back Thursday. "But I don't have much time to talk"—and he wasn't kidding.

The subsequent interview was only 20 minutes long, and most of his answers were as ambiguous as they were brief. I soon discovered that, like many, I had Gallup confused with the tall, blond guy playing a Telecaster (one Russell Willaford) in the Jayne Mansfield movie *The Girl Can't Help It*; I'd never actually seen a picture of Gallup. (After quitting the Blue Caps, Gallup agreed to return to Nashville to cut Vincent's second LP, *Gene Vincent & His Blue Caps*, in October '56. *The Girl Can't Help It* had been filmed in the interim.)

By all accounts, Vincent's band was formed in April '56 and cut their long-playing debut, *Bluejean Bop*, that June. Listen to any of Vincent's sides featuring Gallup (on this or its followup), and it's easy to hear what all the fuss was

CLIFF GALLUP IS ONE OF the most mysterious, enigmatic figures in the annals of rock guitar. Only a sketchy bio can be cobbled together today—some dates and places, the songs he played on, a few quotes—but virtually nothing that gets inside the man himself.

The rockabilly revival spearheaded by acts like the Stray Cats, Robert Gordon, and the Blasters spurred a renewed interest in '50s originators, especially Gene Vincent and the Blue Caps. For a new legion of rockabilly fans, the late Vincent (who'd only scored one Top 10 hit, with two other singles denting the Top 40) was the genre's poster boy—leather-clad, greasy, and most of all, wild.

The newly indoctrinated also discovered a guitar wizard the previous generation of Brits had been salivating over for years: Cliff Gallup. Though he only recorded two albums with Vincent and was a member of the Blue Caps for approximately six months during 1956, his daring guitar work influenced such luminaries as Jeff Beck, Jimmy Page,

about. From the simple but intense "Be-Bop-A-Lula" and "Woman Love" to the high-speed "Cruisin'" or "Race With The Devil"(where Cliff's second chorus introduces a modulation), Gallup seldom took a break that wasn't memorable, and often astounding. Far ahead of his rockabilly contemporaries, Gallup had it all—the bluesy bends of "Bop Street" (which he co-wrote with Vincent), Atkins-style fingerpicking on "Bluejean Bop," and his spontaneous, unexpected solos on "B-I-Bickey-Bi, Bo-Bo-Go" and so many other tunes. He also supplied sensitive accompaniment on ballads such as "I Sure Miss You" and "Important Words" and handled faithful arrangements of the standards "Peg O' My Heart" and "Up A Lazy River."

Born June 17, 1930, Gallup was 26—a bit older than his bandmates and most rock 'n' rollers at the time, and was also married. It didn't take long for him to choose a quieter life back home to life on the road. Only one post-Vincent appearance is known—*Straight Down The Middle* by the Four C's, released in the mid '60s on the local Pussy Cat label. He and the band do an instrumental version of Vincent's #7 hit, "Be-Bop-A-Lula," and several Gallup originals.

In 2010, when I interviewed Albert Lee for *Vintage Guitar*, I asked him who the main building blocks of his guitar style were. "The first one would be Buddy Holly, whose solos were very accessible," he said, "and then I was trying to copy Scotty Moore and Cliff Gallup. I copied all their solos on the Elvis Presley and Gene Vincent records. Cliff Gallup played on two Gene Vincent albums, and I can pretty much remember every one of those solos—along with Jeff Beck, of course; he was in the same boat as me around that time. Scotty was great to copy too, but, looking back, they maybe weren't as complicated as the things that Cliff Gallup was doing. Learning his solos, he was playing in a lot of scales. He was older than the other guys around at that time. He was more experienced—using all of the neck, getting around. So learning those solos, you learned to move around the neck, rather than just staying in one position, like playing Chuck Berry solos."

When Gallup died at 58 (of a heart attack, October 9, 1988), I wasn't aware that my interview was one of the few he ever gave and apparently the only one for a guitar magazine. Jeff Beck was, though. In 1993, he fulfilled a dream by recording *Crazy Legs*, a collection of Gene Vincent songs, casting himself (uncannily) in the role of Cliff Gallup. When I interviewed Beck for *Guitar World* (May '93 issue), I soon realized that he was quoting passages from "Cliff's interview in *Guitar Player* magazine." "That's my interview," I said. "*I* interviewed Cliff Gallup." Suddenly Beck turned into the wide-eyed adolescent who hung onto Gallup's every note. "You did it?" he marveled. "You interviewed Cliff Gallup? Amazing. Have you got his voice on tape? I would love to hear his voice."

Though Beck redefined the role of guitarslinger when he replaced Eric Clapton in the Yardbirds—with envelope-ripping sonic excursions like "Heart Full Of Soul," "I'm A Man," and "Shapes Of Things," and "Beck's Bolero" from his first solo single, as well as more blues-rooted solos on "I'm Not Talking" (with the 'Birds) and "I Ain't Superstitious" (from his solo debut, *Truth*)—traces of his rockabilly hero were seldom evidenced. On rare occasions when the Yardbirds ventured near rockabilly, like the Rock 'n' Roll Trio's "Train Kept A-Rollin'," the resultant "arrangement," Beck chuckled, was "like the blind leading the blind." His tour de force, "Jeff's Boogie," however, mixes Gallup-isms with doses of Les Paul and Chuck Berry—and plenty of Beck's own twists, of course.

Asked where the "Jeff Beck twist" was on *Crazy Legs*, he admitted, "There is none." This time, the motivation was different. "The whole point of it was, 'Hey, this guy Gallup was *it*!"

Not reproducing Gallup's original solos note for note, but using them as a road map, Beck "realized how little I knew." "I figured that each one of his solos is so important, that it should be played just as it was," he explained. "So I had to really sit and listen a bit closely . . . It didn't matter that they were slightly off—except for things like the solo in 'Blues Stay Away From Me.' That has this nagging kind of 7th chord in it that keeps grinding. Once you start that, you've got to pull it off properly; otherwise, it just becomes a half-baked attempt." (For the album, Beck even employed fingerpicks on a '56 Gretsch with DeArmond pickups and flatwound strings, including an unwound G, for "ear-shattering treble with a nice, big, fat low-end—that's the Gallup sound.")

"I see myself like an evangelist," Beck concluded: "'Listen to the gospel of Cliff Gallup.'" But, he added with a laugh, "I'd have made the album just to have it for my car, you know. So I could say, 'Hey, want to hear me play like Cliff?'"

At the time of his death, Gallup was the director of maintenance and transportation for his regional school system, but he continued to play guitar on weekends. His wife, Doris, asked that no mention of his days with the Blue Caps be included in his local newspaper's obituary. That is how Gallup would have wanted it, she said. He was uncomfortable when fans of his rockabilly playing called or sent fan letters. "He never did sign an autograph," she said. "He was not that kind of a person."

The Four C's LP *Straight Down the Middle* on Pussy Cat Records, circa mid 1960s, autographed on the back by Gallup.

But Gallup's influence lives on, and his position in the rock guitar pantheon is stronger than ever. In the July '10 *Vintage Guitar*, I asked Nick Curran, who represents the generation of roots-rockers who came *after* Stray Cat Brian Setzer, to list the half-dozen guitar albums that changed his life. "'Bluejean Bop' by Gene Vincent and his Blue Caps is what got me into '50s rock 'n' roll—or, as some say, rockabilly," he replied. "Cliff Gallup plays some of the coolest solos ever on this baby. He was like a shredder back then—like if Eddie Van Halen was in the '50s!"

Which is as apt a compliment, and summation, as any.

DAN FORTE: Did the Blue Caps consider themselves part of the rockabilly movement? Did you feel a kinship with people like Elvis, Johnny Burnette, and Carl Perkins?

CLIFF GALLUP: That's difficult to answer, because when we first came together with that style of music, why, it just wasn't around. I mean, it wasn't patterned behind anybody that I know of. It all just got started.

DF: So were the solos you played on records completely spontaneous?

CG: Just as they come to mind.

DF: Did you practice a lot?

CG: I guess so. About as much as any young guitar player coming along.

DF: What's amazing about your work with Gene is the level of musicianship compared to your contemporaries in early rock & roll. You must have played in quite a few bands around Virginia before '55.

CG: Oh, yeah. I've been playing music since I was about eight years old.

DF: What type of music did you first play?

CG: Popular music. Then I got into country. And then I got into rock. I played a little bit of everything, I guess.

DF: Did you take up electric early on?

CG: Yeah. I started on electric when I was 12 or 14. That's been so many years ago, I don't even remember what brand my first one was [*laughs*]. I think I got it from Sears & Roebuck.

DF: When you were developing your style, did you listen to blues players much?

CG: No more so than I did anything else. I don't think that many of the electric players were around when I was learning.

DF: Did you have any formal training?

CG: Nope. There were a few guys that showed me a few chords or a lick, so to speak. Like most musicians, you listen to a lot of people—pick up a lick here, a lick there. Pretty soon you originate some kind of a style. I kind of thought Les Paul was the going thing in my younger years, and I used to listen to a lot of Atkins stuff when he first started.

DF: What attracted you to Les Paul and Chet Atkins more than other guitarists?

CG: Well, there just wasn't too many electric guitar pickers around in my younger years. Les Paul was so popular, going so strong, you'd *hear* those things more than anything else. Now, there must be umpteen hundred of them out there, but back in the '40s there was only about a half a dozen major record labels, so there weren't too many. That's just what I happened to hear.

DF: Did you learn Chet's fingerstyle approach?

CG: Yeah, I did that. Still do it now.

DF: Were the solos with the Blue Caps fingerpicked?

CG: Well, I use a combination of a straight pick and two fingerpicks. Most people don't do that. In fact, I don't think I've ever seen anybody do that.

DF: So you wear fingerpicks on your middle and ring fingers and hold the flatpick between your index and thumb?

CG: That's right. And I use the [vibrato] bar with my little finger.

DF: How did you and Gene first get together?

CG: He was living a couple of miles from me, out in the country. I had met him over at the radio station a few times where I staffed. I guess that's how I came to know him. It was primarily country music, and everyone would meet at the radio station and play on Sunday afternoons. Then we cut a dub at the station. Presley had come out on Sun Records and Carl Perkins had "Blue Suede Shoes," and Capitol didn't have a rock artist. So we sent this dub to Capitol, and it got picked out of a thousand-some tapes. That's how it all began.

DF: How old were you when you were in the group?

CG: Oh, I was in my twenties. I don't remember exactly.

DF: What was the personnel of the Blue Caps when you were a member?

CG: The original lineup was Wee Willie [Williams, rhythm guitar], Dickie Harrell on drums, Jack Neal on bass, myself, and Gene. Later on he had various musicians, but I wasn't around then.

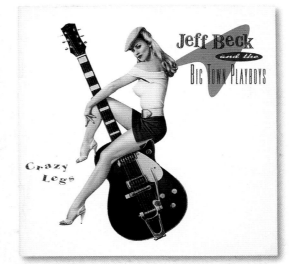

Jeff Beck paid tribute to Cliff Gallup in his 1993 album with the Big Town Playboys, *Crazy Legs.*

DF: What type of guitar did you use on the Gene Vincent sessions?

CG: A Gretsch "pancake"—a black Duo Jet.

DF: Did you ever use Fenders?

CG: No, I never played a Fender. Don't like Fenders. Well, it's not that I don't *like* them. It's just that some people like Fords, some people like Chevrolets.

DF: Do you recall what type of amps you used back then?

CG: I suppose I've been using Fenders for a long time. I used Grady Martin's amplifier in the studio. I think he had a Standel at the time, but I'm not sure what he had, to tell you the truth. He never played on any of those sessions.

DF: Did you ever employ echo units or other devices?

CG: We used echo in the studio—the built-in stuff. But little echo units weren't around. I built the first two echo machines I ever had. I didn't use them on any of Gene's records, but I've used them since. Now they have gadgets by the tons, but back in the '50s you couldn't find an echo machine. So I made the first couple and used them for four or five years before I started seeing the brand names. I used a tape recorder.

DF: Where did you record for Capitol?

CG: Most of the recordings were made in Nashville, at Bradley Studios. A fellow named Ken Nelson produced them.

DF: How rehearsed were the tunes you recorded with Gene?

CG: Most of them were worked out on the road. A couple of songs I wrote with Gene. They were written one night and recorded the next day.

DF: Did you leave the group because of the rough traveling?

CG: Yeah, that was the primary reason. That's a pretty tough life.

DF: What sort of work did you do after leaving Gene?

CG: I've done a lot of staffing for a radio station. They used to bring a lot of country artists here. I guess I've played with half the people in

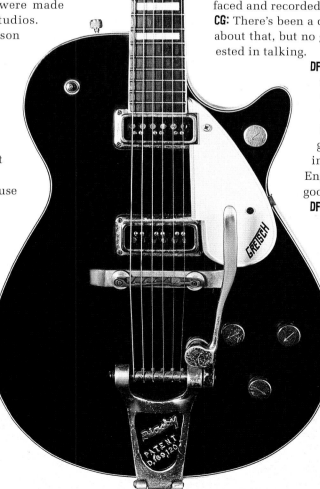

Jeff Beck's 1956 Gretsch Duo Jet, as used on *Crazy Legs.*
Courtesy Nigel Osborne/Jawbone Press

Nashville. Then they put a studio here, but they primarily make commercials. I used to staff there—still do, on occasion.

DF: Have you had a chance to hear any of the current rock players who've been influenced by you—Albert Lee and Jimmy Page from England, for instance, or Dave Edmunds from Wales?

CG: I heard tell that there was a couple of players over there, but I don't know that I've ever heard them.

DF: What type of music do you listen to for your own enjoyment?

CG: I don't know. I like just about everything other than real hard rock. Other than that, music is music.

DF: Do you still play a Gretsch as your main guitar?

CG: Yeah, still play a Gretsch, although it's not a "pancake" anymore. I've been using a Country Gentleman for the past 20 years or so. I've got a Gibson Everly Brothers acoustic that I play in the studio with gut strings on it. It's in mint condition, because I don't use it that much.

DF: Do you play with any of the other former Blue Caps?

CG: No. I see them on occasion, but we haven't played together in many a day.

DF: A lot of the rockabilly players from your era have resurfaced and recorded again. Have you thought of doing that?

CG: There's been a couple of people that have talked to me about that, but no groundwork has been laid. I'd be interested in talking.

DF: You must be aware of the fanaticism that surrounds the records you made with Gene. Have fans located you in Virginia?

CG: People make contact with me. I've gotten letters from people interested in making records in Switzerland and England. You know, Gene got going pretty good over there before he died.

DF: Is the music you play nowadays still rock, or is it more country and western?

CG: It's a combination of everything, even a little gospel. There's several studios in the area now, and lots of places to play.

DF: Do you still do much performing?

CG: Yes, I still play. I never have stopped. I've been goin' since I was a little kid, so there ain't no need for me to stop playing now. I'm still out there beatin' the bushes, mostly local.

Born Albert Lea, Minnesota, on October 3, 1938; died April 17, 1960

EDDIE COCHRAN
Liberty Records

GENERAL ARTISTS CORPORATION
NEW YORK CHICAGO BEVERLY HILLS CINCINNATI DALLAS MIAMI BEACH LONDON

Publicity photo of Eddie Cochran at work, blasting out a song in the 1956 film *The Girl Can't Help It*.

Born in Albert Lea, Minnesota, he was named Edward Ray Cochran. His parents had migrated north from Oklahoma, and he often later proudly told interviewers that he himself had been born an Okie. In 1955, Cochran's family moved to west to Bell Gardens, California, a suburb of Los Angeles. He would be based from California for the rest of his career.

Cochran was a quick musical study. He took lessons in school, but quit band and the trombone to play drums in his own group. He skipped piano lessons and instead taught himself guitar. His first and favorite music as a teen was the country he heard on the radio. Soon, he dropped out of high school and devoted himself to music.

A youthful prodigy, he was performing at an American Legion hall when he met country songwriter Hank Cochran. Though unrelated, they formed a duo as the Cochran Brothers and performed and recorded country music together for the near-forgotten label Ekko. They

DESPITE HIS MATINEE IDOL LOOKS and penchant for cardigan sweaters, Eddie Cochran was the figure of 1950s teenage rebellion personified. His most famous song, "Summertime Blues," was a bold and brash cry, perfectly capturing pent-up teen frustration and desire. With his follow-up, "C'mon Everybody," he took the message further, sending out a call to arms to get up and dance to rock 'n' roll.

Far beyond many of his contemporary rockabillies, Cochran was a consummate musician and performer. He wrote much of his own material; was adept at engineering his sound in the studio, experimented early on with multi-tracking and overdubbing; could both croon out a ballad and scream through a rocker; played a virtuosic and purposeful guitar; was a true rock 'n' roller with all the moves on stage; and performed in several Hollywood films. Had he survived past his 21st year, who knows what future awaited.

"THE COCHRAN BROTHERS"
Eddie and Hank

ekko

The Cochran Brothers in a promotional picture from Ekko Records. Eddie, left, holds his early Gibson L4 with added DeArmond pickup. Hank later moved on to Nashville and became a successful country composer.

split amicably after one year, Hank going on to a career in Nashville, Eddie to rock 'n' roll.

Cochran had heard Elvis' music, and like many a deep South rockabilly, he suddenly got rhythm. Yet his earliest attempts at writing and performing rock 'n' roll lacked fire or conviction.

Based on some of his first rock 'n' roll recordings, Hollywood producer Boris Petroff in 1956 invited Cochran to appear in the big-budget rock 'n' roll comedy film *The Girl Can't Help It*, starring quintessential 1950s blonde bombshell Jayne Mansfield. In the movie, Cochran sang "Twenty Flight Rock" with true rocking swagger, punctuated by stop-time interludes, and a Memphis-style hiccupping vocal. His performance caught the eye of producers from Los Angeles-based Liberty Records.

Cochran began recording in Hollywood's Gold Star Studios, soon becoming a proficient session musician and studio producer. In 1957, he was featured in a second film, *Untamed Youth*, with another platinum blonde, Mamie Van Doren. He also scored his first hit, "Sittin' in the Balcony," which peaked in March 1957 at #18 after thirteen weeks on the charts. This was followed by the singles "Drive-In Show" and the great "Jeannie, Jeannie, Jeannie."

In summer 1958, Liberty released "Summertime Blues," which Cochran co-wrote with his manager Jerry Capehart. The song became his highest-charting hit during his lifetime, reaching #8 on August 25, 1958, on the Billboard pop charts. The song hit #18 on the British charts as well.

During 1958 and 1959, Cochran was often on the road, playing package tours across the United States and Canada, often headlining shows with Gene Vincent.

In January 1960, Cochran and Vincent arrived in Great Britain for a long run of package shows that ran from Scotland to Wales to England. The tour was a screaming success, opening the eyes of overseas fans to the wonders of rock 'n' roll.

On Saturday, April 16, 1960, just before midnight, Vincent, Cochran, and Cochran's fiancée, songwriter Sharon Sheeley, were riding in a taxi after a late show on their way back to London and shortly, home to the United States. Traveling through Chippenham, Wiltshire, on the A4, the taxi crashed into a lamp post on Rowden Hill. Cochran was thrown through the windscreen, and was taken to St. Martin's Hospital, Bath, where he died at 4.10 p.m. the following day of severe head injuries. Both Sheeley and Vincent survived the crash. Cochran's body was flown home, and he was buried on April 25, 1960, at Forest Lawn Memorial Park in Cypress, California.

Poster for the 1956 film *The Girl Can't Help It*, featuring musical interludes by Eddie Cochran Gene Vincent, Little Richard, Fats Domino, and more—not to mention Jayne Mansfield.

159

C'mon Everybody
by EDDIE COCHRAN and JERRY CAPEHART

RECORDED by EDDIE COCHRAN on Liberty Records

METRIC MUSIC COMPANY
Sole Selling Agent
KEYS-HANSEN, INC.
119 West 57th Street   New York 19, N. Y.

John Ritchie Collection

"C'mon Everybody" unashamedly traded on the same type of chord progression as Eddie Cochran's breakthrough, "Summertime Blues." And continuing the theme, it called on teens everywhere to join the rock 'n' roll rebellion and get up and dance.

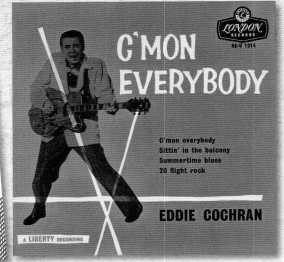

C'MON EVERYBODY

C'mon everybody
Sittin' in the balcony
Summertime blues
20 flight rock

EDDIE COCHRAN

A LIBERTY RECORDING

London Records EP, signaling Eddie Cochran's arrival in the United Kingdom.

Concert poster, Orpheum Theatre, Seattle, Washington, October 25–26, 1957. *Pete Howard/Poster Central*

Singin' To My Baby was Cochran's only album to be cut during his short lifetime. Released as Liberty LRP-3061, it was launched in November 1957.

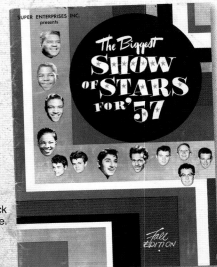

Program for a 1957 package tour including Eddie Cochran, Chuck Berry, Fats Domino, Buddy Holly, and more.

The 1959 film *Go, Johnny Go!* was the story of an Elvis-like singer, albeit whitewashed and smoothed over so none of the hard rockabilly edges showed. But as with many of the early rock 'n' roll movies, the best part was the cameos from Cochran, Jackie Wilson, Chuck Berry, and others.

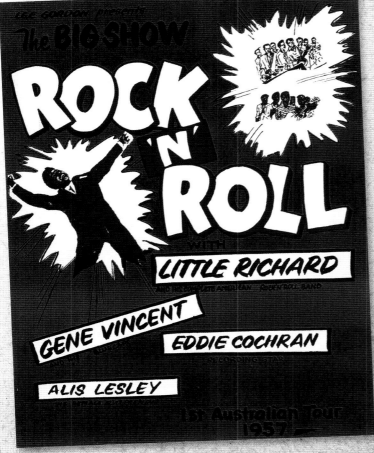

Program for *The Big Show*, the rock 'n' roll tour of Australia including Cochran, Gene Vincent, and Alis Lesley. Little Richard headlined the shows—until he announced on stage that he was renouncing rock 'n' roll and devoting himself to God.

"Last night, Eddie Cochran rocked and he rolled and finally the cows came home. By the time he strummed his last notes on that big, beautiful orange Gretsch 6120 guitar, the audience was worn out and went home satisfied that they had seen the best rockabilly anywhere."

—*The Los Angeles Times*

Cochran with Gene Vincent on the set of British TV show *Boy Meets Girls*.

161

Concert poster, Moss' Empire Theatre, Glasgow, Scotland, February 1, 1960.

HIPPODROME
BRISTOL

Chairman: PRINCE LITTLER   Manager: J. H. CHRISTIE   Telephone 21091

LARRY PARNES presents

AN ANGLO-AMERICAN FOUR STAR ATTRACTION

MONDAY, APRIL 11th
6.25 Twice Nightly 8.40
CLOSED GOOD FRI.

GENE VINCENT
BACKED BY THE
FABULOUS WILDCATS
(by kind permission of MARTY WILDE)

EDDIE COCHRAN
HIT RECORDER OF
"SUMMERTIME BLUES"
"C'MON EVERBODY"

DEAN WEBB
OfT.V.'s "Oh Boy" Recording Fame

PETER WYNNE
The New Golden Voice of the Parlophone Discs

BILLY RAYMOND

TONY SHERIDAN TRIO
FROM T.VS

GEORGIE FAME

From left, Gene Vincent, British rockers Joe Brown and Billy Fury, and Eddie Cochran.

Concert poster, Hippodrome, Bristol, England, April 11, 1960.

Remains of the British taxi from the car crash that killed Eddie Cochran and injured Vincent and Cochran's fiancé Sharon Sheeley. *Michael Ochs Archives/Getty Images*

"Three Steps To Heaven" was Eddie Cochran's last British single issued while he was alive. Released in May 1960, it became a posthumous #1 hit in Great Britain—although it was never released as a single in the United States, which was symbolic of Cochran's status in both countries. And London Records continued to re-release Cochran singles into 1961, cementing his stature in the pantheon of rock 'n' roll greats among British fans.

GRETSCH 6120

It Don't Mean a Thing If It Ain't Got That Twang

THE GRETSCH MODEL 6120 Chet Atkins Hollow Body was the Cadillac of guitars. For rockabillies who dreamed of driving the pink Caddy that Elvis did, it was the guitar to which to aspire.

True, other rockabilly guitarists selected other elite instruments—the Lincolns, Packards, and Imperials of the guitar world. Scotty Moore, once he had some jingle in his pocket after his first gigs with Elvis, traded in his golden ES-295 for the Gibson flagship, a glorious L5CESN. And with his "Blue Suede Shoes" lucre in hand, Carl Perkins set aside his Les Paul for a big, bold, and bodacious ES-5N Switchmaster replete with three—count 'em, three!—pickups.

But for others, the Gretsch 6120 was a Cadillac with all the options, the bells and whistles that glittered in the bandstand lights and made the men envious and women swoon.

It featured gold-plated hardware, natch. A Wild West "G" branded into the body's bass bout and country fashion fretmarker motifs on the earliest models. The 6120 was Gretsch's basic Streamliner model all dressed up for a Saturday night. Which made it perfect for rockabilly.

The fact that it bore Chet Atkins' endorsement was also certainly part of the reason it was adopted by rockabillies. Going with an endorser was a key to selling guitars, then as now: Fender nearly named its new three-pickup solid-body the Jimmy Bryant Model before deciding to stick with its established "-caster" theme and call it the Stratocaster.

Atkins may not yet have made Nashville the country music capitol of America, but he was widely admired by fellow Southern pickers. Legend has it that Atkins started out playing ukulele, but traded a pistol and chores on the family's Luttrell, Tennessee, farm to his elder brother, Lowell, for his first guitar. Inspired by Django Reinhardt and Les Paul, he soon became one of the most influential guitarists. Ever.

Atkins would play on and oversee many a rockabilly session in Nashville, too. He played rhythm on Elvis' "Heartbreak Hotel" in 1956 as well as added his licks to many an Everly Brothers tune.

Detailing the myriad changes made to the 6120 from its debut in 1955 through 1960 is a Herculean task. The changes are so confounding and convoluted, it's almost as if the guitars were built not at Gretsch's famed Brooklyn factory but down the way in a Coney Island funhouse. Edward Bell's

Classic Gretsch rockabilly guitars: A 1955 Model 6120 Chet Atkins Hollow Body accompanied by its solid-body sibling, a Model 6121. *Steve Catlin/Redferns*

GRETSCH 6120

Duane Eddy's original Gretsch Chet Atkins Model 6120, which he used on most of his hit songs, starting in the 1950s. *Courtesy Nigel Osborne/Jawbone Press*

Gretsch 6120: The History of a Legendary Guitar has all the details on the details. Still, there were two key changes that most affected the guitar's playability and sound.

The debut 1955 version featured a Bigsby B6 vibrato tailpiece with a fixed arm, as favored by Atkins. Others, however, soon discovered that the arm got in *their* arm's way. Thus, in 1956, a hinged arm was first tried, then refined with the so-called "Duane Eddy arm" in 1956 and used on all 6120s thereafter.

More importantly, the original DeArmond Dynasonic single coils were upgraded in 1958 to humbucking Filter'Trons. This changeover was long believed to be a reaction to the Gibson humbuckers engineered by Seth Lover. But recent evidence uncovered by Bell shows Gretsch led the way. And the creator of Gretsch's Filter'Trons? None other than Ray Butts, the electrical wizard from Cairo, Illinois, who created the pioneering EchoSonic amplifier with built-in tape-delay echo as used by Scotty Moore in his early days with Elvis—as well as by Carl Perkins and Atkins himself. Butts proved himself indispensible to the sound of rockabilly. Twice.

Atkins had never liked the Dynasonics; he stated in his autobiography *Chet Atkins: Me and My Guitars* that "they were too heavy on bass response, and they hummed terribly." The Filter'Trons featured two sets of pickup magnets wired out of phase and with opposite polarity. This "bucked" the single-coil's hum as it was less prone to picking up extraneous sounds. Beneficial side effects were a louder pickup with a thicker depth of tone compared to the treble-prone DeArmonds.

In later years, Atkins set aside his 6120 in favor of the more-refined Gretsch Country Gentleman and later, the

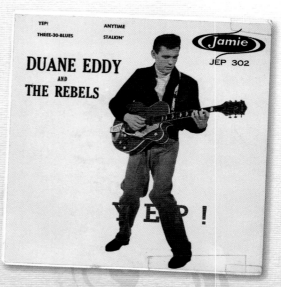

Duane Eddy and the Rebels EP "Yep!"

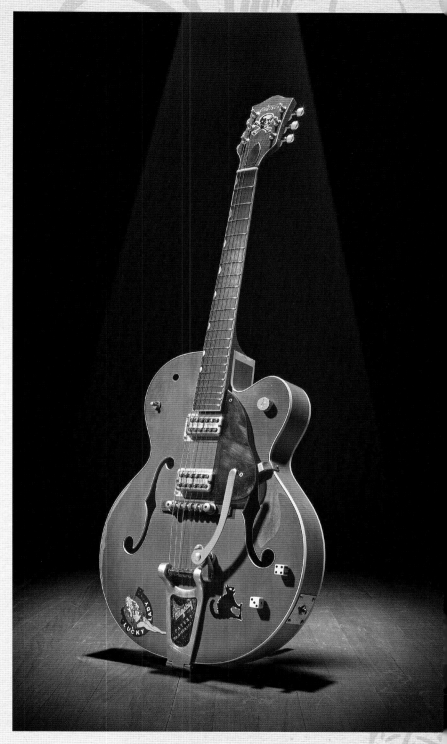

Gretsch's Custom Shop recreated Brian Setzer's famed 1959 Model 6120 Stray Cats guitar. *Fender Musical Instruments Corporation*

Super Chet. But for rockabilly, the original 6120 had all the right stuff.

Eddie Cochran bought his 1955 6120, serial number 16942, from Bell Gardens Music Center in California. He ditched the neck DeArmond pickup and replaced it with a mellower-toned Gibson P-90, as his nephew Bobby Cochran notes in *Three Steps to Heaven: The Eddie Cochran Story*. (And contrary to popular lore, Cochran did not *replace* his gold-colored, Atkins-signed pickguard with a clear version. He simply sandpapered off the underside paint and Mr. Guitar's autograph. Cochran didn't need any ride on Atkins' coattails: he was promoting only himself.)

Duane Eddy bought his 6120 at Ziggie Zardus' Accordion & Guitar Studios in Phoenix, Arizona, on September 20, 1957, for $420 paid off over 24 months, co-signed by his dad. As Eddy remembered, "First time I picked up the red Gretsch, it just took to me, settled right in there. There's times it doesn't get twangy, other times it gets smooth and dragging and menacing."

Given both Gretsch's pedigree and rockabilly's influence, it's little wonder that rockers picked up and plugged in Gretsch hollow bodies, from George Harrison to Brian Jones to Mike Nesmith of the Monkees and beyond.

Still, for all its history, the 6120 may never have achieved its current level of fame, desirability, and value if it were not for rockabilly revivalist Brian Setzer. The Stray Cat proved the 6120's musical essence and class for a modern age that had largely forgotten about the guitar.

Others followed his style. Poison Ivy of the Cramps, Jim Heath of the Reverend Horton Heat, David Lee of the Legendary Shack Shakers—they all played 6120s.

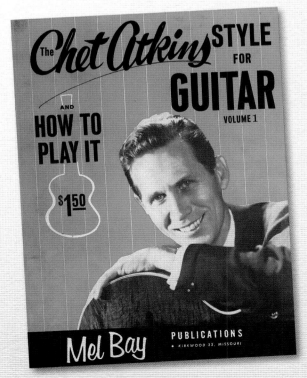

Chet Atkins was a dramatic influence on rockabilly, thanks to his recordings, guitar playing, and his namesake Gretsch guitar.

CHAPTER 6

ROCK 'N' ROLL WAS CLEANED UP, BUTTONED DOWN, COMBED, AND POLISHED AT THE DAWN OF THE 1960S.

Gone were greasy ducktails, pink-and-black slacks, and blue suede shoes. In their place were smooth haircuts, sweaters, and penny loafers.

The hub now was Philadelphia, home, not coincidentally, of Dick Clark's *American Bandstand.* And the new stars were sanitized and trustworthy Fabian, Frankie Avalon, Bobby Rydell, Bobby Darin, Bobby Vee, and more whitewashed, produced teen-idol singers.

Rockabilly was old and in the way. But still it survived in back-woods roadhouses and juke joints. The spirit was also alive in the new surf music of bands like Dick Dale and the Del-Tones, Minne-sota's Trashmen (who began as a rockabilly group), and many more.

AND THERE WAS A NEW MOVEMENT OF GARAGE BANDS THAT KEPT THE BEAT ALIVE.

Ronnie Hawkins and the Hawks with ace guitarist Jimmy Ray Paulman, circa 1960. *Michael Ochs Archives/Getty Image*

Born Huntsville, Arkansas, on January 10, 1935

By Craig Morrison

THOUGH HAWKINS HIT THE *Billboard* charts three times, twice in 1959, with "Forty Days" (Chuck Berry's "Thirty Days") and "Mary Lou" (by R&B singer Young Jessie), and again in 1970, with "Down in the Alley" (an old Clovers song), his recordings rarely do justice to his capabilities. Famous for his spectacular stage shows and the caliber of his highly-rehearsed backup players (one set left to back Bob Dylan and became The Band), in Canada he is an institution, for his music, his wit, his associations with John Lennon and Yoko Ono, and much more. Simply put, he is the man who taught Canada to rock and roll. I'd heard his records on the radio, from early rockers like the scorching "Who Do You Love" to folk songs such as Gordon Lightfoot's "Home from the Forest," a Canadian hit in 1967.

In April 1985, Ronnie Hawkins and his band, with son Robin on guitar, came to play for a week in Le Portage, a night club in the Hotel Bonaventure in Montreal. I went to see the band twice. I had also seen him perform before, in Memphis in 1983, with his own band as well as backed by the Sun Rhythm Section. The interview took place in his room at the hotel, where he would perform that night.

RONNIE HAWKINS: I was born in Huntsville, Arkansas, on January 10th, 1935. I went 'til about the fourth grade in Huntsville then I went to the big city of Fayetteville, a university town. I played through half of high school and all of college. I played a little rhythm guitar at one time. E and A was the two keys we learned and that's all the band knew. I kept getting my hands busted in fights and I kept 'em in casts, so I couldn't keep up with them. Besides I had to book, manage, and baby sit musicians anyways so I didn't have time to learn anything.

I didn't have any [racial] problem until I put the black band together. That was 1957. I went in the army, [like] everybody down there, and did my six months. I did basic in Fort Chaffee, Arkansas, and then went to Fort Sill, Oklahoma, and that's when I met the Black Hawks, in Lawton, Oklahoma, hometown of Leon Russell. We played all the army bases, stayed together for about a year and four months. We did whatever was out at the time: "That'll Be the Day" by the Buddy Holly and the Crickets, songs by Presley, Jerry Lee Lewis. Carl Perkins had "Blue Suede Shoes," "Boppin' the Blues." I was doing that style and the lead guitar player was singing blues. It was the best band I'd ever heard and I'd seen all of them. I'd seen Presley's band,

Ronnie Hawkins' first single was a cover of Chuck Berry's "Thirty Days," which the Hawk retitled "Forty Days." Released on Roulette in 1959, it was backed by the sweetly rocking "Mary Lou."

Jerry Lee's, Buddy Holly's, Roy Orbison had the Teen Kings in Wink, Texas. They weren't nothin', absolutely nothin' compared to these four black dudes. All of them were just gigging, working for five dollars a night too, maybe with the exception of Presley. He might have been making a little more.

We saw all the great black acts, that's what I liked, and we were playing a lot of black bars. Saw Howlin' Wolf, Muddy Waters, Memphis Slim, B. B. King, John Lee Hooker, all of them, coming through for five dollars a night. I saw Ike Turner. Ike was pimping. He had money. The one I liked best was Ray Charles' group with Fathead Newman and Margie Hendricks. God almighty they were good. Ray ain't never been that good ever since.

I knew Billy Lee Riley when he first come out, met him in Memphis. He played with us last time we went down. We learned a set of his songs. He's about 90% Indian. He's slim and he looks good, got the hair dyed black. He looks as good now as he did when he was a kid. He played harmonica and a little guitar. The band you saw [Sun Rhythm Section], man I used to think that was the hottest band in the world. Them poor somebodies can't play nothin' no more. J. M. Van Eaton used to wire a Kotex in the bottom of the snare, under the drum head, to get that thump sound for recording. They had calfskin heads back then, they didn't have plastic. Scotty Moore was one of the first electronic cats down there, like a poor man's Les Paul. An electronic cat made that first [tape] loop echo that Scotty had. Bill Black used to drink that rotten old whiskey, one brand of bourbon that I never even had heard of. Bought it by the case, that's what killed him finally.

I played with the Burnettes, all of them. I still keep in touch with [their sons] Rocky and Billy—"rockabilly"—from Johnny and Dorsey. Rocky Burnette to me is the best rockabilly singer in the world to this day. He's got a throat better than his dad or his uncle. Rocky's a talent but he's laid back. Billy is a good guitar player. Billy's playing with one of them big time dudes. [He was then playing with Mick Fleetwood and would soon join Fleetwood Mac.] Paul Burlison still looks good too. All three of those cats [Johnny, Dorsey, and Paul - the Rock 'n' Roll Trio] were Golden Gloves boxing champions. They had long hair and if four or five rednecks'd call them queer or something, they'd just set their guitars down and kick the shit out of about three tables and come right back on the stage and just keep playing. That was a rough bunch, now boy, they could fight! So their reputation got around, and big guys would come from all over to get on their case. It was like a gun fighter, if word gets out then some kid or tough punk thinks he can outdo it. I never seen them get whipped, and they used to take on two or three each. That was the band Elvis wanted to get in, and they wouldn't. Elvis was a little too cocky for them. They were making a little noise before anybody. Nobody was making any money. If you got three or four dollars a night, you thought you's in the big time. They were at least getting jobs. They had that old official rockabilly sound with no drums. Presley didn't use drums either for a long time. I always liked a drum myself. The drummers that could drum hated rock and roll. That was the big band era, they were used to all that swing.

Me and the Black Hawks decided we was gonna get killed, we better part ways. That's why I came to Canada, like the end of '57. I went back [to Arkansas] and got a phone call from all those session men from Memphis [inviting him to front a band]. By the time I got to Memphis, they had broken up from who's gonna be leader. I took Jimmy Ray Paulman, who had played sessions there and also had been Harold Jenkins'—Conway Twitty's—lead guitar player. Said he had a cousin who played a little bit [of piano] in high school, that was Willard "Pop" Jones. We found a kid

out of Marvell, Arkansas, that Pop knew that played guitar, but he had taken high school snare. That was Levon Helm. We were working out of West Helena, Arkansas, because I got a job there at a place that helped everybody. This guy loaned Elvis money. Elvis had played there, at the Catholic Club, they didn't make enough money to buy gas to get back to Memphis. [Elvis Presley and his band played three times at the Catholic Club in Helena, Arkansas: December 2, 1954, and January 13 and March 8, 1955.] Charlie Halbert was his name. He should be in the books because he helped and fed everybody, ask Carl Perkins and Jerry Lee.

Sonny Burgess and the Pacers were out of Newport. I knew Sonny well, I played in the band with them lots of times. He had a cat that later on became Conway Twitty's bass player: Big Joe Lewis. Jack Nance played trumpet in Sonny Burgess and the Pacers, and he played drums for Conway Twitty and he wrote half of "It's Only Make Believe."

CM: So you gigged in Canada before you moved here?

RH: Yeah. We had a summer and we had a chance to play in a little bar that paid us 400 dollars a week, but we didn't know we had to pay an agent and a union out of it.

CM: Did you usually do your own bookings?

RH: I did all my own stuff. They had those Memphis agents that'd make Al Capone look like a boy scout. Bob Neal was one of them. I saved his life when a friend of mine was getting ready to kill him. I had a club there in Fayetteville and Neal sent Eddie Bond. He had one [record] that was halfway rockabilly. That little club we had was a rocker. You couldn't sing no hillbilly shit in there unless you could fight. They sent Eddie Bond, a disc jockey who played on the

side. Bob Neal said he was one of the rockinest cats up there. He booked all of them. Jerry Lee, Carl Perkins, all of them come through there because it was a stop off going to the Red Foley Show in Springfield, Missouri, The Ozark Jubilee, and that was good because it was networked too. Then from there, you either did Ed Sullivan or Perry Como [television shows]. That's when Carl Perkins had the bad wreck. He played two days for us then he went to the Ozark Jubilee and then he had the car wreck going to the Perry Como show. I don't think he played again for three or four years.

So Eddie Bond started that hillbilly shit, and the students were geared for like Sonny Burgess and the Pacers, they rocked. All those: the Burnettes rocked, Carl Perkins,

"Ruby Baby" was penned by Jerry Leiber and Mike Stoller, and originally recorded by the Drifters to become a major R&B hit in 1956. Ronnie Hawkins' version was sublime rockabilly.

Jerry Lee. They'd come all the way from Memphis for a hundred dollars a night, many a time. Jerry Lee was the one who was the rockinest back then. He got pilled up and fired his band on stage in Memphis the night before he came to Fayetteville and all he brought was a drummer, Russ Smith from Newport, Arkansas. Had arms about that big around, eating them pills and he also did a couple of Z class movies with "Great Balls of Fire" and "Breathless." Just drums and piano. My friend said "that ain't gonna work." And he was late to start with. You know Jerry Lee's crazy—he says, "I'll tell you what, get me a six pack of beer, and I'll take a couple of these yeller jackets" as he called them, some kind of pill, "and we'll go on and if the people don't like us, you don't have to pay us." The university had a special meeting the next day, because the girls had ten o'clock curfew, but nobody left. Jerry Lee must have played *eight* straight hours. He never left, they just kept bringing him beer and every now and then he'd pop a yellow jacket. That drummer, he played bumblebee music, I mean fast rocking. That piano was worth what it weighed when Jerry Lee got through with it. He beat the shit out it. But boy he mesmerized everybody. He did it, I don't know how. Jerry Lee pounded every number and sung every song I'd ever heard of.

I first heard "Mary Lou" from Roy Orbison. "Mojo Man" was written for me by Norm Riley, the guy that took me, Gene Vincent and Eddie Cochran to England. [Hawkins performed on British television in January 1960.] He hooked me. It was a famous story. He checked himself into a mental institution, couldn't remember where all the money was that he owed Gene Vincent and Eddie Cochran. He didn't owe me

Hawkins did his trademark Camel Walk decades before Michael Jackson revived the dance as the Moon Walk.

much, I spent most of mine. I didn't get but 1,500 dollars. I wasn't based in Canada until about 1963. I just came to Canada and played, went back to Arkansas. I lived on the road. I became a landed immigrant, because they started putting some rules on the border. We chiseled out a little small time circuit in Ontario and it was going over pretty good. We were making a living, it was easier than working out of Memphis.

I had cut a few things in Memphis that didn't do well, audition tapes. Buddy Holly also auditioned for Sun. But they had four artists going at that time and he had already locked up every pressing plant. Sam Phillips had Carl Perkins, Elvis Presley, Johnny Cash, and Jerry Lee Lewis. They were selling more records than anybody. They had all they could handle with the four heavies. It just flooded everything and nobody else got anything. They turned down Buddy Holly. I used a couple of boys there, J. M. Van Eaton played with me a few times, and Roland Janes. I cut two blues numbers, they came off pretty good. They wanted songs they could get the publishing on, so we cut old public domain songs or changed them. That was Sam's idea. Sam has made more money than God. Sam invested in two little motels in Memphis, and that was [the start of the] Holiday Inn [chain]. Sam didn't exactly need to be fightin' an 18-hour day on pilled-up musicians.

I wasn't in Memphis a lot, but I was down there every time I could afford to stay. I stayed for a month once and ran out of money, and our guitar player got his guitar repossessed. They were too lazy to work, afraid it would hurt their hands. So I painted the Memphis Queen [riverboat], me and another guy. I had more paint on me than I got on the Memphis

Queen. But they paid me, that's when I cut a few little things there.

There was a disc jockey there that made Presley. He was a hot disc jockey, and got on TV: Dewey Phillips. Killed hisself finally. He went crazy, lost his job. But Dewey was one of them redneck hip cats. He was popular and he loved Presley. Boy, he just crammed [Presley's records] down so Presley started getting bigger and bigger, and he hit the *Louisiana Hayride*. Colonel Tom [Parker] managed Hank Snow, they were partners actually, and Elvis went out as opening act on that first little tour. Before it was over, Hank Snow was opening for Elvis, because there wasn't anything left when Elvis went on. Then Colonel Tom pulled a little scam in, said, "I think I'll just semi-retire," and sold the other half of his business to Snow. He said, "I'll just keep this kid," so that Hank Snow didn't get half of Presley.

CM: Was the term rockabilly derogatory, a negative connotation?

RH: You ain't shitting, it's negative down there, as negative as you can get. Two pegs below a prisoner of war, and every preacher in the world was on your case, just playing that devil's music.

CM: When did you first hear "My Babe"?

RH: I learned that from my first cousin, Dale Hawkins: "Suzy Q," "La-Do-Dada" and all that, he was on Chess. I didn't know him well, except Dale came back up to Hawkins Holler in Arkansas and stayed two or three summers.
I've known Ray Smith forever. Ray killed himself, Ray blew his head off right in front of his wife and family. He was crazy, he had that Jerry Lee Lewis touch, always carried guns. He shot a cat in Kingston. I don't know how he got out of it, he managed to beat it somehow. I knew Warren Smith. When I couldn't go to England that time [in 1977], I got Warren Smith and Ray Smith to go in my place. They were both dead a year later. So not too many people want to still go play that rockabilly for me anymore! I've known Jim Dickinson forever. Jim played with me. He came into Muscle Shoals, Alabama, when I was using Duane Allman. I'd met him a few times before.

CM: Were you ever pressured by producers to do songs you didn't want to do?

RH: Oh yeah, in those days you did what they said. They were the boss. Whoever puts up the money usually tells you what to do. Back then, they'd work a week on a song. "Blue Suede Shoes," I bet it took months. Putting egg crates and old rusty microphones around that dinky Sun [studio]. It's about the size of this room, the whole building. Sam Phillips had an ear. He knew how to get a sound that was commercial, when he did it himself.

I stayed in Canada. I had several opportunities to go back to Nashville and to Memphis and to New York, but I liked it up here, it was an easy gig. I'm just doing my thing, don't make big money but it's steady.

Mr. Dynamo, Ronnie Hawkins' second LP on Roulette.

Born Windsor, Ontario, on January 24, 1936

By Deke Dickerson

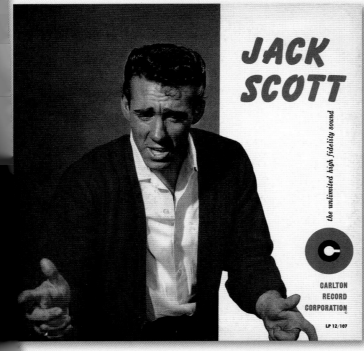

Jack Scott's debut LP, on Carlton Records. As the back cover text reported, "At age 22, the lean, handsome, serious Jack Scott has embarked on a record career which will inevitably lead to the glamour worlds of television, cinema and theater."

ROCK 'N' ROLL AND ITS WARPED cousin rockabilly were mostly the property of the South in the 1950s, with nearly all the big stars coming from states within driving distance of Memphis. However, it makes sense that the city of Detroit spawned a real honest to goodness rock 'n' roll legend, Mr. Jack Scott of Hazel Park, Michigan.

While Detroit was as far north as any major American city, the population was for the most part made up of hillbillies and African-Americans who moved up from South to work in the automobile industry.

From the 1930s to today, this diversity has made Detroit a spawning ground for many interesting musical combinations, from John Lee Hooker, Little Willie John, Hank Ballard and the Midnighters in the R&B field; Casey Clark, Lonnie Barron and the York Brothers in the country western field; the entire Motown Records clan and Atlantic Records super star Aretha Franklin in the soul world; and of course a whole slew of gritty rock bands from the MC5 to Iggy and the Stooges to present chart darlings the White Stripes. Even current-day rap-rock star Kid Rock is a Detroit mix of Black hip-hop and redneck country influences.

Somewhere in that mix came Jack Scott. He was a Canadian-born Italian, real name

Giovanni Dominico Scafone Jr., who was raised in Windsor, Ontario, just over the border and across the bridge from Detroit. At the age of 11, Jack's family moved to Hazel Park, Michigan, a hillbilly (read: white) suburb of Detroit.

Jack's father was a musician and played guitar for the kids (Jack was the oldest of seven children), putting a guitar in Jack's hands at the tender age of eight. Jack loved country music and would strum his guitar around the house and listen to country music on the radio, dreaming big dreams about the Grand Ol' Opry and Nashville.

During his teenage years, Jack worked a number of odd jobs while continuing to play guitar. He formed a local hillbilly band called the Southern Drifters at the age of 18.

Jack was obsessed with music from an early age. He imitated Hank Williams, Webb Pierce, and many others. His aspirations from this early age were fully formed, and in fact he changed his name from Giovanni Scafone Jr. to Jack Scott on a suggestion from local WEXL disc jockey Jack Eirie that he might be more successful with an easier to pronounce, more anglicized name.

Like many other teenagers of the mid 1950s, when Elvis came along everything changed, and Jack realized he might have some potential with the new sound of rock 'n' roll. The Southern Drifters began working Elvis and Bill Haley songs into their country repertoire.

It's doubtful that Jack had any idea that he would soon be at exactly the right place at the right time, a place where a good-looking, greasy-haired Italian kid who played the guitar could be a famous rock 'n' roll musician, but that's exactly what happened.

In early 1957, the group decided one night after a dance, to rent some late night studio time, and laid down two tracks, "Baby She's Gone" and "You Can Bet Your Bottom Dollar." "Baby She's Gone" was influenced heavily by Elvis' version of "Money Honey," but has proved to be a classic in its own right, with Jack's original vocal delivery hinting at the style he would make his very own in the upcoming few years.

The group consisted of Jack's cousin Dominic on drums, Stan Getz on bass, and Dave Rohillier on lead guitar. Their fiddle player, Wayne "Arkansas" Sudden came to the session, but didn't play. It's interesting to note that Stan Getz (not the famous jazz musician) would also play on the other phenomenal Detroit rockabilly masterpiece, "Long Blond Hair"/"Rock Rock" by Johnny Powers, showing what a small rock 'n' roll community Detroit had at the time.

The group took their acetate around to all the local record shops, trying to find a label that would put it out. One local record store man named Carl Thom played the dub for the local ABC–Paramount rack jobber, who then mailed the acetate to New York City for the label bigwigs to hear. Like many other labels, ABC–Paramount was keen on getting new rock 'n' roll records on the market, and leased quite a few regionally recorded tapes for release. They released "Baby She's Gone"/"You Can Bet Your Bottom Dollar" straight from Jack's demo tape, not bothering to do a big studio re-cut of the tracks, in April 1957 on ABC–Paramount.

The record was a small local success, but not a hit, so ABC–Paramount tried again with a second release, "Two Timin' Woman"/"I Need Your Love," released in November 1957. Although "Two Timin' Woman" was another classic rocker, this record sold even less than the first release and Jack was soon dropped from the label.

By early 1958 Jack had composed two new songs, which he felt were hit material. He recorded acetate dubs of the new songs in order to pitch them to record labels. The rocker was a blast of a number about a friend he had who was always getting into trouble. The problem was that it was called "Greaseball," surely an apt title, but one which didn't fly with the record company executives, who felt "Greaseball" might insult the Mexican-American community. After the record company told him to change the title, Jack went into the studio bathroom and saw that someone had written "Leroy was here" on the wall, and the song title immediately was changed to "Leroy."

The flip side was another ballad, entitled "My True Love." Legend has it that Jack wrote it for his first girlfriend. As ballads go, it was the first fully realized number that epitomized the Jack Scott ballad style—a near dirge tempo, with simple teenage lyrics delivered by Jack in a plaintive, drawn-out drawl, a style that became a favorite of greasers, teddy boys and rockers around the globe. Jack Scott would work this ballad style for years.

Although some have stated that "Leroy"/"My True Love" was issued first on the Detroit based Brill label, several Detroit area record collectors vouch that there was no such release. It's possible that it may have been put out on another acetate dub record with the Brill label, which would explain the confusion.

What is known is that a song plugger from New York, Jack "Lucky" Carle (brother to Frankie Carle, the easy-listening musician) heard the record, and took

it to Murray Deutch in New York City, who was the general manager of Peer–Southern Music Publishing Company.

Deutch contacted Joe Carlton, who purchased the two cuts along with an option on Jack Scott's career, for $4,800 and soon released "Leroy"/"My True Love" on his own Carlton label in June 1958. Deutch snagged song publishing as his cut on the deal, and Jack "Lucky" Carle assumed a management role in Jack Scott's career.

"Leroy" became an immediate hit, and Jack Scott was suddenly a rock 'n' roll star, although he was still a kid living at home with his parents. After "Leroy" peaked at Number 25 on the charts, the disc jockeys turned it over and began playing "My True Love," which eventually peaked at Number 3 on the charts and became one of the biggest hits of 1958.

Jack Scott had indeed arrived. Unfortunately due to his multi-tiered management/publishing/record label arrangement, he was also soon to learn all about the vagaries of the music business, and how everybody managed to get a big chunk of the money except for the artist. He was a young 22 year old, though, and at the time was just happy to have a record that was played every morning on the radio in his mother's kitchen.

Jack's band had made some adjustments, too, bringing in the talented Al Allen on guitar and George Kazakas on saxophone. Jack had also brought in a vocal backing group from across the border, a young group of Canadian singers named the Chantones.

The Chantones were from Windsor, Ontario, Jack's original hometown, and they brought a unique sound to the Carlton Recordings. Their name came from the French phrase "*nous chantons*," which simply means "to sing." Although their influence was strictly white-bread vocal groups like the Crew Cuts and the Four Freshmen, their harmonies were somewhat ragged, not polished, and there was a heavy accent on the bass singer. It was a unique sound that no other group had, and the Chantones input on the classic Jack Scott rockers can't be overemphasized.

After the success of "Leroy," Jack Scott was off and running. A series of excellent tracks followed, including "Geraldine," "With Your Love," "Save My Soul," and another classic Jack Scott ballad entitled "Goodbye Baby," which rose all the way up to Number 8 on the charts.

The next single, "I Never Felt Like This"/"Bella," was another great effort that failed to chart, though it was a perfect distillation of all the right elements, with a cool Magnatone vibrato effect on Al Allen's guitar, a memorable melody, and excellent mood backing vocals by the Chantones.

The next release, which only reached Number 35 on the charts at the time, without question became the song that

"Leroy" was Jack Scott's first single, released by Carlton in 1958. It reached #11 on the charts.

LEROY
(Jack Scott)

462
Peer International
BMI
CRO-148 · 2:07

CARLTON

JACK SCOTT
with Orchestral
Accompaniment

GOODBYE BABY
Words and Music by JACK SCOTT
PRICE 50¢

as Recorded by
JACK SCOTT
on CARLTON RECORDS

STARFIRE MUSIC CORPORATION
Sole Selling Agent: PEER INTERNATIONAL CORPORATION, 1619 Broadway, New York 19, N. Y.

has defined Jack Scott ever since—the greaser classic "The Way I Walk," backed with another good rocker entitled "Midgie."

"The Way I Walk" is perhaps the ultimate in greaser bravado, a song that means little to the casual listener but reaps volumes to the hipster who can relate to such lines as "The way I walk is just the way I walk." Greaser existentialism at its finest, it was a language that could not be understood by the older generation, but which fully connected with the kids.

Jack Scott had his own style—not a frantic, out of control way of rocking, but instead something that bordered on a slow burn. It was menacing, but in the way that a mean look or a slight gesture was, instead of a fist to the face. As those who have studied horror films or film noir know, sometimes these implied feelings are more compelling and hold more power than an explosion of violence. Jack Scott's finest moments, like "The Way I Walk," are perfect examples of this.

Jack recorded several of his new Carlton singles in true stereo, which had just come out commercially in 1958. After Elvis' binaural stereo recordings of 1957 (which were not released until the 1980s), Jack Scott's stereo recordings of 1958 and 1959 were the first stereo recordings to be released by a white rock 'n' roll artist. The only downside to this achievement was that when the stereo version of his first album, simply titled *Jack Scott* (Carlton LP 12/107) was released, half of the album was remixed in re-channeled "fake" stereo, taking away from the

fact that half of the album was indeed breaking new ground being released in true stereo.

Jack was drafted in January 1959, and immediately began applying for deferment based on the grounds that he was supporting his parents and siblings. That didn't fly, so Jack applied for a medical discharge on the grounds of a chronic ulcer. The ulcer freed him from his service, and he was out by May 1959.

A feud between Peer–Southern music publishing and Joe Carlton at Carlton Records resulted in Jack being wooed away from Carlton to record for a new American wing of the British label Top Rank. In retrospect, Jack wished he had remained with Joe Carlton, but it was a management decision and he went along with the party line.

Jack was just beginning to learn that he was a product, being bought and sold by men in suits on the East Coast, each of them taking a piece of him, leaving Jack with lots of glory but no songwriting, publishing, or performance royalties. It was a classic sad tale of the music business.

Top Rank entered the game with a fantastic two sider, "Baby Baby"/"What In The World's Come Over You," both of which sounded like a continuation of what Jack had been doing over at Carlton. *Baby Baby* was another great rocker in the "Leroy" tradition, but the ballad side, "What In The World's Come Over You," turned out to be the hit, and ruled the airwaves in the first few months of 1960. It peaked at Number 5 on the charts.

About this time, Joe Carlton exercised his right to release Jack Scott material. Carlton's buyout stated that he could not release new singles, so Carlton put out a new album sneakily titled *What Am I Living For* to subliminally capitalize on the success of "What In The World's Come Over You" (leasing the four 1957 sides from ABC–Paramount to round out the album), as well as a number of singles on a new label he started, Guaranteed.

As far as Jack's career was concerned, it was terrible timing to have these new releases clogging up the marketplace when he was releasing new material on Top Rank. Of course, many years after the fact, fans were grateful that such rockers as "Go Wild Little Sadie" and others were released and not left in the vaults.

Really, Jack had little to complain about in 1960, however, as his next release on Top Rank, "Burning Bridges"/"Oh Little One," became a Number 3 hit and "Burning Bridges" became the biggest selling record of his career.

Top Rank released no less than three Jack Scott albums in less than a year and a half. *What In The World's Come Over You* was a collection of his hit singles and cool album tracks like "Good Deal, Lucille." Strangely enough Top Rank released two specially recorded concept albums, *I Remember Hank Williams* (a collection of mid-tempo Hank Williams tributes with rather milquetoast production), and a gospel album called *The Spirit Moves Me*. The latter two are rarely discussed among the greasers that hold Jack Scott near and dear to their hearts.

Again the music business dealt Jack like a pawn in a chess game that he had little control over. In 1961 Top Rank Records went out of business and Jack's contract along with all the old Top Rank masters were sold to Capitol. Jack wanted to investigate other avenues but the suits in charge of his career made the decisions for him, which he ultimately regretted, especially the move to Capitol.

Whereas the sessions for Carlton and Top Rank had been loose, informal, and creatively controlled by Jack himself, the Capitol records were formulaic productions where Jack walked in the studio and they already had the backing tracks recorded to songs he didn't write or choose.

Jack was told time and time again, by the people who "owned" him, that these songs were the new "in" sounds, and the new direction in music, so Jack recorded whatever they put in front of him. The sad thing is that they took away the originality Jack Scott had brought to the table with his own brand of Detroit rock 'n' roll. As such, the Capitol Records are far inferior to the ABC–Paramount, Carlton and Top Rank recordings, though a few good rockers and ballads escaped, such as "Grizzly Bear."

More than anything else, the record business was literally changing around Jack Scott, rather than the other way around. To his credit, Jack Scott never really changed his style to suit a new fad or craze—he was always just Jack Scott. When the Beatles took over in 1964, he did what a lot of previous rockers did. He began recording pop-influenced country music that essentially was a continuation of what he'd been doing all along.

When his Capitol contract expired in 1963, Jack phoned RCA Records in Nashville, and wound up with Chet Atkins himself on the phone. Chet was coming up to Detroit to do a demonstration for Gretsch Guitars, and asked Jack to pick him up at the airport and loan him one of Jack's flattop acoustic guitars for the performance. Jack shuttled Chet around Detroit, and played him a few songs. The next morning, when he took Chet back to the airport, Chet asked Jack to record for RCA Records, or more accurately, their Groove subsidiary.

Jack's releases on Groove (and beginning in 1965, RCA proper), starting with his first single in December 1963 all the way to his last in 1966, were eerily timed with the Beatles massive takeover of the music industry. That being said, Jack kept plugging along, making good records that failed to click with the country music audience.

There were a few very good 1950s style rockers recorded at RCA/Groove, which must have seemed terribly out of place in the British Invasion marketplace, but today they are enjoyable, if slightly awkward, to listen to. Tracks like "Meo Myo'," "Wiggle On Out," and "Flakey John," are almost like a greaser's last stand, but again, enjoyable songs in retrospect. Even Jack states that these records didn't have any "balls" (his word) but for 1965 and 1966 they are great stabs at keeping real rock 'n' roll alive.

Although to the greater record buying public it must have seemed like Jack Scott was retired from the business after his RCA/Groove contract ended in 1966, he kept releasing singles that didn't connect, first for ABC–Paramount, the label he'd started with in 1957, then Jubilee, then GRT, then one last major label stand in 1973 and 1974 on Dot Records. These records were all good enough attempts at current country and pop music, but there wasn't a song in the bunch that was hit material, and by the mid-1970s Jack Scott was back to playing the local bars around Detroit.

Jack kept demoing new material, thinking the opportunity would arise for a new career, but he had no idea where that opportunity might arise. As it so happened, it turned out to be Europe, where a new crop of greasers and teddy boys who had discovered Jack's 1950s classics were clamoring for the man himself to come and make personal appearances and new records.

Essentially, that's the path Jack Scott's career has taken since then, playing local shows around Michigan as Jack Scott the local hero, and touring over in Europe several times a year, as Jack Scott, rock 'n' roll legend.

At the very least, Jack Scott has secured a niche for himself in the history of rock 'n' roll. As he likes to point out, he had more hits than Gene Vincent and Eddie Cochran combined. His sound endures to the present day, loved by "greaseballs" the world over. Greaseballs of the future will look to Jack for inspiration, for the mold can't be bettered.

ROCKABILLY, EUROPEAN STYLE

CHAPTER 7

IN EUROPE, ROCKABILLY LIVED ON WHILE IT DIED BACK HOME.

Gene Vincent and Eddie Cochran were the music's great ambassadors, spreading the style to Great Britain, where it was disseminated throughout the continent and even to Japan and beyond.

England embraced the music. Home-brewed British rockabillies toured the country, revamping American songs and writing some of their own. And the music rubbed off on young fans who started their own bands, groups that would have names like the Beatles (in honor of Buddy Holly's Crickets, of course), the Who, the Yardbirds.

France, too, had its rockabillies. Johnny Hallyday became the gallic Elvis, followed by Eddy Mitchell's Chaussettes Noires as well as the English-American import Vince Taylor, and others.

THROUGHOUT THE 1960S AND 1970S, ROCKABILLY WAS ALIVE, WELL, AND ROCKING ON FOREIGN SOIL.

Anglo–American–Franco rockabilly singer Vince Taylor does it up right in concert in Paris in 1961. *Roger Viollet Collection/Getty Images*

Born Isleworth, Middlesex, England, on July 14, 1939; died August 28, 1991

By Garth Cartwright

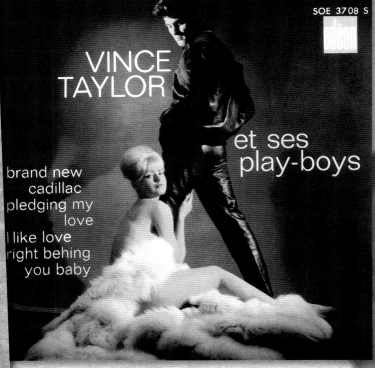

Vince Taylor would be best known for his tune "Brand New Cadillac" due mostly thanks to the Clash's cover of the song on *London Calling*. But Taylor's version rocked with equal abandon, proving that punk was invented with rockabilly.

MAD, BAD, AND DANGEROUS to know, Vince Taylor stands as one of the strangest tales in rock 'n' roll. Taylor's legend largely rests on his 1959 recording of "Brand New Cadillac" – often cited as the greatest British rockabilly record ever made, "Brand New Cadillac" retains its thrill and in 1979 was covered by The Clash on their *London Calling* album. The Clash gave "Brand New Cadillac" (and Taylor) a hip kudos. Yet Vince, while still alive, was unable to capitalize on the resurgent interest from a new generation of fans. He was simply too far gone.

Vince Taylor was born Brian Holden in Middlesex, England, in July 1939. In 1946 his family immigrated to the US, settling in New Jersey. His older sister Sheila married Joe Barbera of Hanna–Barbera animation fame in 1955 and the Holden family followed her to Los Angeles. Brian enrolled at Hollywood High School and quickly became enamored with rockabilly. He attempted to launch a singing career with Joe Barbera as manager. In 1958 Barbera invited the teenager to accompany him on a business trip to London to check out the local music scene. Brian was directed to the 2i's Coffee Bar on Old Compton St. in Soho. The 2i's was the launch pad for many of the British rockabilly singers and local musicians were impressed by this tall, handsome American. Brian formed a band, quickly won a Parlophone recording contract and changed his name to Vince Taylor, christening his band The Playboys.

Vince Taylor & The Playboy's initial 1958 singles "I Like Love," "Right Behind You Baby" and "Pledging My Love" failed to trouble the British pop charts and Parlophone ended his recording contract. The B-side of "Pledging My Love" was "Brand New Cadillac", an original song written by Taylor that rocked as hard as the best US rockabilly records and featured a sizzling guitar solo from Joe Moretti (who would also play the solo on Johnny Kidd & The Pirates's phenomenal "Shakin' All Over").

Taylor, dressed in black leather and extremely confident, proved to be a talented live performer and drew loyal audiences across the UK. Yet something was not quite right – Taylor suffered from paranoid delusions and this meant he would often fail to turn up for concerts (regularly rushing back to London to check whether girlfriends were cheating on him being a particular obsession) and act irrationally toward band members. Having signed to Poretti Records Taylor & The Playboys released the dynamic 1960s single "I'll Be Your Hero"/"Jet Black Machine." They appeared on British TV and Taylor remained a dynamic live performer. Yet his eccentric behavior became too much for The Playboys and they fired him. The Playboys remained on good terms with Taylor and when, in 1961 they were booked to perform at a rock 'n' roll event at Paris's Olympia Theatre, Taylor accompanied them. The concert promoters witnessed Taylor performing with The Playboys at soundcheck then announced the British band (with Vince) were now the event's headliners. So strong was French reaction to Taylor that he largely based his career there. Signed by Barclay Records, Taylor began releasing a series of EPs and an album. While he still wrote some of his material he increasingly relied on covering US hits. His recordings of "My Babe," "Twenty Flight Rock," "Memphis, Tennessee" and others proved he had lost none of his prowess.

By 1962, The Playboys were again unwilling to work with Taylor and he became reliant on French musicians including those who backed Johnny Hallyday. At one point his percussionist was Prince Stanislas Kosslowski de Rola, the son of celebrated painter Balthus and later to become a Rolling Stones insider. Kosslowski actually made initial contact with the Stones at their 1964 Parisian debut when Taylor opened for them. This concert signaled how quickly rock music was changing but by then Taylor was acting increasingly bizarrely and taking LSD altered his behavior for the worse. At one UK concert he announced he was the reincarnation of a Biblical prophet. Serious mental health problems dogged Taylor throughout the rest of his life. In France he retained a devoted following yet he recorded and performed irregularly.

Having learnt to fly as a teenager, Taylor later worked as a plane mechanic in Switzerland. He died there of cancer in 1991, a largely forgotten figure. David Bowie noted that he based Ziggy Stardust on Taylor. In 2009 London's Ace Records issued *Jet Black Leather Machine*, the first CD to gather Taylor's essential recordings.

70 394 Ⓜ

SWEET LITTLE SIXTEEN
LOVE ME
C'MON EVERYBODY
TWENTY FLIGHT ROCK

VINCE TAYLOR

et ses play-boys

70 395 Ⓜ SO GLAD YOUR MINE · LONE TALL SALLY
BABY LETS PLAY HOUSE · LOVIN' UP A STORM

VINCE TAYLOR et ses play-boys

Photo Herman Léonard

Born Paris, France, on June 15, 1943

By Garth Cartwright

The man in the spotlight: France's beloved rock 'n' roller Johnny Hallyday shows his best Elvis pose in concert in September 1960. *Lipnitzki/Roger Viollet/Getty Images*

IN FRANCE JOHNNY HALLYDAY is a living legend. Courted by politicians and considered by many of the populace to be the greatest rocker ever, Hallyday can attract 500,000 fans to a single concert. To the non-French speaking world, Hallyday is either unknown or the eternal wannabe. The truth falls, actually, somewhere between both claims.

Johnny Hallyday helped popularize rockabilly in France. His striking looks made him a youth icon. He went on to champion Jimi Hendrix and Otis Redding when both artists were largely unknown internationally. His popularity across Francophone Africa means everyone from Algeria's Khaled to Congolese rumba bands rate Hallyday. Today, aged 67, he remains a superstar in France, performing stadium concerts of maximum bombast while every uprising in his private life—problems with women and health being common Johnny occurrences—is documented. For better or worse he is the French Elvis and that nation's enduring love of American music of the 1950s can, in many ways, be traced to its original affection for local boy Hallyday.

French teenagers began catching the rockabilly bug in the late-1950s by tuning into AFN, the American Armed Forces Network. American singles were available at NATO bases across France and select Parisian record shops imported rockabilly—just as they had imported jazz decades earlier. Initial French attempts to record rockabilly were inept but the music kept getting more and more popular and by 1959 Radio France had its own rock 'n' roll show. This lead to a spate of youths wanting to sing the music.

One of them was a skinny teenager with striking cheekbones, fulsome lips, and a wistful look. He was Johnny Hallyday and by December 1959 he was performing live on Radio France. In March 1960, he had his first release on Vogues Records. This wasn't a hit but his follow-up, "Souvenirs, Souvenirs" was. In 1961, he signed to major label Phillips and played Paris's prestigious Olympia Theatre. He undertook military service in 1964 so disproving the naysayers who had argued Hallyday was a bad influence on French youth. Just as Elvis had moved from indie to major label, served in the army and become a mainstream entertainer so would Johnny. Unlike Elvis he's turned into a decent actor.

Johnny Hallyday was born Jean-Philipe Smet in occupied Paris in June, 1943. His parents separated the following year and he spent much of his youth being passed around relatives until he ended up living with his uncle, Lee Ketcham. Ketcham worked as a dancer and had Americanized his name to Lee Hallyday. Jean-Philipe took his uncle's surname and later added "Johnny" to sound more rock 'n' roll. By the mid-1950s he was enamored with American movies and music and wore a golden pompadour. Teaching himself English, he began singing songs by Elvis, Eddie Cochran, the Everly Brothers, Little Richard, Carl Perkins, and others, often singing in a hodgepodge of French and English.

Hallyday looked the part—girls screamed and boys admired his sharp clothes and penchant for big US motorbikes. He moved well but his initial recordings were less than convincing. Hallyday was more enthusiastic than talented when it came to singing rockabilly. By the mid '60s he was married to Sylvie Vartan (France's Queen of Pop) and regularly recording in London (a lack of talented French rock musicians had hampered his initial recordings). Here he developed his sound with help from the likes of Jimmy Page, Mick Jones (later of Foreigner), Brian Auger, and the Small Faces. He saw Jimi Hendrix's early London concerts and booked him to support his French dates. He also recorded with Otis Redding's touring band (consisting of such celebrated Muscle Shoals musicians as Jimmy Johnson, Tommy Cogbill, Roger Hawkins, and Spooner Oldham). King Curtis helped out on saxophone while Otis looked on, initially bemused then appreciative. This era is now regarded as Hallyday's musical highpoint.

During the 1970s Hallyday's music became less adventurous and his blatant borrowings from popular American singers attracted contempt. Young French rockabilly fans would refer to those they considered "plastic" as "Johnnies" i.e. not capable of performing real rockabilly. Other French rockabilly singers of the early '60s like Eddy Mitchell, who lead the band Les Chaussettes Noires (The Black Socks), and Dick Rivers, who sang with Les Chats Sauvages (The Wild Cats), made more compelling records.

No matter: Johnny Hallyday took rockabilly's wild American pulse and gave it a distinctly Gallic flavour. To his millions of fans he is "Le Roi de French Rock 'n' Roll".

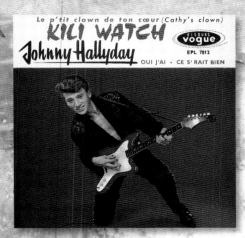

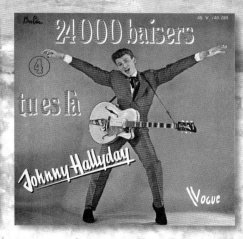

Born London, England, on November 10, 1940; died June 16, 1999

By Garth Cartwright

SCREAMING LORD SUTCH STORY

Jack The Ripper
Black And Hairy
Purple People Eater
Dracula's Daughter

OF ALL THE BRITISH ROCKERS to arise out of the United Kingdom beat boom, David Edward Sutch should be noted for several things: he was the most outrageous performer of his generation; he had an eye for escapades that would grab media attention; he recorded several 45s with Joe Meek, the brilliant, doomed UK pop producer; his band The Savages provided a training ground for many future British rock stars and, most tellingly, he possessed almost no talent as a singer or songwriter.

Sutch was born in November 1940, and as a teenager became enamored with American rock 'n' roll and the UK's Hammer horror movies.

Frequenting the coffee bars in Soho, central London, Sutch began taking to the stage and singing with bands. That he had precious little vocal talent was obvious. That he had a huge enthusiasm to entertain and great love of rockabilly and rock 'n' roll also came through. Sutch borrowed "Screaming" from American R&B singer Screaming Jay Hawkins and adopted "Lord" as a tease—this working class oddball pretending to be part of the aristocracy was the first of many jokes he would play on the British establishment.

In the late 1950s, British rockabilly and rock 'n' roll was largely defined by handsome if bland Elvis imitators. Sutch was already an extrovert and, with his hair over his shoulders, stood out. To help him stand out even further he began employing all kinds of outrageous props—wearing a motorcycle helmet with huge buffalo horns attached, attacking the audience with fake knives, axes and guns, coming on stage in a coffin, driving around in a hearse. To British teenagers hungry for trashy, American-style entertainment, Sutch provided a mix of Grand Guignol theatre mixed with loud rockabilly and rock 'n' roll.

Sutch's infamy in Britain's tabloid newspapers brought Joe Meek down to check out his act.

Meek liked what he saw, sharing as he did with Sutch a love of horror movies, spectacle and American rockabilly and r&b. Meek produced Sutch's 1961 debut single "Til The Following Night"/"Good Golly Miss Molly" so setting the format for Sutch's 1960s 45s—one side a horror song, the other a cover of an American song Sutch performed in his concerts. The single was not a hit—the BBC found Sutch too outrageous for their timid playlists—but it and those that followed were great fun, with Meek's innovative, effects heavy productions and Sutch's nutty performances harking back to the most eccentric American rockabilly of the 1950s. Sutch followed with a series of gloriously over the top singles: "Jack The Ripper" (banned and a highlight of Sutch's performances), "Monster In Black Tights," "Dracula's Daughter" and "She's Fallen In Love With The Monster Man."

Few brought them but Sutch was unconcerned with hit singles—he was one of the UK's top drawing live acts and teenage musicians Ritchie Blackmore, Jimmy Page, Jeff Beck, John Bonham and many others played in his backing band The Savages at some point before going on to greater things. Sutch's 1965 take on Johnny Burnette's "The Train Kept A Rollin'" finds The Savages tearing up the song with wild guitar duels of the sort later developed by The Yardbirds (who would also cover Burnette's song).

Sutch shifted to the US in the late-1960s where he could be noted driving around in a Rolls Royce painted in Union Jack colors. In 1970 he released his first album, *Lord Sutch & Heavy Friends* (Atlantic).

Essentially demos cut featuring ex-Savages who were now very famous rock stars (Page, Bonham etc.), *Heavy Friends* snuck Sutch into the Top 100 US album chart. Follow-up album *Hands Of Jack The Ripper* found him in concert backed by the likes of Keith Moon and Ritchie Blackmore.

Sutch returned to the UK and focused on politics—he had wittily stood for Parliament in 1963 as leader of the Teenage Party; he now became leader of The Raving Loony Monster Party and would stand at every by-election going, enjoying adding levity to the proceedings.

His influence on 1980s psychobilly acts was noted when The Cramps booked him as support for several UK dates while The Meteors invited him to record with them.

Sutch suffered from manic depression and this lead to him committing suicide in June 1999. His influence on the likes of the Sex Pistols—Malcolm McLaren studied Sutch's media guerrilla tactics and always kept his 45s on the jukebox—and later The White Stripes and The Horrors (both perform "Jack The Ripper") mark him out as a British eccentric whose appeal has yet to wane.

By Deke Dickerson

IN ITS ORIGINAL, PURE, undiluted form rockabilly was gone before most people knew it was even there.

If you ask collectors, musicians who lived in the original 1950s era, and scholars familiar with the genre, no one can give you a conclusive answer of when exactly rockabilly started or ended—or even what exactly constitutes "rockabilly" per se.

What can be agreed upon is that rockabilly existed for a very brief time, perhaps two to three years in the mid 1950s, and that at the time, nobody called it rockabilly—it was just called rock 'n' roll (although to be fair, there are a number of references to "rockabilly" in the 1950s, but generally in trade magazines and other outside sources. And a handful of records do exist using the term, such as the Johnny Burnette Trio's "Rock Billy Boogie," Hayden Thompson's unreleased "Rockabilly Gal," and "Rockabilly Rhythm" by Gene McKown—but by and large, all the musicians who played what we now call rockabilly only called it rock 'n' roll at the time).

The thing, that certain "Ingredient X" that makes it rockabilly to the fans that came later were things of which the original makers were completely unaware. If a mumble-mouthed peckerwood from Tennessee went to approximate a rhythm and blues song (or to goose up a hillbilly number with electric guitars), they had no idea they were forging something completely unique with a wild-ass take on their influences. The electric guitars, the slap bass, the wild abandon on the drums, the slapback tape echo used in the studio—those were simply organic elements surrounding these people at the time.

Like any good forest fire, rockabilly was a music that had lots of dry tinder (millions of postwar bored teenagers looking for something new and exciting), a lit match (Elvis Presley bucking out of the gate like a bronco), and sufficient time for the forest fire to rage out of control before being forced into submission (1955–1958, when small, upstart labels like Sun and King and Chess were able to have large national hits without the promotional muscle of the large record labels). By the end of the 1950s, the large labels had stepped in, taken control, put out the fire, and the weird Southern freak music known as rockabilly was no more.

Americans have a funny relationship with their own culture. When something is invented, be it a gadget or a fashion or a dance or a musical style, Americans buy it, play with it for a while, and then discard it with alarming speed. In the 1960s, rockabilly had been all but forgotten, save for a few juke-joint performers like

Charlie Feathers whom somebody had forgotten to tell that the Beatles had landed.

Something funny happened to rockabilly on its path to obscurity, however. Beginning in the early 1960s, a small group of obsessed English and European collectors (and an even smaller group of Americans, it should be noted) started going to the South and buying up these obscure records, raiding the jukebox distributors, the old record warehouses, and often the original artists themselves. These collectors brought these records back to England and Europe and started a new revival of what they started calling "rockabilly."

One man in particular—a Welsh Teddy Boy named "Breathless" Dan Coffey—is often given credit for being the original source for American music of the 1950s being reintroduced to the British Isles. The Teddy Boy culture was a working-class gang culture that dressed in an odd mishmash of Victorian-era clothes and 1950s greaser chic, and they worshipped American rockabilly music. The more primitive it was, the more basic the beat, the more caveman and sing-a-long the lyrics were, the better.

There has never been a more energetic and excited music fan in the history of the world than "Breathless" Dan Coffey. His tireless promotion of the kind of music that he loved undoubtedly helped spread rockabilly's popularity overseas during those wilderness days of the 1960s and 1970s. To this day, Coffey will send out hundreds of postcards a week to the people he deems important (this author felt honored when he began to receive postcards from Coffey), written in a furious scrawl, cramming thousands of words onto a tiny postcard, always raving about the latest incredible music he had just discovered, or rediscovered.

In the early 1960s, Coffey began bringing back 45rpm records from America to the United Kingdom, and songs that he had played at his disc jockey record hops began to gain popularity with the local Teddy Boys. Soon, impossibly rare original discs like "Boppin' High School Baby" by Don Willis and "Tongue-Tied Jill" by Charlie Feathers began to sell for a collector's premium, and a new pipeline was established. Before long, thousands of original American records were imported overseas. Soon after that, bootlegs and compilation albums of the rarest and most expensive originals made the music even more accessible to the average music fan.

The Teddy Boys themselves grew absurdly long sideburns, wore the Confederate Rebel flag on just about everything, and in general began to exaggerate a grotesque cartoon image of their perception of American 1950s culture—an American culture that never really existed.

In those early days of what can be called the Rockabilly Revival, there were bands recreating the old sounds, but these bands were few and far between, so a network of DJs and record hops began to emerge on the scene. There were most certainly record hops in 1950s America, but they were always secondary to live music and generally used as filler. This was not the case with the English and European Rockabilly Revival.

EUROPEAN ROCKABILLY

Eddy Mitchell and les Chaussettes Noires—the Black Socks—were darlings of the French rockabilly scene. Christened Claude Moine upon his birth in Paris on July 3, 1942, Mitchell took his stage name from American expatriate tough-guy actor Eddie Constantine, later the star of Jean-Luc Godard's *Alphaville*. He became a French rock 'n' roll institution, touring and recording to this day.

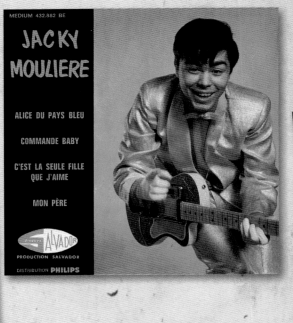

An interesting confluence of technology and the times happened in the 1970s Rockabilly Revival. Disco music was becoming the new thing in the mainstream club culture. People began to go to clubs merely to listen to DJs playing disco records, played at deafening volumes over newly improved sound systems that were vastly louder than anything available in the 1950s or 1960s.

Though the Teddy Boys and others in the Rockabilly Revival scene despised disco, they co-opted many of the basic tenets of the music. DJs played records at obscenely loud volumes, had a preference for records that fit a certain beat or dance pattern, and stuck to a rigid formula. To this day, European DJs must play records in a series that includes three boppers (records with a 2/4 beat good for "bopping"), three jivers (records with a swinging 4/4 beat good for "jiving" or swing dancing), and two strollers (records with a straight 4/4 time to which women do a formulaic, robotic "stroll"). All these dances were invented in the United States, but co-opted to this rigid form by European DJs during the disco era.

During the punk rock and New Wave era of the late 1970s and early 1980s, a new style of rockabilly emerged, particularly in London. The style has become known as Neo-Billy, and was represented by such acts as Levi and the Rockats, the Polecats, and the Stray Cats, who gained fame first in England before returning to their native New York.

The Neo-Billy era coexisted with punk rock, New Wave, and the synth-pop pretty-boy era of such acts as Duran Duran and Depeche Mode; 1950s fashion merged with eyeliner, lipstick, earrings, and other accoutrements of the day. Authenticity was never considered, and attire such as bowling shirts with sleeves torn off were even sold at department stores as "rockabilly" garb.

Several of the Neo-Billy acts got signed to major record labels in the 1980s. Bands such as the Polecats and the Shakin' Pyramids made brazen attempts at pop stardom by adding synthesizers and drum machines to their sound. These efforts were rejected by radio stations as well as the fans, and the records didn't sell. The rockabilly groups that tried to achieve pop stardom suffered major credibility problems afterwards.

One exception to the rule was the Stray Cats, who broke through the English charts and a few years later became huge stars in the American mainstream. The Stray Cats were marketed as a boy band by their record label, with articles in teenage newsstand magazines detailing how dreamy each member was, and embarrassing videos showing the band in hair-spray coiffed and eyeliner glory. Their records, however, were carefully crafted, extremely well produced songs that turned on an entire new generation to the exciting sound of rockabilly music.

Brian Setzer's guitar playing and singing ability transcended the need for synthesizers or added gloss. The band's best records, including their breakthrough hit "Rock This Town," had an energy that bordered on punk with pop hooks that borrowed from the best original 1950s rock 'n' roll, a combination that proved to be a winning ticket for chart stardom. Of all the groups in the 1980s era, the Stray Cats were the chosen ones who achieved mainstream stardom.

As the 1950s became further distant in the past, an interesting thing happened in the English and European rockabilly scenes.

In the late 1980s and early 1990s, a new generation of kids became obsessed with rockabilly. Unlike the earlier generations, the new generation rejected the cartoon-like imagery of the Teddy Boys and the Neo-Rockabilly cultures.

"Authentic Rockabilly" or the "Hep Cat Scene" became the latest in a series of trends. The authenticity of original 1950s culture became a slavish obsession—not only in the clothes, hairstyles, and music: this obsession extended to the cars, music, and recording equipment used by the bands. In essence, these rockabilly fans sought to recreate a complete 1950s womb-like existence, as though life were always a July day in 1956.

The Authentic Rockabilly scene soon became an extremely dedicated, and extremely exclusive, sect. Prices of vintage gabardine clothes rose to the point that no young kids discovering the music for the first time could afford to buy the clothes to join the clique.

Although the Authentic Rockabilly scene held great promise, ultimately the movement wound up imploding on itself due to the lack of young blood coming in.

The Authentic Rockabilly movement would be the last organic happening in rockabilly circles throughout the world. Beginning in the mid 1990s, the Internet changed everything. The World Wide Web and the Global Village it had to offer soon united rockabilly fans all over the world.

The English and European Rockabilly movements have left their mark on the world. Today, all of the Rockabilly festivals from Las Vegas to Moscow use the English/European DJ format, filling dance floors with thousands of young and old fans that bought their outfits on eBay.

Perhaps the most interesting vantage point on how the English and Europeans have changed Rockabilly comes from the original 1950s rockabilly performers. Often, these performers are in disbelief at what they see at these festivals—women with tattoos, DJs playing music at deafening levels, and enthusiasm over what they would consider mundane things, like gabardine shirts and double-stitched dress shoes. These aspects of the rockabilly music scene are things these performers never witnessed in the original era.

Larry Collins from the Collins Kids had a priceless quote when a reporter asked him about minute details from the 1950s: "Go ask those kids out there. They study this stuff; I just lived it."

Undoubtedly rockabilly music will continue into future generations where the 1950s will seem as distant as the Civil War seems to today's reenactors. What is interesting is the fact that a music and style so American became so co-opted by English and European influence—an influence that kept the music from disappearing into the abyss; but an influence that also changed it forevermore.

EUROPEAN ROCKABILLY

Crazy Cavan and the Rhythm Rockers rock a 1971 gig in the hall of the Fishmonger's Arms public house in Wood Green, North London. The band included at the time vocalist Cavan Grogan, lead guitarist Lyndon Needs, rhythm guitarist Terry Walley, bassist Don Kinsella, and Mike Coffey on drums. *Ray Flight*

Billy Fury (born Ronald William Wycherley) was one of several British rock 'n' rollers produced by impresario Larry Parnes. Parnes was also the mover behind Marty Wilde (born Reginald Leonard Smith), Vince Eager (born Roy Taylor), Dickie Pride (born Richard Charles Knellar), Lance Fortune (born Chris Morris), Duffy Power (born Ray Howard), Johnny Gentle (born John Askew), and Georgie Fame (born Clive Powell).

Singer Cliff Richard performs with the Shadows, including bassist Brian Locking and Hank Marvin with his famous red Stratocaster, on the *Sunday Night at the Palladium* TV show in London in 1960. Marvin's stinging guitar was strongly influenced by Buddy Holly and other early American rock 'n' rollers—and in turn inspired a whole generation of British musicians.
Popperfoto/Getty Images

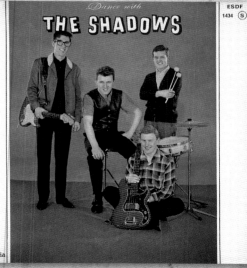

IN RETROSPECT, IT'S ONLY RIGHT THAT THE ROCKABILLY REVIVAL WAS REVVED UP DURING THE EARLY DAYS OF PUNK.

The ethos of the two musical styles were near identical: three chords, instruments turned up to eleven, a scream—and let the mayhem begin.

Both rockabilly and punk were born rebels. And both sparked a culture, lifestyle, and fashion sense that was equally rebellious.

As with the original rockabilly's origins, the revival can be pinpointed to one group of musicians—here and now, the Stray Cats. But again, the story's not so simple.

The groundwork for the revival had been laid by the faithful, many of whom were located far from the American South, in Great Britain, France, Germany, the Netherlands, Scandinavia, and Japan. Those who kept a candle burning for Gene Vincent. Those like Screaming Brian Coffey who tirelessly collected the old recordings. Those who re-released albums of the music to spread the good word.

And the Stray Cats were not the only band to spark the revival, although they were the most prominent. Robert Gordon, Crazy Cavan, Lonnie Donegan, Shakin' Stevens, and more were all there at the beginning of the new era of rockabilly.

AS CARL PERKINS SANG SO LONG AGO, "RAVE ON, CHILDREN I'M WITH YOU . . . !"

Brian Setzer of the Stray Cats rocks and rolls at the Theaterfabriek in Munich, Germany, in July 1989. *Bernd Muller/Redferns*

BRIAN SETZER AND THE STRAY CATS

Born Massapequa, New York, on April 10, 1959

By Garth Cartwright

The Stray Cats rock London's Lyceum on December 15, 1981. From left, Slim Jim Phantom, Brian Setzer, and Lee Rocker. *David Corio/Redferns*

MORE THAN ANY OTHERS, the Stray Cats were responsible for re-launching rockabilly as hip, youth music. The Cats possessed the right look and were both fortunate and ambitious enough to ensure they were in the right place at the right time. That bandleader Brian Setzer was a phenomenal guitarist, handsome as hell, and wrote good original songs all helped. But their music, look, and timing were what won them attention.

Setzer was a musical prodigy. At an early age, he joined his elder brother Gary's arty new wave band the Bloodless Pharaohs, which played New York City's underground music venues and were recorded by Marty Thau (former manager of the New York Dolls and Suicide) for Marty Thau Presents 2 X 5. In 1979, Setzer formed the Tom Cats with brother Gary and bassist Bob Beecher (also of the Pharoahs) as a side project. Setzer's idea was for the trio to play rockabilly parties around Long Island when the Pharoahs didn't have gigs in New York City. Setzer soon became more enthusiastic about 1950s rockabilly and less interested in the Pharoahs' art rock. This lead to him splitting with Gary and Bob.

Setzer reshaped the Tom Cats when he met two Massapequa teenage rockabilly fans who had recreated the 1950s look and were intent on forming a group—Lee Rocker (Leon Drucker) and Slim Jim Phantom (James McDonell). The Tom Cats' raw approach to 1950s songs and willingness to blend the style of 1950s rockers with a punk-inspired look made them stand out. Setzer's magnificent guitar playing—only twenty, he played a hollow-body Gretsch that allowed him to unleash twangy, reverb-heavy notes—also attracted attention and the Cramps, having lost their crazed guitarist

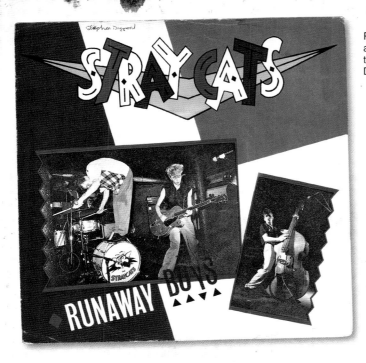

Rockpile roots rocker and producer Dave Edmunds met the Stray Cats after a London gig and offered to record the group. In November 1980, the band released its first single in England, "Runaway Boys"/"My One Desire," climbing to #9 on the charts.

look straight out of *The Wild One* and recording Vince Taylor's rockabilly anthem "Brand New Cadillac" on their 1979 album *London Calling.* Welsh rockabilly revivalist Shakin' Stevens began enjoying British chart hits in early 1980 while the Cramps had given rockabilly the kind of hip cachet that blues enjoyed in the 1960s. The Stray Cats—so young and so pretty!—were perfect for this scene and, with their retro tattoos, vintage clothing, and supersized quiffs attracting attention from London's beautiful people. The band quickly became the toast of the town.

The influential weekly music paper *New Musical Express* put the Cats on the cover before they even had a record deal, thus ensuring a bidding war from various labels. Veteran British rocker Dave Edmunds introduced himself after one concert and agreed to produce the band. Their debut single "Runaway Boys" came out on Arista Records in November 1980, and made it clear that the band were more than hype and haircuts. "Runaway Boys" was a Setzer original that celebrated youths who flee home to a place "where the cops don't know" over a descending bass line and layers of reverb-heavy guitar. It is a classic single, perhaps the best song Setzer has ever written, and made the Stray Cats instant stars, reaching #9 in the UK charts.

To British teenagers tired of punk and new wave's minimalist, asexual look, the Cats were a dream—dressed in tight jeans and leather jackets with cool hair. The band's next single, the anthemic "Rock This Town," also

Bryan Gregory, offered Setzer the position. He considered it—by now the Cramps commanded a large cult following in Europe—but turned it down, considering Lux and Ivy's band too primitive for his playing. He also believed that the Cats would make it.

The Cramps' success in Europe encouraged the Tom Cats to look across the Atlantic. While they had a following in New York City and Long Island, it looked unlikely that the band would get much attention from an American record industry in thrall to the likes of Foreigner and Journey. Once famous, the Cats liked to tell of how they sold all their musical gear to buy one-way plane tickets to London. Following Jimi Hendrix's lead, the band—now renamed the Stray Cats—began performing in London bars and clubs and, as with Hendrix, word quickly spread about the American hot shots. Where Hendrix's trio were pushing rock music's boundaries, the Stray Cats proudly looked back to the music's mid 1950s origins.

A rockabilly revival had been gathering steam in London over the past eighteen months with many music fans, disillusioned both by punk's devolution into thug music and new wave's reliance on synthesisers, heading into clubs frequented by Teddy Boys, the british youth cult that swore by 1950s rockabilly. The Clash had picked up on this as a way out of punk's impasse, adopting a greaser

Concert poster, England, 1981.

BRIAN SETZER AND THE STRAY CATS

The Stray Cats released their first, eponymous LP in England in 1981. The album reached #6 on the British charts.

were going to self-produce their next album and extend their range, a warning signal should have flashed. Their sophomore album, *Gonna Ball*, was released in late 1981, packed with jump blues, R&B, doo-wop, and rock. The band stretched out and played well, but the magical rockabilly flavour they had made their own was missing.

The Cats relocated to the United States and signed to EMI. The label compiled *Built For Speed* from the band's first two albums, launching it in 1982. EMI didn't expect that the Cats would repeat their UK success in the US—few American radio stations were playing music with a distinctive 1950s flavor—but the Cats made a handful of strong videos and won MTV rotation slots. Suddenly, American teenagers were enamored. *Built For Speed* reached #2 in the US charts and made the band instant American stars.

Not only did the kids love the Cats, several famed musicians praised them. In the UK, they were championed by the Rolling Stones and Robert Plant; in the US, they found Bruce Springsteen jumping on stage to jam with them while veterans of the 1950s championed their style: rockabilly guitar legend James Burton praised Setzer's guitar technique. The Cats were the biggest band in America and seemingly could do no wrong. A full-scale rockabilly revival took hold in the United States with many punks dropping their ripped clothes and spiky haircuts for quiffs and vintage clothes.

reached #9. Their third single, "Stray Cat Strut," launched in April 1981, was a sultry striptease of a song that demonstrated Setzer as the hottest young guitarist working. "Stray Cat Strut" reached #11 and coincided with the band's eponymous debut album.. *The Stray Cats* album featured a mix of powerhouse covers—Warren Smith's crazed Sun Records holler "Ubangi Stomp," Eddie Cochran's pulsing 1958 rocker "Jeannie Jeannie Jeannie"— and Setzer originals.

Album tracks "Rumble in Brighton" (about the mods and rockers riots in the British seaside town) and "Storm the Embassy" (about the Iranian hostage drama) showed Setzer willing to write beyond genre limits.

The Stray Cats' debut album went gold in Great Britain and they were declared one of the hottest bands of the new decade. Success quickly followed internationally with France and Japan both developing Stray Cat fever. Everything was happening so fast—Rocker and Phantom were still teenagers and Setzer only 22—that when the band announced they

Promotional poster for the band's United States debut with 1982's *Built For Speed* LP. The album featured eleven songs extracted from the band's first two British albums plus the new title track. It reached #2 on the American pop charts.

Yet the Cats failed to capitalise on it all. Their 1983 album *Rant N' Rave with the Stray Cats* (paired again with producer Dave Edmunds) found the band dangerously close to a *Happy Days*–style parody. The band scored a US hit with "(She's) Sexy and 17" but album sales failed to match those of *Built For Speed*. Critics and the public began to look on the group as a novelty act. Again, fame proved fickle.

Setzer began performing guest sessions for Bob Dylan and Robert Plant's retro supergroup, the Honeydrippers. The Stray Cats dissolved in 1984, and Setzer then set off on a solo career crafting roots rock music that was well reviewed. Phantom and Rocker teamed up with former David Bowie guitarist Earl Slick for Phantom–Rocker–Slick, releasing two hard rock albums.

Inevitably, the Cats had to reform, and launched 1986's *Rock Therapy* album. In 1987, Setzer portrayed his hero Eddie Cochran in *La Bamba*, the biopic about doomed teenage Chicano rocker Ritchie Valens. While his cameo lasted but a short time, Setzer's incendiary version of "Summertime Blues" was a highlight of the film.

In the 1990s, Setzer formed the Brian Setzer Orchestra, helping spur a swing revival. The big band's 1998 album *Dirty Boogie* went platinum and spawned the hit cover of Louis Prima's "Jump Jive An' Wail." As with the rockabilly revival, the swing revival soon lost its commercial momentum, but Setzer continued to tour and issue stellar albums that sold solidly.

Along the way, Setzer has won three Grammys and become a "Simpson" alongside Mick Jagger, Keith Richards, and Tom Petty on *The Simpsons*. He received Gibson Guitar's Lifetime Achievement Award and his artist signature guitars are the best-selling line for Gretsch. Oh yes, and the Brian Setzer Orchestra has played the White House.

Sitting with him in London several years ago, I asked Setzer about the Stray Cats' glory days. He recalled how poor they were initially in London yet how enthusiastically London audiences—and girls—welcomed the band. I wondered if he really was the scrapper he sings about in the Cats' hits. "No," he laughed. "I'm not aggressive at all. I don't know why so many of those songs go on about fighting because I never get in fights!"

I then noted that the Cats were one of the first bands to advertise tattoos as an emblem of cool and Setzer admitted he

Rockabilly Riot! was Brian Setzer's tribute to Sun Records, released in 2005. It featured some of his best traditional rockabilly tracks ever.

was bemused by how these days every band appeared to be heavily tattooed. "Tattoos have always been part of rockabilly culture," he said. "I don't know if we helped kick off the thing of bands being tattooed. For us they were as essential as our hair and clothes."

Concerning rockabilly's brief 1980s resurgence into a Top 40 music format, he smiled and said he had no idea why the music suddenly had such appeal and then went back to being an underground sound. That he helped get rockabilly's primal sound back on the radio and to a new generation of teens was something he was happy to have been associated with. He then emphasised that he had always listened to a great variety of music—from the jazz of Duke Ellington and Django Reinhardt through country music and rock—and with his Orchestra and playing solo, he could explore these forms. With the Cats, he could and would only perform rockabilly and that's why he chose to keep the reunions brief.

Since then, the Stray Cats have reformed twice with the live CD and DVD *Rumble in Brixton* being a fine document of the Cats on full throttle. In 2008, the Stray Cats toured Europe on what they called a Farewell Tour, extending it to Japan, New Zealand, and Australia.

Melding the Brian Setzer Orchestra with the Stray Cats, Setzer's 2010 double-CD set *Don't Mess With A Big Band* was a great blend of big-band swing and rockabilly.

Brian Setzer's Top 5 Rockabilly Guitarists

By Brian Setzer

#1 CLIFF GALLUP: Back in the '50s, music was more regional. I believe Cliff would have grown up in Virginia listening to local country music, blues, and jazz that was being broadcast from New York. You can certainly hear this in all of his guitar playing. When he applied it on those first two Gene Vincent albums, it became pure magic. Its amazing that he only cut those two albums, never toured, yet had such a great influence on future generations of guitar players.

#2 SCOTTY MOORE: Scotty, being from Memphis, was less prone to have a jazz influence. You can easily hear the big influence Chet Atkins had on him. Even though Scotty was influenced by Chet, his playing was uniquely original. Here's another player who really only played for about four years . . . but oh, those four years!

#3 JAMES BURTON: Here's a totally different style from the above two players, yet he fit uniquely into the rockabilly niche. James' Louisiana swamp boogie perfectly spiced up Ricky Nelson and Elvis Presley records.

#4 EDDIE COCHRAN: Eddie made some of the first "produced" rock 'n' roll records. He was overdubbing guitars way before the Beatles came along and he wrote his own songs. Damn good ones! Eddie was the man.

#5, ETC. JIM HEATH, DARREL HIGHAM, AND PAUL PIGAT: Here are three great current rockabilly guitarists. Just like the original guys from the '50s, they have been influenced by the greats, yet have their own unique style. Check them out. You won't be disappointed.

Brian Setzer's 1955 Gretsch White Falcon guitar.
Nigel Osbourne/Redferns

Brian Setzer and Slim Jim Phantom of the Stray Cats perform on stage at the Enmore Theatre on February 23, 2009, in Sydney, Australia. *Gaye Gerard/Getty Images*

Born Bethesda, Maryland, on March 29, 1947

By Garth Cartwright

Robert Gordon and ace guitarist Danny Gatton perform at the Berkeley Square in Berkeley, California, on May 10, 1981.
Clayton Call/Redferns

ROBERT GORDON is rockabilly's missing link. In the late 1970s, he arrived as a disciple reintroducing rockabilly to a wide audience.

Gordon claims that upon hearing Elvis sing "Heartbreak Hotel" in 1956, he knew what he wanted to do. His passion for Eddie Cochran, Gene Vincent, Jerry Lee Lewis, and other less-famous singers of the era has never faded. As a teenager, Gordon's deep baritone voice meant he could sing in a manner similar to Elvis at his best. Forming a band in high school, Gordon sang rockabilly and soul hits, but disliked the British Invasion bands, claiming, "The 1960s passed me by."

Rather than growing his hair and taking LSD, Gordon married and began raising a family. Still interested in attempting to make it as a singer, he shifted to New York City where his dark, moody looks, bristling quiff, taste for 1950s gear, and hatred of 1970s stadium rock meant he fitted in perfectly with the new bands who were taking shape around Bowery club

Robert Gordon's eponymous debut LP from 1977 featured Link Wray on guitar.

CBGB. Fronting Tuff Darts, a band that played rock 'n' roll with punk attitude, they appeared on the *Live at CBGB* album that featured the likes of the Ramones and Blondie. Journalist-turned-A&R man Ben Edmonds went to CBGB to sign Tuff Darts but was so impressed by the support band, Mink DeVille, that he chose them instead. Mink DeVille's vocalist Willy DeVille also sported a quiff and retro tastes but he possessed a remarkable selection of original songs—something Gordon lacked.

Richard Gottehrer, a songwriter and producer best known for penning such 1960s New York hits as "My Boyfriend's Back" and "I Want Candy," auditioned Tuff Darts but pronounced himself only impressed by Gordon. Finding Gordon could sing a huge number of 1950s songs, Gottehrer arranged a recording deal with independent label Private Stock and paired him with guitarist Link Wray. The duo cut two fine albums and toured widely. European rockabilly fans immediately embraced Gordon and in 1977, after Elvis died, he received major American airplay with his recording of Billy Joe Riley's "Red Hot." Bruce Springsteen gave Gordon his song "Fire" to record in 1978, but problems at Private Stock meant the album it was on, *Fresh Fish Special*, tanked. Gordon and Wray then split acrimoniously, and Gordon began working with British guitarist Chris Spedding.

Gordon signed to RCA and released the album *Rock Billy Boogie* in 1979. Several songs off the album won wide radio play, and as the rockabilly revival was just gathering steam, Gordon looked to be a movement figurehead. Yet his 1980 album *Bad Boy* bombed. The 1981 album *Are You Gonna Be the One* sold well, but Gordon then fell out with RCA over the budget for his next album and found himself dropped. By then the likes of the Stray Cats and the Cramps had outstripped Gordon with their more leftfield take on rockabilly while Gordon, with his straight renditions of Elvis hits, appeared rather staid to the youthful audiences suddenly in thrall to cat music.

In 1982, Gordon had another opportunity at stardom when he was cast opposite a young Willem Dafoe in *The Loveless*, an unintentionally camp biker film. Gordon was originally hired to provide the soundtrack but his handsome features and retro look found him cast in a lead role. *The Loveless* is not a very good film—although it has a cult reputation—and Gordon did not enjoy the early mornings and actor egos (at one point he punched Dafoe). The film is now best remembered for being the debut feature of Katherine Bigelow, who went on to win an Oscar as director of *The Hurt Locker*.

Gordon maintained a low profile for a long time, rarely performing or recording. More recently, he began touring again in Europe and the United States, issuing a new album and live DVD. His voice remains strong. Gordon's devotion to rockabilly helped raise interest in the music and his refusal to go the way of novelty bands like Sha Na Na meant he is taken seriously by fans and musicians.

Fresh Fish Special arrived in 1978, again teaming Robert Gordon with Link Wray.

Robert Gordon's cover of Bruce Springsteen's "Fire" proved his biggest hit, melding rockabilly with pop music.

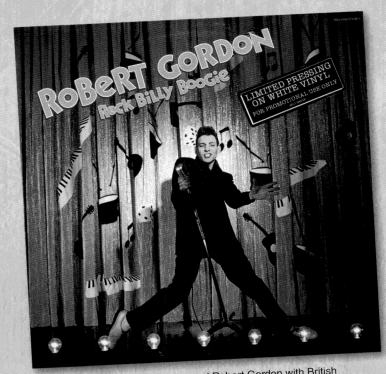

Rock Billy Boogie from 1979 teamed Robert Gordon with British rockabilly guitar ace Chris Spedding.

199

SLEEPY LABEEF

Born Smackover, Arkansas, on July 20, 1935

By Peter Guralnick

Sleepy LaBeef playing a working man's Gibson J-45 in an early band in Houston, Texas, circa 1957. D. Knipe backed him on lead guitar with thirteen-year-old Wendell Clayton on bass.

IF YOU FREQUENT THE HONKY TONKS, you may very well have run across the music of Sleepy LaBeef. For a number of years he worked the area around Atlanta. Before that it was Port Huron or Kansas or the circuit of NCO service clubs where there is three or four hundred dollars to be made for a night's work and a string of bookings to be lined up—if you go over. When I first met him in the spring of 1977, Sleepy LaBeef had been working Alan's Fifth Wheel Lounge, about an hour north of Boston, for nearly three months on a pretty regular basis. There he had been laying down the original rockabilly sounds of Sun six nights a week, five sets a night, to an appreciative audience of truckers, regulars, factory workers off the late-night shift, and just plain Sleepy LaBeef fans who may have caught him on talk-master Larry Glick's two A.M. phone-in broadcasts from the truckstop.

How in the world, the question naturally arises, did a six-foot-six, 265-pound, basso

profundo, first-generation rockabilly from Arkansas ever end up at Alan's Truckstop in the northeast backwater of Amesbury, Massachusetts? In the case of Sleepy LaBeef the answer lies in a series of mischances and coincidences. He had spent much of the previous summer fixing up a 1948 Greyhound Silverado, which was intended to carry him on his nonstop touring of thirty-nine states and which bore the true legend "Sun Recording Artist." (Sleepy was the *only* artist then recording for that seminal label, a distinction that he took as a compliment when new owner Shelby Singleton first proposed to reactivate Sun for something other than reissues—"At least I thought it was a compliment at the time. I don't know, maybe he thought I was prehistoric.") That bus caught fire and burned up on the Maine Turnpike on New Year's Day, 1977. Sleepy's clothes, tapes, and record collection were all destroyed, and the bus was left a charred shell. He played his gig that night at Alan's anyway, and when the opportunity arose, he welcomed the chance to settle in. The result was that for the next year he would use Alan's as his base, booking out of the club, living in the motel unit behind it, working intermittently at restoring the bus for resale, and establishing Sleepy LaBeef as New England's number one name in rockabilly and country music.

I'll never forget the first time I went up to Alan's to see Sleepy perform. A friend and I had noticed an item in the local paper that made reference to Sleepy's extended engagement in Amesbury, virtually next door to the small town in which we lived. We drove up to the truckstop and parked out back where the big semis were idling, then ventured into the bar with some trepidation, since Alan's had

had a shaky local reputation even before its owner, Clifford Titcomb, a former Amesbury selectman, pulled a gun on an IRS agent (he was subsequently sentenced to a year's alternate service doing hospital work). Sleepy was tuning up on the bandstand, the waitresses were wearing cowboy outfits, the PA crackled with CB lingo, and we got swept up in another world.

"Call them honky tonks if you want," wrote *Country Music* editor Michael Bane, "but for the Saturday-night regulars, that raunchy, neon-lit bar with its cheap beer and even cheaper solace is called *home*. The honky tonk is as American as apple pie; as deeply ingrained in our collective subconscious as the prostitute with a heart of gold. A working-class pit stop between today and tomorrow; a buffer zone between exhaustion and despair; soft lights and hard country music—a good honky tonk is all that and more.

"A honky tonk is a magical place where all the rules are, however temporarily, suspended. . . . Sure, you can dance at a honky tonk, but it's more than a dance hall. You can hear live music at a honky tonk, but it's more than a listening room. And you can drink yourself blind at a honky tonk, but it's more—much more—than a bar. A good honky tonk is the American dream shrunken to beer, broads, and a bunch of loud music. . . ."

To some this might not sound like much of an advertisement, and admittedly for a nondrinker and nonsmoker like myself there are distinct disadvantages to the honky tonk environment, but taken all in all, finding Alan's (and Sleepy LaBeef) was for me like finding the bluebird of happiness on my back door. I had traveled thousands of miles to hear music like this, played in just this kind of setting, and as Sleepy ran through what must have been a typical set (featuring everything from Muddy Waters to Webb Pierce to Elvis Presley and Little Richard), I turned to my friend, whose expression mirrored my own, and we both silently asked the question: could this really be for real?

Over the next few months we would come back again and again. For a while my friend joined Sleepy's band, and we became friendly with Cliff and June, who owned the Truckstop complex (twenty-four-hour diner, all-night garage, motel, and club), denounced Taxachusetts with all the zeal of the most ardent conservative civil libertarians, and eventually—despite a prior lack of experience with any aspect of the music business, save for the club, and with nothing but their unstinting enthusiasm for Sleepy and his music (which they learned was called rockabilly) to serve as qualifications—came to manage Sleepy, until the Fifth Wheel was closed down for nonpayment of taxes. We heard Sleepy run through a good portion of the

six thousand songs he estimates to be in his repertoire. ("I don't know why, I used to just listen to a song twice on the jukebox, and I'd have it. I don't like to boast, but I honestly think you could put me in a room trading songs with just about anyone you could name, and I could keep going longer than they could.") We learned to recognize and greet the regulars in one fashion or another. We nodded to the Bird Woman, whose slacks hung loose on her rather brittle, skinny frame but who always seemed to find a trucker twenty or thirty years younger than she; we always appreciated the cheerful confidence of the Glider, a rather stout young woman who commandeered her partners around the dance floor with a masterful stride; we even learned to enjoy the singing of PBL (this was her CB handle—her real name was Nancy), another stout young woman, who stepped out from behind the cash register occasionally to warble "You Ain't Woman Enough (To Take My Man)." There were no distinctions of age or class at Alan's Truckstop; everyone was accepted as a fellow refugee of the night. And over it all hovered the towering presence of Sleepy LaBeef.

In the space of an evening with Sleepy LaBeef you can get a short course in the history of rock 'n' roll, from Jimmie Rodgers to Jimmy Reed, encompassing Woody Guthrie, Chuck Berry, Joe Tex, and Willie Nelson as well. A multi-instrumentalist who plays the guitar with all the gut-wrenching fervor of a bluesman like Albert King, Sleepy is possessed not only of an encyclopedic knowledge of the field but of the flair, originality, and conviction to put the music across as well. At this point I can't count the number of times I've seen him perform, but I've never seen Sleepy do a set that was less than entertaining, nor have I known him to play the same set twice. You could come out to Alan's on occasion and catch what Sleepy would call a mechanical performance, but though he himself had certain reservations about the venue ("Let's face it, a lot of these truckers have one thing on their mind. They could care less about music"), a spirit of hearty informality, stubborn eccentricity, and great goodwill always prevailed.

Every night at the Fifth Wheel was a little bit different, and Sleepy always adapted to the occasion. On weekends he wore his wide-lapeled, white western tuxedo with ruffled shirt. If there was a trucker in the audience who could pick—or even one who just thought he could pick—Sleepy gave him his moment on stage. For birthdays, the band responded appropriately. If the crowd was dead, it would be mainly sad songs, fast waltzes, and mournful country standards. For Monday night Fifties Night —when the waitresses exchanged their black cowboy pantsuits and hats for saddle shoes, rolled-up jeans, and sloppy shirttails—Sleepy would take on a more imposing look in T-shirt and black leather jacket, his lip curled, hair slicked back, surveying the room good-humoredly from under hooded fifties eyes.

The one constant was that Sleepy always put on a good show. The crowd might change, Sleepy's mood certainly varied, the band underwent radical changes of personnel (in the first two years I knew Sleepy, only the drummer, Clete Chapman, who signed on in Iowa in 1974, stayed for any length of time), but the feeling remained the same. He would go through phases when he would play the fiddle (actually Sleepy saws away on fiddle, which is a recently acquired enthusiasm) almost every night for several weeks running; then he might not pick it up again for months. The same with piano, which he attacks with the rough enthusiasm, if not the skill, of Jerry Lee Lewis. Some nights he might inject a heavy dose of blues; other nights it was non-stop sets of rockabilly free association in which Sleepy would shift from song to song—often after no more than a verse—with no sign to the band other than his own booming vocals and guitar, and with a decided taste for obscurity, which could make a Jerry Lee Lewis medley out of songs no one would ever think to associate with Jerry Lee, but done up in the Killer's inimitable style.

All this was great fun, as indeed it was to hear Sleepy's rumbling voice churning out rockabilly (Sleepy is probably the only rockabilly baritone, and listening to him sometimes, one is almost tempted to believe that Howlin' Wolf, a singer Sleepy admires and resembles both in stature and in physical presence, has come back to life as a rock 'n' roller), but it was nothing compared to the thrill of the rare occasions when Sleepy would really catch fire. This would generally come on older, gospel-influenced material like "Worried Man Blues" or Roy Hamilton's "You Can Have Her," but there was no predicting when it would happen or if it would happen at all. When it did, Sleepy would almost go into a trance, singing and swaying in an irresistible, rock-steady groove, going on like Wolf for ten or fifteen minutes at a time, extemporizing verses, picking lyrics out of the air, savoring the moment until he had extracted every last ounce of feeling from it, and then shrugging off-handedly as he went back to his table. "You don't," he apologized, "want to get too wild." And then he might recall the first time he saw Jerry Lee Lewis, in Galena Park, Texas, when a whole football stadium walked out on Jerry Lee while the fiery piano player was chewing out his drummer. You can't get too wrapped up in your own performance, says Sleepy, who always pays the utmost attention to

Sleepy LaBeef strikes a rockabilly pose, circa 1957.

his audience, feeds them fast songs or slow songs depending upon their mood, but, like the consummate showman that he is, never lets them go away unsatisfied.

"When I first started off in nightclubs and things, it just scared me to death. My legs would shake, and I would be sweating all over. But then I said to myself one day, 'Hey, I like this, so I've got to get through this stage fright. I've got to relax and feel out people, get to know them, get some kind of communication going.' That's pretty much the way it goes. I don't plan anything. It's all trial and error, I guess. If the first two or three things don't work, then we just move around and try something else."

He was born Thomas Paulsley LaBeff (the family name was originally LaBoeuf) on July 20, 1935, out in the country from Smackover, Arkansas, where he grew up on a forty-acre farm, which his father eventually sold for $300 to go work in the oil fields. He remembers his mother singing "Corinna, Corinna" as she walked behind the plow. Sleepy was the tenth of ten children and was nicknamed at an early age, on his first day of school, as a matter of fact, because—here he pulls out a frayed picture showing a six-year-old with heavy-lidded eyes almost glued shut. He started listening to Groovey Boy, a disc jockey on station KWKH out of Shreveport, who played a mixture of hillbilly boogie and rhythm 'n' blues and, according to Sleepy, developed the Bo Diddley beat years before it actually became popular, with his radio theme song, "Hambone." He listened to Lefty Frizzell, too, who was broadcasting on KELD in nearby El Dorado in the early forties (when Lefty himself was only thirteen or fourteen), injecting a lot of blues into his performance.

Unlike most rockabilly singers, though, Sleepy does not cite black music per se as being the preeminent influence on his work. He himself was well acquainted with black music both from the radio and from selling watermelons with his father in the black section of town. He feels strongly, however, that rock 'n' roll, black and white, came primarily from the church, and indeed that is both where he started out singing (United Pentecostal) and where he lists his strongest influences: Vernie McGee, a guitar-playing deacon, and the Revered E. F. Cannon, pastor of his Norphlet church. He also cites Martha Carson, whose "Satisfied" became a white gospel standard, but above all it was Sister Rosetta Tharpe, the great black gospel singer (she originated "This Train," among other classic gospel numbers), who he feels provided the bedrock for rock 'n' roll. Jerry Lee Lewis, he is positive, derived his piano style from Sister Rosetta's blithely bluesy guitar work, particularly on the highly influential "Strange Things Happening Every Day" (cited also by Johnny Cash and Carl Perkins as one of their most vivid musical memories). As far as Elvis goes, Sleepy's first reaction when he heard "Blue Moon of Kentucky" on the radio was the shock of recognition. "'Cause I knew exactly where he was coming from. I thought, this is really something. Here's somebody singing just like we have in church for years. Only he was putting that gospel feeling to blues lyrics—that was what was so different about him."

Sleepy quit school in the eighth grade over a misunderstanding with the teacher, though "I never did give up on learning." At fourteen he traded a .22 rifle to his brother-in-law for a guitar and "liked it so well I was playing in church within two weeks." Then at eighteen he left Arkansas ("Around the time it started to happen in Memphis I headed west, I guess") and ended up in Houston, where he went to work as a land surveyor, a job he has always liked (he had earlier worked for the Arkansas Highway Department and even after he moved to Nashville, he continued as a civil engineer for several years) because "it gives you a chance to meditate on lots of things." He also started singing with his first wife, Louise, in various gospel duos and quartets

around town (George Jones, the current country superstar, was an occasional participant), mostly on "family-type shows" like the Houston Jamboree. That was where he met Elvis for the first time and where his wife made the mistake of lending Elvis her guitar after he had broken the strings on his own. "After he did the show he came back and said thank you, real nice and polite, but the front of the guitar was just about defaced, it was all scratched up and every string was broke—we sold it for, I think, $90, and that was an $800 guitar."

It was shortly thereafter that Sleepy switched over to secular music and started making records for Pappy Daily—one of the most colorful of a colorful line of Texas entrepreneurs and George Jones's discoverer—both under his own name and under various pseudonyms, for border stations like XERF in Del Rio. The records for XERF were cover versions of popular hits of the day, sold by mail order and made to look and sound as close to the original as possible. According to Sleepy, he did everything from the Everly Brothers to Fats Domino, though it seems difficult to imagine him fooling anyone with that booming bass voice today. The records he made under his own name or variants thereof—as Tommy LaBeff, for example, on Wayside—included frenzied classics like "Tore Up" and a "Baby, Let's Play House" that came complete with Presley-like hiccupping vocals. He recorded for Gulf, Finn, Picture, Crescent—all with little or no commercial success—and crossed paths frequently with Mickey Gilley, Kenny Rogers, Glen Campbell, all of whom were hanging around Bill Quinn's busy Gold Star Studio (where Sleepy got to know blues singer Lightnin' Hopkins as well). Like Gilley (whose long-time drummer, Michael Schillaci, Sleepy raised from the time he was thirteen), Sleepy established a name for himself around town, investing in a couple of clubs and a hamburger drive-in and playing the rough Channel joints seven nights a week ("We didn't wear helmets back then, but it might have helped if we had"). Then one night, while he was waiting to go on at the Wayside Lounge, "The waitress said, 'There's a telephone call from Columbia Records in Nashville.' I went to the phone and said hello. A man said, 'Sleepy? This is Don Law. I want to sign you up.' He sounded serious. It was hard to believe."

So, while Gilley was still stuck on local labels, Sleepy signed with Columbia in 1964, moving to Nashville shortly thereafter. In 1968 he signed with Shelby Singleton, whom he had met originally on the *Louisiana Hayride* a decade before (this was in fact the last time that Shelby saw Sleepy perform) and who acquired the Sun catalogue from Sam Phillips the following year. With the exception of six months he spent playing the role of a swamp monster in the movie *The Exotic Ones,* Sleepy has been on the road ever since.

It's very likely that Sleepy has never made any money from any of his records. Except for "Blackland Farmer," a country chartmaker in 1971, he's never had anything resembling a hit ("I believe anyone could have had a hit with 'Blackland.' I didn't do anything special with it"), and certainly Shelby Singleton has never been lavish with his financial support. "I have a little different philosophy than most people in the business," declares Shelby, who has been highly successful in his own highly unorthodox way. "My methods of merchandising are entirely different. I just print up ten or fifteen thousand copies of a record, and then if it doesn't sell I can dump it for schlock for more money than it cost me. I don't buckshot the market like the big companies do, because I believe that any artist, in the beginning at least, is the victim of the song." In other words, the song starts the artist, the artist doesn't start the song.

Unfortunately Sleepy's song hasn't arrived yet—at least not so far—and, without any promotional money behind him or income from writing or record royalties, Sleepy's whole living is on the road. Still, he manages to make the best of it in his own imperturbable way. About six months after his bus burned up, Sleepy acquired an almost-new Banner motor home through a helpful automobile dealer, just one in his legion of New England acquaintances, and between that, and a little Vega, and a high-backed trailer to bring up the rear, Sleepy's entourage (his wife Linda, a three-piece band, and occasionally his twenty-one-year-old son, Harmony Paul) manage to make it from gig to gig in comfort, if not in style.

Everywhere Sleepy goes, he has what he calls his "following." It changes from venue to venue, but it takes in all ages and all walks of life, from policemen to wealthy businessmen to college students, truckers, Swedish rockabilly fanatics, and Navy men off the nuclear submarine base in Groton, Connecticut. There is no one with whom Sleepy is not at home and at ease, as he moves diplomatically between sets from table to table, announces the presence of an old friend from the bandstand, and placates the divergent tastes of the various segments of his audience

with a characteristically eclectic and impromptu selection of material. There's always a Big Event coming up, there's always an occasion to celebrate, even if it's only the band's imminent departure for Port Huron, one of Sleepy's more frequent ports of call. Throughout the confusion of booking changes, personnel changes, automotive breakdowns, and personality clashes that are bound to crop up, Sleepy remains absolutely unflappable ("You know me, I don't ever get too excited") and somewhat inscrutable besides. You can't really direct Sleepy, even towards something unquestionably to his advantage, if Sleepy doesn't want to do it himself. Whatever he does do, though, proceeds from the warmest of impulses, and Sleepy always proves the most gracious of hosts. The only qualities which he will not tolerate are drug use among band members (this has cost him a number of musicians, needless to say), bad language, dirty jokes, and racial slurs. In this, as in everything else, though, Sleepy can be so oblique in his disapproval that the offending party is sometimes not sure just what he has done—but will do almost anything to make sure he doesn't do it again.

When the Truckstop was closed down by the state tax commission in October of 1977, it seemed as if an era had come to an end. A story I wrote on Sleepy, along with numerous stories by Steve Morse of the *Boston Globe*, had generated further media interest, and Alan's had become a kind of central headquarters for all the displaced rockabillies in the New England area. I had dinner a few times with Cliff and June after the closing, and we played around with various schemes to thwart the government and get the Truckstop back in business. Sleepy's life didn't change much. June was still booking him, and he and Linda continued to live at the motel—which had also been closed down—so we would get together socially, to listen to tapes or just to talk, fairly often. Sleepy still had his books (he is an avid reader, and a born-again Eldridge Cleaver, whose *Soul on Ice* he had admired, was his great enthusiasm that winter); he had his collection of Sister Rosetta Tharpe, gospel singer Claude Ely, and, of course, his rare rockabilly records; he studied the Bible assiduously as always; and whenever he got in a tape of a new religious "debate" (a fundamentalist dialogue between two preachers like the Reverend R. E. Bayer, a Florida evangelist known as the Walking Bible, and the Reverend Marvin Hicks of Corpus Christi), he would eagerly play us portions.

For a while, though, it seemed, he was oddly dispirited—subdued, preoccupied, some nights he seemed almost distracted on the bandstand of whatever club he was playing. We speculated that perhaps Sleepy's religious convictions were leading him to question the nature of his vocation. A long-time teetotaler, he had recently quit smoking, too (Sleepy, a man of prodigious appetites, had been smoking five packs a day for most of his adult life), and maybe, I thought, he was now giving serious consideration to his stated intention of taking up preaching some day. ("I'm not a hypocrite. I don't live it, but I know it's the best thing.") I never found out what was on Sleepy's mind, and I don't think I'll ever know. He went out of town for a couple of months on tour, and when he came back he was his old self again, singing and playing with all his old vigor and enthusiasm. Only he wasn't playing at the Truckstop any more, which had reopened after eloquent testimony by Sleepy before the Amesbury board of selectmen. And June was no longer booking him. I don't think Cliff and June were ever quite sure what had happened either, but, whatever the cause of the estrangement, Sleepy patched things up socially with his former employers, and before long everyone was going out for Chinese food once again.

After that, surprisingly, things started picking up for Sleepy. He played New York and was invited to appear at England's prestigious country festival at Wembley. More stories appeared on him; he was runner-up for *Country Music*'s Silver Bullet Award for promising newcomers (forty-seven-year-old Jack Clement won the award); even Shelby Singleton began to wonder if Sleepy's time hadn't finally come, though as far as Shelby was concerned, such thoughts were speculative only and did not necessitate any kind of rash financial commitment.

Sleepy, of course, remained calm in the midst of the storm, although "storm" might be a misnomer for what could still turn out to be just another trade wind. Talking with Sleepy is always an education in historical perspective anyway, and his conversation is studded with references to the great and near-great, the almost weres and never wases—Charlie Rich at Houston's Sidewalk Café, Elvis at the Magnolia Gardens, Willie Nelson clerking at a record store in Pasadena, Texas, Johnny Spain and Frenchy D., Rocky Bill Ford, Bobby Lee Trammell, and Charlie Busby, the guitarist from Red Shoot, Louisiana, who he says taught James Burton how to play. "I think if they'd gotten the breaks," says Sleepy ruminatively of these last, "they could have been just as great as the ones who made it."

I don't doubt it. At one point in our acquaintance I gave Sleepy the *Rolling Stone Illustrated History of Rock & Roll*, to which I had contributed several chapters. Sleepy found the book interesting, as I thought he would, recognizing many old friends and supplying a good number of anecdotes.

In the chapter I had written on rockabilly, though, I had included his name in a list of obscure artists I had thought as forgotten as Frenchy D. and Johnny Spain. "They cultivated," I wrote, "the look, the stance, the sound of their more celebrated colleagues. All they lacked was the talent." Had I, Sleepy asked me, puzzled and a little hurt, really meant what I wrote? No, I tried to apologize, not about *him* anyway,

since I had never really had the opportunity to hear him, except on a stray cut or two, when I wrote the piece. "I don't know," he said with characteristic imperturbability, "I guess you could still think that."

Well, as it should be abundantly clear by now, I don't. In many ways Sleepy is as great a performer as I've ever seen, and when you see the way that people respond to his music, you wonder why, and if, rockabilly ever went away. Sleepy has a theory on that ("I didn't ever see it change. The people were still digging it, and the musicians liked playing it, but the big companies figured it was a fad and they took it away from the kids"), but in any case it is no exercise in nostalgia for the people who have come out to see Sleepy LaBeef at Alan's Fifth Wheel or the Hillbilly Ranch; they couldn't care less that it was John Lee Hooker who originated "In the Mood" or Scotty Moore whose licks Sleepy duplicates note for note on "Milkcow Blues Boogie." Sleepy's records may not do him justice, but Sleepy knows how good he can be.

"I never sold out," he can say with pride. "Nobody owns me. I know I'm good. I wouldn't be honest if I didn't tell you that. I've been around long enough to know that if I get the breaks I can still make it—Charlie Rich was older than me when he finally did. And if I don't get the breaks—well, when I started in this business I didn't even know you could make a dime out of it. And I think I'd still be doing it tomorrow, if there wasn't any money in it at all. That's just the way I feel."

By Garth Cartwright

Lux Interior and Poison Ivy of the Cramps bring rockabilly to CBGB in New York City on December 10, 1993.
Ebet Roberts/Redferns

THEY SAY YOU CAN'T REINVENT the wheel, but in the late 1970s the Cramps came close by reinventing rockabilly. Back then few imagined rockabilly as anything but kitsch nostalgia à la *Happy Days*. The Cramps conjured up rockabilly's primal spirit, understanding that back in 1955 Elvis, Jerry Lee and co. were punks creating a raw, new sound that offended many. Appropriately many of that era's greatest rockabilly recordings sound demented, primitive, the stuff of hillbilly psychos.

The Cramps oozed out of New York's punk clubs playing rockabilly as swampy throb music and in doing so reminded the world that here was a true American folk art. "I'm Cramped" they sang and soon we all were. What a name! What a band! What a sound! Let us now pay tribute to the Ohio misfits who returned rockabilly to its righteous place as bad music for bad people (as The Cramps liked to say).

Centred around vocalist Lux Interior (born Erick Purkhiser) and guitarist Poison Ivy Rorschach (born Kristy Wallace), the Cramps took shape in New York punk clubs CBGB and Max's Kansas City 1976–1978. While many would imitate them and "psychobilly" – a genre they unwittingly invented after using the term to describe the Cramps' sound – would become a mutant genre of its own; there could never be another band quite like the Cramps.

The Cramps issued two 45s on their own Vengeance label in 1978. These 45s, "The Way I Walk"/"Surfin' Bird" and "Human Fly"/"Domino," were recorded at Sam C. Phillips Recording Studio in Memphis with pop legend/cult icon Alex Chilton at the controls. Aged 16, Chilton went from being a Memphis schoolboy to pop star as lead singer of the Boxtops ("The Letter," "Cry Like A Baby"). He then lead cult rockers Big Star before arriving ragged in New York. Hearing the Cramps' elemental rockabilly enthused him to bring the band to Memphis. Lux and Ivy, being aficionados of discarded American pop culture, loved Memphis, especially with the maverick Chilton guiding them around.

How did the Cramps in Memphis sound? Lux hiccupped like a hillbilly on helium while Ivy plucked twangy guitar over a fat wall of distortion. Of the songs only "Human Fly" was an original – and what an original! – while the band's reinterpretation of Detroit rockabilly icon Jack Scott's 1959 anthem "The Way I Walk" was unbelievably potent.

The Vengeance 45s attracted rave reviews in New York's rock press, being punk-contemporary while possessing a hillbilly pulse no one else came close to. Their cult status was enshrined when they played a 1978 gig at Napa State Mental Institute. Filmed on grainy 8mm b&w, this concert has become the holy grail of Cramps outsider activism. Signed to the IRS label in 1979, the Vengeance singles were repackaged as the 12-inch vinyl *Gravest Hits* EP and the band sent out as support on the Police's European tour. The Cramps began spreading the rockabilly gospel and many were converted.

Nick Kent astutely observed, "beneath the slogans there's a musical essence—The Cramps are after all the first and foremost exponents of a new form of rockabilly that could rejuvenate that particular very potent pulsebeat in a way that—and here I take a deep breath and go way over the top— Marley & The Wailers did for reggae." Kent continued with, "Right now, The Cramps are out on their own but their music has spiritual connections with similar maverick and under-marketed works by the likes of the incredible Roky Erickson and Captain Beefheart." Wow! This was heavy praise and Kent proved right both times: The Cramps took rockabilly to a broad youth audience while their failure to score pop hits meant they, like Roky and Beefhart, would end up with a loyal cult following.

But let's rewind to Cramps origins: Erick and Kristy met in 1972 when both were studying Art & Shamanism at Sacramento City College. 24-year old Erick and 19-year old Kristy were quickly smitten, both sharing a taste for offbeat music, movies and culture alongside a loathing of the corporate rock mainstream. How better to express their aesthetic than form a band? Erick, tall, thin and very gaunt, was vocalist. Kristy guitarist: she just had to first learn to play guitar. The next three years saw the couple living in Ohio, doing all kinds of menial jobs (and some less than legal – drug dealing for Erick; working as a dominatrix for Kristy), sifting junk shops for old records and clothes and plotting the Cramps' evolution. Erick renamed himself Lux Interior after an advertisement for a car boasted of its "luxurious interior" while Kristy chose Poison Ivy Rorschach after it came to her in a dream.

In August 1975, they landed in New York. Working in a record store alongside Gregory Beckerleg, Lux invited him to join the Cramps. Beckerling, who changed his name to Bryan Gregory, was chosen for his distortion driven guitar playing and strange looks – Nick Kent reported that he wore a necklace made from human bones (chicken, actually) and "a long bleached swathe of hair totally covering one side of a face so gaunt it looks like his cheeks were connected by one medium-size voodoo pin . . . , a pair of eyes so venomous-looking that, replete with the gamut of tattoos covering his arms, Gregory looks like he walked out of the human snake-pit of a Todd Browning film." Cleveland

music fan Miriam Linna was co-opted into shifting to New York and drumming for the band—even though she had never drummed before—from late 1975 until mid 1977 when she retired and was replaced by Nick Knox, another Ohio musician. Linna would later co-found *Kicks* magazine and reissue label Norton Records—both magazine and label champion retro music/trash culture.

Playing CBGB, the Cramps were considered heirs to the Ramones: Both bands shared a love of 60s trash culture, strong image, dry wit and were inspired by the New York Dolls and the Stooges. Yet where the Ramones emulated the Dolls and Stooges penchant for wild hedonism, Lux and Ivy preferred a quiet life of record collecting and watching 1950s horror movies.

European success lead the band back to Memphis with Chilton producing their 1980 debut album *Songs The Lord Taught Us*. The album consisted of original Lux and Ivy songs and covers; one song, "The Mad Daddy," celebrated the maverick early 1960s Ohio DJ whose tastes for crazed records and outlandish stunts had a lasting influence on Lux. Artists covered included Johnny Burnette, Dwight Pullen, Jimmy Stewart, the Sonics, and stripper anthem "Fever." Burnette, Stewart, and Pullen were all original rockabilly artists while the Sonics were Seattle's fiercest mid '60s garage band. Rockabilly remained the template for the Cramps sound yet they blended this with surf music, primitive rock instrumentalists (especially those of Link Wray) and '60s garage bands: on "Human Fly," Lux sang "I got 96 tears and 96 eyes" so referencing Question Mark & the Mysterians' legendary 1966 hit "96 Tears."

Just as the Cramps were about to start their first U.S. tour, Bryan Gregory fled with the band's van and equipment. It was suggested he had joined a Satanic cult but Ivy later admitted Gregory's heroin addiction caused his implosion. Relocating to Los Angeles, the Cramps plucked teenage guitarist

Bad music for bad people

Kid Congo Powers (born Brian Tristan) from the Gun Club, an LA punk-blues band they had befriended. This line-up recorded 1981's *Psychedelic Jungle*—their most coherent album—then entered into a legal dispute with IRS Records due to non-payment of royalties and tour support. Prohibited from recording until the case was settled, the Cramps missed out on the rockabilly goldmine as the Stray Cats, Polecats, and Shakin' Stevens all charted.

It's now possible to view the legal battle as the Cramps' crux—finally freed from IRS they appeared to lose creative momentum: Kid Congo was fired and the band became guitar-bass-drums-vocals; the original songs now sounded less fun and more forced and the covers uninspired. Nothing on 1986 comeback album *A Date With Elvis* matched previous recordings. From then on the Cramps were a band to catch in concert rather than on vinyl. Regular touring saw Lux develop into one of rock's most crazed performers: he threw himself into audiences, fellated microphones and stripped to "Fever" while Ivy played fierce guitar. I caught the Cramps twice: first, in Auckland in 1986 (this concert was released in 1987 as Rockinnreelininaucklandnewzealand) where they put on a frantic show let down only by their over reliance on *A Date With Elvis* material; secondly in London, 2003, where they rocked as hard as any band I've ever seen.

Prior to the 2003 concert, I got to interview Ivy. This proved something of a shock: I expected a tough, rock 'n' roll bad girl, all cynicism and bad language. Instead I met the politest, most quietly spoken woman I have ever interviewed. "Oh gosh" and "pardon me" were two expressions she regularly employed and when talking of her and Lux's then 31-year-long relationship she chuckled when I called them alt.rock's Paul and Linda McCartney: like the McCartneys Lux and Ivy were strict vegetarians. This, she admitted, caused some difficulty when touring in France, a nation that loved the Cramps but saw requests for meat-free meals as sacrilege.

"Everything in music and art is so safe these days," said Ivy when I enquired as to her thoughts on such Cramps-influenced bands as the White Stripes. "When we started it was literally 'do this or go to jail!' Now there's all these bands trying to sound deranged but rock music's just become so conventional. The music scene today— pop, rock, R&B and country, especially country, there's nothing hillbilly about those acts anymore— generally sucks. It's all so bland."

Ivy did admit that the Cramps were finally benefiting from the mainstream's sudden embrace of all things gothic and psychobilly: The Cramps appeared twice on teen TV show *Beverly Hills 90210* while their tunes were licensed to sell Miller Beer and soundtrack hunky vampire Angel's angst. The couple's smart business sense meant they now only toured occasionally, preferring to live comfortably in a mock-Moorish castle in LA's suburbs. Here they raised their cats, played old 45s, collected 3D cameras, corresponded with jailed serial killers, made folk art for one another and continued to celebrate old American trash culture as that nation's greatest achievement. Ivy proudly told me that Lux had brought her a Liberace peanut warmer. "It's shaped like a peanut, painted yellow and covered in rhinestones. It's really scary and cool. Just like Liberace." They loved Hollywood but avoided the sun and were refused entry to Disneyland for being "too strange"—this disappointed Lux. Ivy then suggested she and Lux were "too retarded to do anything else. We can only play rock 'n' roll."

What, I wondered, was the secret of their enduring romance?

"It's destiny, maybe. When we talk to other couples they may dislike something about the other person while we like almost everything together. We share the same values and it just seems natural to us. There's something karmic about our relationship. I feel like I've known Lux my whole life— perhaps I knew him in another life—and I just feel very, very lucky that we are together."

They would remain together for five more years: Lux Interior died suddenly in 2009 of an aortic dissection in February 2009. By then the Cramps had slowed to a halt: no new music since 2002's mediocre *Fiends Of Dope Island* album and no concerts after 2006. Nick Knox had left the band in 1991 and Bryan Gregory died in poverty in 2001 while the primitive pop vision that once made the Cramps so fresh had staled. 1950s' rockabilly was made in brief spurts by hormonal teenagers; the Cramps were well into their twenties when they reinvented the genre and while they sustained it for several years the primitive magic informing rockabilly slowly ebbed away. That said, the Cramps' best recordings still sound fabulous and should inspire any listener to check out wild, crude American music. As Lux Interior stated, "rock 'n' roll is so great that everyone in the world should think it's the greatest thing that's happening. If they don't, they're turds."

FOR MUCH OF HIS CAREER, Hasil Adkins was a one-man rockabilly band. He remembered hearing Hank Williams on the radio, listening to the wide range of instruments, and figuring it was all Hank. So, he too learned a little bit on a lot of instruments and played as many of them as he could all at once.

The Haze claimed to have a repertoire of more than 9,000 songs out of which 7,000 were originals. He recorded sporadically over the years until Billy Miller and Miriam Linna started New York City-based Norton Records to keep his legacy alive and loud.

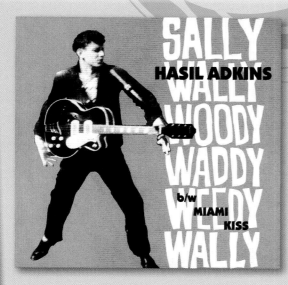

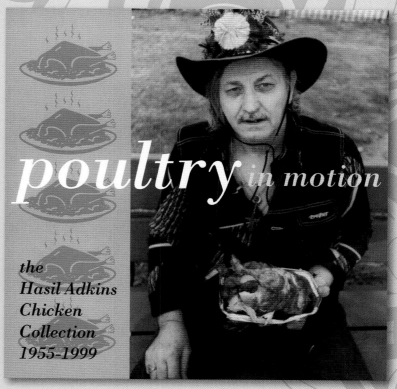

A classic—and perhaps the only—album ever devoted to the lowly chicken, *Poultry In Motion: The Hasil Adkins Chicken Collection 1955–1999*.

TAV FALCO AND PANTHER BURNS

By Tav Falco

Tav Falco and Ron Miller one day in Memphis in May 1980. *buZ Blurr*

THEY'RE ALL GHOSTS NOW . . . the mythic ones whom we, as ditch diggers in American music, learned from and from them concatenated the rustic song and dance of Panther Music. The crazy hiccupping belch of the Feathers touch, the romping Arkansas strut of Sonny Burgess, the unholy howl of bull cow Chester Burnett who took Highway 49 off of Dockery Plantation at age 39. . . . The inventory of antics seems epic, but in reality the list is short.

Outside of their legacy of recordings, nothing palpable remains of *the* mythic ones except meagre hands full of photographs and lurid mementoes. Those of us who knew them as devil's disciples, who tried to understand them, who worshipped at their alter, who maybe angered them, were enchanted by them and sometimes despised by them, who ever sought that ineffable spark of invention and humanity that seemed to ignite from them 90 miles in all directions . . . those of us who were awed by their celebration of swagger tempered by lonesome and rueful poetic darkness were in the end left with nothing, other than a mystique more infectious than a nest of spitting vipers.

There was Muddy Waters, the Rolling Stones, Howling Wolf, and then there became the Panther Burns—a notion elevated in the pastoral painting by Carroll Cloar as *Panther Bourne*. As in the painting, the band is founded upon legend . . . it is the legend of the unapproachable Panther Burns that surrounds a plantation still thriving off of Highway 61 near Greenville, Mississippi. When in the late 19th Century land was being cleared in the delta for further cultivation of cotton, rumor had it a cunning panther stalked and terrorized the local population around the plantation that would become known as Panther Burn. The wildcat howled savagely all night and it raided the chicken coops of the farmers. The planters formed a posse to track down the forlorn creature. They set traps, but the animal eluded their traps. They tried to shoot it, but it evaded their rifle fire, and the shooters missed. Finally, they corralled the critter into a cane break and set it aflame. According to witnesses, the screams coming from the panther were an unholy amalgam of animal lust and divine transubstantiation, which continue to curse the plantation. Thus Panther Burns would become the name most fitting a rock 'n' roll band.

Yet what is an RnR band without an aesthetic? Before I had ever picked up a guitar, I began to cultivate mine. Within the sphere of deep blues, I learned no one is more esteemed than a sissy blues singer. Bobby "Blue" Bland grew up in the church in Memphis, and he had it all: the pipes, the aching effeminate tonalities, and the mistreated heart that had been trampled by a legion of abusers. To please his lover he had to work in the white folks' yard, and as he sang, *that kind of work is real hard.*

What can I tell you about the aesthetic of an artist like Charlie Feathers? A man who was at one with the world that surrounded him. In harmony, yet in his hillbilly stance he was totally against the grain in adherence to his own interior and often-esoteric vision. An illiterate artist whose liberation from print stress only enhanced his audial sensitivity and his sense of vocal mimicry: a sensibility that surpassed even the talents of American Indians who in their native state could mimic the calls and tonal screeches and grunts of the birds and animals of the forests.

Charlie was obsessed with the purity, the incendiary lyricism, and the rhythmic sensuality that infused

Charlie Feathers and Harley-Davidson. *Falco*

the synthesis of cotton patch blues and hillbilly mountain music that he and radio engineer, Sam Phillips, had stumbled upon. In a converted radiator repair shop at 706 Union Avenue, Charlie and Mr. Phillips underwent months and months of experimentation in this makeshift pre-Sun Records studio.

For there to be great artists, there must be great audiences, and it was the voodoo of radio and jukeboxes that brought the new music to the ears and feet of post war beboppers in the Mid South. No one knew what to call it, whether it were fish or foul, but Dewey Phillips understood it instinctively. He talked that down home hipster jive and jumped to radio right out of a record shop on Beale Street. He never learned how to operate a control board, but his show *Red Hot and Blue* was a smash hit with the public. WHBQ put George Klein in the control room gopher slot for him and to make sure that Dewey didn't wreck the studio on his night time slot. Dewey had the white audience and the black audience, and he got his hands on new releases right from the distributors before anybody else. Every declaration, expletive, hoot and holler Dewey spewed on the air was infused with rollicking tribal power. He played the rocking guitar picking, gospel shouting Sister Rosetta Tharpe right along side of the corn whiskey and amphetamine fuelled pumping piano of Jerry Lee Lewis. He and Sleepy Eyed John on WHHM broke Sun Records so hot around Memphis that it was pitiful. Around Arkansas, Louisiana, Mississippi, Alabama, and Tennessee the records got into the hands of DJs with the compliments of Sam's brother, Jud Phillips, who followed the same circuit he had previously travelled with his gospel quartet while still in the US Marine uniform from the Korean War. Jud is thought of as the greatest RnR promotion man of all time. Everybody liked Jud. He had the personal charm and conversant gifts that drew people to him from every level of the business, and he always kept the welfare of the artist as No. 1 priority. Due to the promotional efforts of Jud Phillips, the Sun label broke across the Mid South hotter than a fresh fucked fox in a forest fire.

When Charlie Feathers wasn't listening to demo tapes in the old Chevrolet parked in front of his house, he was sitting on the couch chain smoking Viceroys and watching baseball on TV. Sometimes he would pull his Martin guitar out from under the couch and strum along to the baseball game. Watching him in this was how I learned to play, "One Hand Loose." Charlie understood and fostered the musical form that he and radio engineer, Sam Phillips, "discovered" in only one context: slapback echo on the vocals, acoustic rhythm guitar, electric lead guitar, percussive slapping contrabass, and no drums. For him, this and only this instrumentation, could produce pure rockabilly. Charlie also had a few simple words of advice: "Tav," he said, "you got to scare them a little bit—the audience, you got to scare 'em just a little." Followed by, "If you ain't doing something different, you ain't doing nothing at all."

Cordell Jackson, 1980.
Falco

TAV FALCO AND PANTHER BURNS

Cut from the same cloth was Cordell Jackson who claimed to be the first lady recording engineer and who started her label, Moon Records, in the 1950s in Memphis. Cordell was quite a guitar thrasher on her red Hagstrom, and she saw something in the thrashings of Panther Burns that stirred up the restless waters in her own libido. Hardly opposed to renegade rockers, she embraced Lux and Ivy when the Cramps came to town to record.

While he was recording the Cramps, Alex Chilton was playing on stage with the Panther Burns as he had done from the beginning as a founding member of the band. Different as they were, Cordell adored both groups and was cognizant of how the Cramps expanded and electrified rockabilly, while Panther Burns deconstructed the genre.

By virtue of persistence and enduring mystique, Panther Burns have now become *the last steam engine left on the track that don't do nothing but run and blow*. Yes, art is long, and life is short. The list of hillbilly cats and blues stompers around Memphis seems like it could go on forever, but the list of mythic ones from whom we descend is far more tenuous than you might imagine.

Lux Interior and Bryan Gregory at Phillips Studio in 1980. *Falco*

Alex "LX" Chilton with Panther Burns. *Falco*

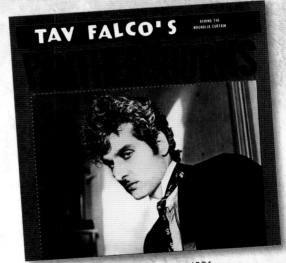

The debut Panther Burns LP from 1981.

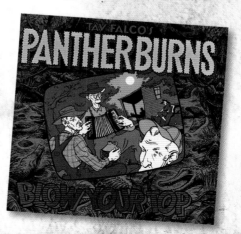

THE METEORS

By Garth Cartwright

THE CRAMPS LIFTED THE TERM "psychobilly" from Johnny Cash's 1976 US Country hit "One Piece At A Time" and stuck it on flyers promoting their late-1970s New York concerts. In 1979 the term followed them across the Atlantic and in the United Kingdom, where their swampy rockabilly instantly won a large audience; "psychobilly" began to be muttered by hipsters, record labels and music writers as a hot new musical genre.

Of the many British bands who suddenly began describing themselves as "psychobilly" it is the Meteors who most genuinely represent the genre. Indeed, the Meteors and their fans are known to use the phrase "Only The Meteors Are True Psychobilly." Considering both the band and their fans tend to resemble extras from a Mad Max movie it's not often someone loudly disagrees with them about this. The Cramps—lovers of art, cats and obscure old records—wanted no truck with the testosterone crazed psychobillies; Poison Ivy explicitly stating that they disliked most of the bands trading as psybs and had never considered the noun anything more than "a carny term to drum up business."

Business is what the Meteors have done ever since they formed in south London when guitarist/vocalist P. Paul Fenech and double bassist Nigel Lewis—both veterans of the British rockabilly scene—teamed up with punk drummer Mark Robertson. The trio attempted to fuse rockabilly's hiccupping rhythms with punk guitar aggression. Their initial performances at London rockabilly clubs found audiences less than enthusiastic. Fenech recalled that before one performance he was told "the drummer can't play here—he's got green hair!" Relocating to music venues that booked punk bands, the

Meteors quickly won a loyal following for their aggressive playing. Fenech's songs often favored horror and sci-fi themes and in concert he would spit mouthfuls of chicken blood across stage and audience. Inevitably, the Meteors attracted a following as aggressive as their music and fans were first called "the Crazies" and then "the Wrecking Crew." These psychos developed a dance style known as "wrecking" that essentially involved brawling at the front of the stage. Both the English music press and the tabloid newspapers took an interest in the band, the former briefly championing the Meteors as the UK's wildest new band while the latter went in for "shock-horror" exposes on the "violent youth cult that is psychobilly."

Island Records signed the Meteors in 1981—an odd pairing seeing Island largely recorded black music and had never courted punk or rockabilly bands—released their debut album, *In Heaven*, then quickly dropped the band. From there on The Meteors would release dozens of singles and albums on tiny indie labels and tour constantly. Quickly it was established that The Meteors were P. Paul Fenech and whatever rhythm section dared back him. Fenech's appearance—bald, burly and heavily tattooed—meant the Meteors were never mistaken for rockabilly pinups the Stray Cats or the Cramps' arty chic. Indeed, psychobilly's predominantly male fans thrived on the band's celebration of chaos. In interviews Fenech swore allegiance to Satanism and Charles Manson so provoking further controversy. Yet he insisted that all Meteors concerts were a "politics and religion free zone." This came about after witnessing British punk divide into warring factions of hard left and extreme right.

Never developing their UK audience beyond a small cult, the Meteors found larger audiences in continental Europe, Southern California and Japan. Across different continents The Meteors sang the psychobilly gospel with such anthems as "Hymns For Hellbound," "Hell Train Rollin'," "My Daddy Is A Vampire," "Mutant Rock," "Psychobilly Stomp" and the tender "Corpse Grinder." Fenech's tongue is firmly in cheek when he sings such songs: the campy aggrieved English horror rock they create is similar to that pioneered by Screaming Lord Sutch in the early 1960s. While the Meteors looked back for influences their gory songs predated much of the goth punk/black metal that would issue forth in the 1980s and 90s. That the Meteors' relentless mix of rockabilly twang and punk power chords never won over wider audiences—as the Cramps, Misfits, and White Zombie all managed to do—reflects both the band's dedication to psychobilly and the limits of their appeal.

Fenech began releasing solo albums— six so far— in 2000. Having studied recording technology at university he now runs his own studio in Swindon, England. Yet when the full moon rises Fenech takes the Meteors out to play, singing those ole psychobilly blues to small, loyal audiences. Some of whom still like to wreck.

Spreading the Good Word

The Reverend Horton Heat heat up the stage at Sala Apolo in Barcelona, Spain, on April 6, 2010. From left, Jim Heath, Paul Simmons, and Jimbo Wallace. *Jordi Vidal/Redferns*

JIM HEATH: "In the late seventies, I began to figure out that rockabilly was *the* coolest music. Of course, living in Texas, I had been exposed to the normal rockabilly stuff (although I'm pretty sure that the term 'rockabilly' wasn't really widely used to describe the fifties mix of country and R&B music until the late seventies). Early Elvis, Carl Perkins, Johnny Cash, Bill Haley, and Gene Vincent were familiar to most every guitar player growing up in Texas. What wasn't really known to me until the late seventies was the expansive amount of labels and bands that were part of that sound.

"Hearing all those different styles of more obscure fifties artists like Warren Smith, Al Ferrier, Joe Clay, Johnny Carroll, Charlie Feathers, and scores of others made me realize that there was room in this genre for me to formulate my own sound—and make it work in modern realms.

"Another thing that brought me to this idea was the fact that rockabilly was kind of the kicking dog of musical styles. I knew that it was not getting the respect it deserved. And, that it would someday rise up and get noticed as a musical style to rival its other American counterparts—the blues, jazz, and country western.

"Rockabilly actually had these other styles beat in a couple of ways. The energy of those up-tempo wild men (and some wild-women, too) was off the charts. Plus, rockabilly was not only a musical style, it was a lifestyle too. Fast cars, mid-century design, switchblade knives, pompadour haircuts, and stuff like that. I realized that rockabilly would have its day, and that I could maybe be a part of that.

"One of my favorite things about rockabilly is how the musicians had a lot of different kinds of roots. Swing, jazz, country, and blues . . . sometimes all at once. Rock 'n' roll beats, blues shuffles, jazzy swing beats, and bluegrass stomps. Kid guitar players like Cliff Gallup or Gene Vincent and the Blue Caps and pro guys like Mickey Baker were all relevant and well . . . hot!

"Little did I know that my career in rockabilly would lead to playing gigs backing Gene Summers, Sid King, and Screamin' Jay Hawkins, recording at Sun Studios (sight of the original Memphis Recording Service) with Johnny Powers, Malcolm Yelvington, and Barbara Pittman, opening for Johnny Cash and Carl Perkins, doing gigs and jams with Brian Setzer, Scotty Moore, and Phil Alvin and getting to talk for a bit with Sam Phillips, the founder of Sun Records. There's lots of other things too, but you get the picture.

"Little did I know that what I thought about this music, hillbilly bop, rockabilly, or whatever you-a-call it, was right on target, and my dream of it becoming way more than the short-haired, ugly duckling of all musical styles would come true with a vengeance.

"From the original revival with the likes of the Stray Cats, Robert Gordon and the Blasters, to the modern-day realization that there's a pretty good slap bass player or three in every town (once not long ago, slap bass was a dying art everywhere . . . even music writers asked about Jimbo's 'cello'), it seems pretty evident that rockabilly will make it into the realm of legitimate music genres—and it is a genre to be reckoned with."

REVEREND HORTON HEAT

PSY-HO BILLY FREAK OUT
by Rev. HORTON HEAT
with Guitar

Guitar, Vocals: Rev. Horton Heat
Drums: Pat (Taz) Bentley
Bass: Jimbo Wallace
Snapshot by Charles Peterson.
Design by Art Chantry.
Recorded at Reciprocal
by Jack Endino.

SINGLES CLUB
DEC 1990
EDITION OF 6,500

© 1990 Horton
House Publishing
Time: 2:37

SUB POP

Psychobilly Freakout
(Rev. H. Heat)
THE REVEREND
HORTON HEAT

© 1990 Sub Pop
SP98 A

Revival
REVEREND
HORTON
HEAT

THE FULL-CUSTOM GOSPEL SOUNDS OF

THE ★ REVEREND ★ HORTON ★ HEAT

Reverend Horton Heat

THE REVEREND HORTON HEAT
and RUN WESTY RUN
with special guests
FLAT DUO JETS
FIRST AVENUE 701 FIRST AVE. NO.
MINNEAPOLIS, MN
MONDAY • MARCH 14, 1994
DOORS OPEN 8:00 PM • SHOWTIME 9:00 PM
MUST BE LEGAL AGE. I.D. REQUIRED.

0303 SEAT
SEC. ROW
GEN. ADM.
MAR 14, 1994

REVEREND HORTON HEAT
MONDAY DEC 30TH 2002
WITH SPECIAL GUEST: UNKNOWN HINSON
HOUSE OF BLUES - LAS VEGAS
3950 LAS VEGAS BLVD. / MANDALAY BAY / (702) 632-7600

ARTWORK, LAYOUT, AND DESIGN ©JOHNNY ACE STUDIOS. WWW.ACEKUSTOMS.COM. SPECIAL THANKS TO T.J. O'GRADY / THROTTLE JOCKEY ORIGINALS. VISIT WWW.REVERENDHORTONHEAT.COM

THE REVEREND HORTON HEAT
with special guests
SUPERSUCKERS
and HAGFISH
FIRST AVENUE 701 FIRST AVE. NO.
MINNEAPOLIS, MN
THURSDAY • SEPT
DOORS OPEN 8:00 PM
ADMIT ONE THIS DATE ONLY

0262 SEAT
SEC. ROW
GEN. ADM.
SEPT 14, 1995

215

HEAVY TRASH

Jon Spencer of Heavy Trash performs at the Pistoia Blues Festival in Pistoia, Italy, in 2009. *Alessandro Laporta/Alamy*

WELCOME TO HEAVY TRASH, the rockabilly your mother warned you about. If truth be told, however, it's doubtful she could even have imagined the depths of this music—the depravity of the guitar tones, the wickedness of the riffs, the sensuality of the singing.

Heavy Trash is Jon Spencer and Matt Verta-Ray. Describing the band's music, however, is difficult, but fun. Think Tom Waits crossed with the Rock 'n' Roll Trio. Or the Velvet Underground fronted by Hasil Adkins. In a word, unique. And cool. Purists, plug your ears. But if you're into experimentation, innovation, and sheer soulfulness, you have to give this a spin.

Most folk know Jon Spencer from his Pussy Galore, Blues Explosion, and Boss Hog exploits. Matt Verta-Ray is tougher to pin down. He's been in the bands Madder Rose and the fabulous Speedball Baby, a foray into deconstructed rockabilly and *alternative* alt rock.

"Jon and I are both very open-minded when it comes to being affected by any musical vein when we are coming up with stuff of our own," Verta-Ray says. "The same applies to the recording process—we don't have many rules and if a weird or anachronistic idea asserts itself, we'll certainly consider it."

Verta-Ray also runs a studio, NY Hed, famous for its menagerie of tube amps and old-school effects and echo machines. And while Spencer is the band's frontman, Verta-Ray is the mad scientist behind its sound

"Sam Phillips' recording style looms large with us as he was one of the real innovators at making great records," he says. "We generally will roll the tape all the time if we're tracking. Sometimes we'll keep recording even if we feel we have a good version on the reel just to see if any interesting variation or happy mistake happens. After we're confident (or too tired) we knock off and come back the next day to figure out which takes are the best. I'll often get out the razor blade and edit between takes to get a whole one that just leaps out at us. It's amazing how many records we all know and love that were the product of splicing-block madness. It ends up being more like filmmaking than sound capture."

Spencer's rig is simple: for recording, he's true to his acoustic stage guitar, a 1960s Gibson LG-2. But Verta-Ray chooses between an array of classic rockabilly gear: a 1959 Gretsch 6119, 1955 Gibson ES-295 fitted with a Bigsby, and an old Frankenstein's monster of a Telecaster. "Seems like the Teles like an early '60s neck, old body with the finish—sadly—belt-sanded off by a previous owner." And they spice the tracks with the tones of a reissue Danelectro baritone guitar.

Among other amps, Verta-Ray is inspired by his elderly Magnatone, especially on the tune "Good Man." "The main riff was inspired by the cool tremolo sound coming out of my Magnatone amp—it doesn't vary the volume like with a Fender, it varies the pitch. I guess it's what they call 'true tremolo.' In any case, it's a really creepy sound and brings up all kinds of emotions. Ike Turner, Mickey Baker, and Bo Diddley all made good use of that Magnatone tremolo."

IMELDA MAY & DARREL HIGHAM

THE MARRIED TEAM of guitarist Darrel Higham and singer Imelda May blend good old rockabilly with an Irish twang, thanks to Imelda May's heritage and bodhrán playing. Under her maiden name of Imelda May Clabby, she released a debut disc in 2003, *No Turning Back*, which was later re-recorded and reissued under her current stage name. Her followup album, 2008's *Love Tattoo*, hit #1 in Ireland, while her latest, 2010's *Mayhem*, hit #1 in both Ireland and Great Britain.

IMELDA *May*★
Love Tattoo

IMELDA *May*★
IS PURE DYNAMITE! IN...
MAYHEM
IT WILL MAKE YOU SCREAM FOR MORE!
FEATURING DARREL HIGHAM   AL GARE   STEVE RUSHTON   DAVE PRISEMAN

let's rock tonight
Darrel Higham

Darrel Higham
The Cochran Connection
Vol. 2
With guests
The Jets, Imelda Clabby, James Compton and Al Nichols

The golden dress: Irish rockabilly diva Imelda May.
Courtesy Decca Records

WORLDWIDE ROCKABILLY REVIVAL

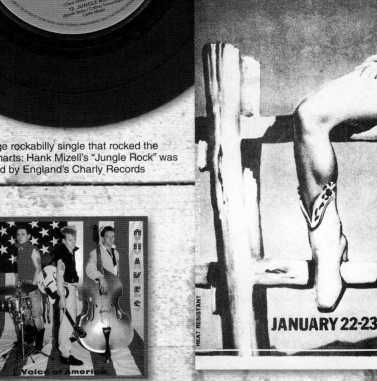

THE WORLD FAMOUS ROCKABILLY CATS

FRI. SAT. NITE

THE RANCH
14850 TELEGRAPH
(Just S. of Fenkel)
534-0877

JANUARY 22-23

The vintage rockabilly single that rocked the modern charts: Hank Mizell's "Jungle Rock" was re-released by England's Charly Records

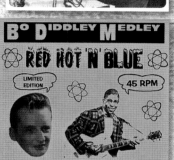

Hot Rod Cruise-In Starts At 6!

$12 advance

WorldWideRetro.com Presents The Seventh Annual

ROCKABILLY PROM™

March 27, 2010

Featuring:

The Queen of Rockabilly
WANDA JACKSON

Texas Sensations
TWO TONS OF STEEL

& Honkey Tonkin'
LUCKY TUBB

One More Hour
And I'll Be At
The Prom!

PLUS!:

Retro Prom Photos!

King and Queen Crowned!

Door Prizes!

Dance Off!

Pabst Blue Ribbon BEER

Accept No Substitute!

KNUCKLEHEAD'S SALOON

2715 Rochester. Kansas City, Missouri - (816) 483-1456 - RockabillyProm.com

Slammer 2010

The ROCK'n'ROLL WEEKENDERS TEAM presents

HEMSBY 30

Britains BIGGEST Rock'n'Roll Weekender!!!

6th 'til 12th MAY 2003

Star USA ACTS at YOUR request...

A True Rock'n'Roll Star...
JACK SCOTT
& his fantastic ALL American Band

"BRRRR....Black Slacks!"
First time together in Europe...
JOE BENNETT
& the SPARKLETONES
(The ORIGINAL 50's line-up)

Still Stranded in the Jungle' the dynamic
JACKS/CADETS

The Rockin' Rollin'...
MARVIN RAINWATER
(T.B.C.)

From Louisiana to the 'Promised Land'
A rare appearance for...
JOHNNIE ALLAN
'The Swamp Rocker'

HOWLIN' HOUND DOGS (CANADA) EVA EASTWOOD & the MAJOR KEYS (SWEDEN)
THE SATELLITES (AUSTRALIA) MISCHIEF (HOLLAND) MARIA VINCENT & the MILLIONAIRES (UK)
ERVIN TRAVIS & the VIRGINIANS (FRANCE) THE TEXABILLY ROCKERS (PORTUGAL)
THE HICKSVILLE BOMBERS (UK) SMOKEY MOUNTAIN BOYS (UK)
BOPPIN' STEVE & THE PLAYTONES (SWEDEN) MEMPHIS (UK)
and THE HOUSEROCKERS' BIG BAND (UK)

PLUS... AN INTERNATIONAL LINE-UP OF TOP ROCK'N'ROLL D.J.'s

FANTASTIC VALUE...
£67.00 per person
(based on 6 people sharing)

ROSIE FLORES

ROSIE FLORES
Rockabilly Filly

Claude Bleses
&
Big Beat Records
présentent

FREDDIE FINGERS LEE
en France

20/10 ROANNE : Théâtre municipal
21/10 BOLOZON (01) : Club St-Éloi
22/10 CLERMONT-FERRAND : L'Aquarius
23/10 EGLETON (19) : Le Grill
24/10 BELLEGARDE (30) : L'Antre
26/10 ST-ETIENNE : Salle Jeanne d'Arc
27/10 LE PUY : Théâtre municipal
28/10 CAHORS : Le Sherlock
29/10 NOISSAC (82) : Le Nirvana
30/10 ALES (30) : Le Cyclope
31/10 LYON : Le Palladium
04/11 NANTES : Le Macumba
05/11 DINAN : Le New Pop Club
06/11 PARIS : Forum des Halles

distribution MUSIDISC EUROPE
publishing YOU YOU MUSIC

CRUISE

David Perry

JUEVES VIERNES SABADO
9 10 11
NOVIEMBRE
LA ARENA · MADRID | LA CAPSA · EL PRAT DE LLOBREGAT | JAM · BERGARA
Horo: 22H en todas las salas. Entrada Anticipada: 4000 Pts./Entrada en Taquilla 4500 Pts.

¡¡FIESTA 10º ANIVERSARIO BLOODY MARY!! 2ª Parte ¡¡EN DIRECTO!!

LINK WRAY
¡¡POR 1ª VEZ EN NUESTRO PAIS.
EL GENUINO REY DEL INSTRO ROCK!!

DEKE DICKERSON
& THE ECCO-FONICS
LIDER DE LOS INCREIBLES
UNTAMED YOUTH

THE PHANTOM SURFERS
¡¡LOS PRINCIPES DEL SURF!!

THE CHURCH KEYS
ROCK & ROLL PRIMITIVO
CON MIEMBROS DE LOS A-BONES

+ EXPOSICIÓN DE FOTOS ROCK & ROLL POR J. A. ARETA "J..."
PINCHA DISCOS: IDOIA & JUXE (BLOODY MARY) + THE PROFE (MA...)

Boss Tweed

New Set Of Rules
The Jime

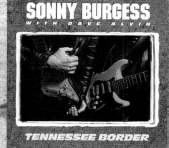

SONNY BURGESS
WITH DAVE ALVIN

TENNESSEE BORDER

The Sun Rhythm Section
Old Time Rock 'N Roll

DANNY AND
THE FAT BOYS

AMERICAN MUSIC

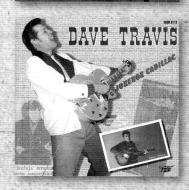

DAVE TRAVIS
JUKEBOX CADILLAC

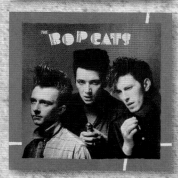

THE BOP CATS

BIG SIX
get off it and rock it...

WORLDWIDE ROCKABILLY REVIVAL

still on a winning streak!

DEKE

MELODY by deke dickerson

NEW ALBUM OUT NOW!

appearing:
Friday, April 29th 10pm
W/ The Casket Draggers

Deke Dickerson and Crazy Joe Tritschler perform on stage at Sala Apolo in Barcelona, Spain on March 13, 2008. They play a Danelectro twin necked guitar. *Jordi Vidal/Redferns*

Kim Lenz
and the Jaguars

BIG SANDY
AND HIS
FLY-RITE BOYS

appearing

Feelin' Kinda Lucky

BIG SANDY
and his
FLY-RITE BOYS

LOSER'S BLUES
THREE YEARS
BLIND
WHAT'S IT TO YA?
STRANGE LOVE
AND OTHERS!

HIGHTONE RECORDS

Artist: Vince Ray

WORLDWIDE ROCKABILLY REVIVAL

Phil Alvin of the Los Angeles punk rockabilly band the Blasters rocks Texas in 1980. *Janette Beckman/Getty Images*

The Rivers Rockabilly Trio break loose: Bassist Bradley Keough, guitarist Stu Frederick, and drummer J. B. "Memphis" Smith.

The Reckless Ones: From left: guitarist and lead vocalist Kevin O'Leary, drummer Dylan Patterson, and bassist Adam Boatright.

Artist: Vince Ray

VIVA LAS VEGAS
APRIL 1-4 2010 13 ORLEANS HOTEL LAS VEGAS
VIVA 13 ROCKABILLY WEEKEND
©Vince Ray
ROCKABILLY WEEKEND
www.vivalasvegas.net

The Hillbilly Delights rock out in front of the former Love Me Tender rockabilly shop in Tokyo in 2006. From left, guitarist Yasuhide Horii, singer Shinji Tamura, bassist Takaaki Fueda, and drummer Satoshi Ishitsuka.

Feel Like Rockin'

PUMPIN' PIANO
MABO &THE88

Japanese rockabillies dance away a Sunday afternoon in Tokyo's Yoyogi Park.

WORLDWIDE ROCKABILLY REVIVAL

David Perry

By Luc Sante

The unknown rockabilly band.

AFTERWORD

WE ARE ASSEMBLED HERE at the tomb of the unknown rockabilly band, somewhere on the shores of the Great American Sea. The rain is coming down slantwise, destroying our pompadours and making our string ties hang down like cooked spaghetti. We can barely hear the preacher over the torrent, but we know he is invoking the ghosts of all the failed bands from all the teenage campaigns of ages past—the doo-wop quintets who never settled on a name, the mod combos who couldn't afford matching suits, the psychedelic groups who slept through their one scheduled recording session, the punk outfits who lost key members to cough syrup or Jesus or manslaughter charges before they ever got a chance to play out. Their uneasy spirits stalk the land, infecting aspiring young players with fatal doubt, stalling the cars of talent scouts, shorting out amp connections, foreclosing on record stores.

And that is why we come here once a year to lay a wreath at the tomb of the unknown rockabilly band: to persuade them to rest, and lay off the young. But just have a look at them—they were never meant to be! They should never have tried occupying the same stage, and they should have left music to find its own way home. The piano player, with his incipient Mickey Mouse ears, was clearly destined for a career working with puppets. The twins on guitar and bass were natural-born casino greeters. The other guitarist has the fine tapered hands of a pest-control agent specializing in silverfish. And the drummer—he was meant as an example. What happened to him should have been shown to driver-safety classes in every high school in the country.

So that is perhaps the true meaning and significance of the unknown rockabilly band. There is a reason why they and their fellows trip up young musicians and dash hopes nurtured since childhood! They act out of kindness, based on their own sad experiences. They want to save the young from mediocrity and failure—or far worse, mediocrity and success. They are like Flannery O'Connor, who when asked whether she thought university programs discouraged too many writers, replied that they didn't discourage enough of them. But pop music has no university programs. At least not yet.

We should gaze upon the image of the unknown rockabilly band, captured in all their semblance of glory by Maurice Seymour of Chicago, and savor the fragile pantomimed ambition, the jackleg bravado, the rented instruments, the press-on smiles. We should earnestly thank them that they favored us with stage fright and bad haircuts and imperfect pitch at the right time and saved us from a lifetime of bitter regret if not one of endless lawsuits. One day, when all music is made by combinations of small and unassuming oblong boxes, the unknown rockabilly band will at last be able to sleep.

SIGRID ARNOTT is a textile artist, historian, and writer.

New Zealand-born, South London-based, and oft'wandering **GARTH CARTWRIGHT** is an award-winning journalist and critic who regularly contributes to *The Guardian*, *The Sunday Times*, *fRoots*, and the BBC's website. He is the author *Princes Amongst Men: Journeys with Gypsy Musicians* and *More Miles Than Money: Journeys Through American Music*.

Singer and guitarist **DEKE DICKERSON** performs with his band the Ecco-Fonics throughout Rockabilly-loving parts of the Earth. In his spare time, he is a historian, writer, producer, and collector.

Dutch-born **PETER DIJKEMA** works as a civil servant and plays guitar and sings as a hobby. His passion for the sounds and history captured on early rockabilly records (including the artists and the instruments they used) sent him on a quest culminating in the meticulous reproduction of rare amps of the era.

DAN FORTE has written for numerous publications and annotated dozens of records in a career spanning 35 years. An ASCAP/Deems Taylor Award winner for excellence in music journalism, he has interviewed such legends as George Harrison, Duane Eddy, Frank Zappa, Eric Clapton, Buck Owens, Jimmy Reed, James Jamerson, Carlos Santana, and Stevie Ray Vaughan.

ROBERT GORDON is the author of *It Came From Memphis* and *Can't Be Satisfied: The Life and Times of Muddy Waters*, among other books. His films include *Johnny Cash's America*, *Respect Yourself: The Stax Records Story*, and William Eggleston's *Stranded In Canton*.

VINCE GORDON is a guitarist, singer, and songwriter with his rockabilly trio, The Jime. He is also editor of The Rockabilly Guitar Page with historic information on rockabilly guitar players and their gear. He has two educational eBooks available on rockabilly guitar playing.

PETER GURALNICK has been called "a national resource" by Nat Hentoff for work that has argued passionately and persuasively for the vitality of this country's intertwined black and white musical traditions. His books include *Feel Like Going Home*, *Sweet Soul Music*, *Searching For Robert Johnson*, and the novel, *Nighthawk Blues*, as well as a prize-winning two-volume biography of Elvis Presley, *Last Train to Memphis* and *Careless Love*. His latest book, 2005's *Dream Boogie: The Triumph of Sam Cooke*, was hailed as "an epic tale told against a backdrop of brilliant, shimmering music, intense personal melodrama, and vast social changes." He is currently at work on a biography of Sam Phillips.

Historian and critic **GREIL MARCUS** is the author of *Bob Dylan by Greil Marcus: Writings 1968–2010*, *When That Rough God Goes Riding: Listening to Van Morrison*, *Mystery Train: Images of America in Rock 'n' Roll Music*, and other books.

DAVID MCGEE is the author of biographies of Carl Perkins (*Go, Cat, Go! The Life and Times of Carl Perkins, The King of Rockabilly*), Steve Earle (*Restless Heart, Outlaw Poet*) and B.B. King (*There Is Always One More Time*), is a contributing editor at *The Absolute Sound*, and founder/publisher/editor of the online roots music and culture magazine, TheBluegrassSpecial.com.

RANDY MCNUTT is the author of *King Records of Cincinnati*, *The Cincinnati Sound*, and *We Wanna Boogie: An Illustrated History of the American Rockabilly Movement*.

Montreal ethnomusicologist, musician, and professor **CRAIG MORRISON** is the author of what has been called "the definitive history of rockabilly": *Go Cat Go!: Rockabilly Music and Its Makers*.

LUC SANTE is the author of *Low Life: Lures and Snares of Old New York*, *Kill All Your Darlings: Pieces, 1990-2005*, *The Factory of Facts*, *No Smoking*, and the photography collections Evidence and *Folk Photography: The American Real-Photo Postcard 1905-1930*, among others.

On page 2: Classic RCA ribbon mic. *Konstantin Sutyagin/Shutterstock*
On page 3: Danny Gatton's 1954 Gibson ES-295. *Thomas Gage/courtesy Arlen Roth and the Gatton Estate*
On the contents page: 1950s American automobile. *John De Bord/Shutterstock;* Blue suede shoes. *Richard Fleischman;* Sun Studios, Memphis, Tennessee. *Stephen Burrows/Alamy;* 1950s American automobile. *John De Bord/Shutterstock*

First published in 2011 by Voyageur Press, an imprint of MBI Publishing Company, 400 First Avenue North, Suite 300, Minneapolis, MN 55401 USA

Voyageur Press titles are also available at discounts in bulk quantity for industrial or sales-promotional use. For details write to Special Sales Manager at MBI Publishing Company, 400 First Avenue North, Suite 300, Minneapolis, MN 55401 USA.

To find out more about our books, visit us online at www.voyageurpress.com.

ISBN: 978-0-7603-4062-2

Editor: Michael Dregni

Design Manager: Katie Sonmor

Cover and book designed by: John Barnett / 4 Eyes Design

Printed in China

PERMISSIONS
All quotes in "Carl Perkins: Original Cat" are from the author's interviews for his biography of Carl Perkins, *Go, Cat, Go! The Life and Times of Carl Perkins, The King of Rockabilly.*

"Sleepy LaBeef: There's Good Rockin' Tonight" copyright © 1979, 2011 by Peter Guralnick. A version of this essay first appeared in Lost Highway: Journeys and Arrivals of American Musicians by Peter Guralnick. Reprinted by permission of the author.

"Cliff Gallup: Crazy Fingers" copyright © 2011 by Dan Forte. Portions of this interview previously appeared in *Guitar Player* magazine. Reprinted by permission of the author.

"The Lost Boy" copyright © 2005 by Greil Marcus. Reprinted by permission of the author.

David Perry